SOCIETY FOR NEW TESTAMENT STUDIES

MONOGRAPH SERIES

General Editor: G. N. Stanton

D0087473

54

THE OLD TESTAMENT PSEUDEPIGRAPHA
AND THE NEW TESTAMENT

The Old Testament Pseudepigrapha and the New Testament

Prolegomena for the Study of Christian Origins

JAMES HAMILTON CHARLESWORTH
George L. Collord Professor of
New Testament Language and Literature
Princeton Theological Seminary

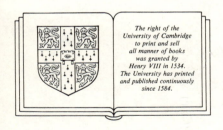

*The right of the
University of Cambridge
to print and sell
all manner of books
was granted by
Henry VIII in 1534.
The University has printed
and published continuously
since 1584.*

CAMBRIDGE UNIVERSITY PRESS

CAMBRIDGE

LONDON   NEW YORK   NEW ROCHELLE

MELBOURNE   SYDNEY

Published by the Press Syndicate of the University of Cambridge
The Pitt Building, Trumpington Street, Cambridge CB2 1RP
32 East 57th Street, New York, NY 10022, USA
10 Stamford Road, Oakleigh, Victoria 3166, Australia

First published 1985

Printed in Great Britain at
the University Press, Cambridge

Library of Congress catalogue card number: 84-29367

British Library cataloguing in publication data
Charlesworth, James H.
The Old Testament pseudepigrapha and the New
Testament : prolegomena for the study of
Christian origins. − (Monograph series/Society
for New Testament studies; 54)
1. Apocryphal books (Old Testament) − Criticism,
interpretation, etc. 2. Christianity − Origin
I. Title   II. Series
229'.91   BS1700
ISBN 0 521 30190 4

WG

CONTENTS

Preface   *page* vii
Abbreviations   xi

Introduction   1

**1 The Pseudepigrapha: New Opportunities and Challenges
for the Biblical Scholar**   6
  Introduction   6
  The Modern Study of the Pseudepigrapha   6
  New Opportunities and Challenges   18
  The Canon, Inspiration and the Pseudepigrapha   25
  Conclusion   26

**2 The Pseudepigrapha, Early Judaism and Christian
Origins**   27
  Introduction   27
  Dating the Evidence   31
  Methodology: A Search for the Essence of Early
   Judaism   47
  Perceptions of Early Judaism and Christian Origins   58
  The Cosmic Theology of Early Judaism   65
  The Eschatological Anthropology of Early Judaism   67
  Conclusion   68

3 The Pseudepigrapha and the New Testament   70
  Introduction   70
  Scrutinizing the Literary Relationships Between the
   Pseudepigrapha and the New Testament   70
  The Pseudepigrapha and Dating the New Testament   80
  Messianism and Christology: A Major Problematic
   Term   87

103431

Conclusion 91

**Appendix: The SNTS Pseudepigrapha Seminars from 1976
        to 1983** 94
    1976 (Durham, N.C.; Duke University): The Testaments
        of the Twelve Patriarchs 94
    1977 (Tübingen; Eberhard-Karls-Universität): The
        Books of Enoch 102
    1978 (Paris; Châtenay-Malabry): 1 (Ethiopic) Enoch and
        Luke and the Dating of the Parables of Enoch 106
    1979 (Durham, England; University of Durham):
        Methodological Issues − The Messiah, 'Christos',
        and the 'Anointed One' 111
    1980 (Toronto; Trinity College): Hymns, Odes and
        Prayers 119
    1981 (Rome; Domus Pacis): The Pseudepigrapha and
        the Apocalypse 123
    1982 (Leuven; Paus Adriaan VI College): Joseph and
        Aseneth 132
    1983 (Canterbury; University of Kent): 1 Enoch, Jude
        and the Canon 137

Notes 142
Glossary 188
Select Bibliography 193
Indexes 201

PREFACE

The present reflections represent some thoughts that have evolved since 1958, when I first became interested in Early Judaism. During these years my understanding of Early Judaism has changed significantly. Most importantly, I gradually abandoned the idea that first-century Palestinian Jews were mostly activistic and non-reflective; now I know that many of them were well-educated not only in Israelite and Jewish traditions but also in the achievements of other cultures, notably, Roman, Greek, Syrian, Egyptian and Iranian (in the old broad sense). First-century Judaism was shaped by the Great Revolt, which ended in the Romans burning the Temple; but it was by no means a culture devoid of creative new compositions.

With the recovery of the Dead Sea Scrolls and related manuscript discoveries, and with the number of documents now in the Old Testament Pseudepigrapha comes a quite new awareness of the vast amount of Early Jewish literature we now possess. Many of the texts we now consider paradigmatically important for the study of Early Judaism and Early Christianity were simply unknown to such erudite and indefatigable scholars as M.-J. Lagrange and W. Bousset. With each new discovery of an old document should also come the question, 'How much more has been irretrievably lost?' (see chapter 2, n. 51). First-century Judaism was intellectually alive, new compositions poured forth from many segments of that complex we misrepresent by the overworked word 'religion', as if we have a categorical container into which we pour our undigested data.

For more than a decade I have been trying to contribute to the study of Early Judaism and Early Christianity by editing and translating manuscripts studied in many of the famous libraries, including the Vatican, the British Museum, the John Rylands University Library of Manchester, the Bodleian Library, the Bibliothèque Nationale and the Bibliothèque Bodmer. My past work has been primarily analytical. Now I have begun an attempt to struggle with the essential meanings and functions of the hundreds of documents that are our primary sources. While avoiding the error of attempting to construct a system out of some of the data, I have reflected on the meaning of our texts for the phenomena that qualified and defined Early Judaism and Early Christianity. The move, therefore, is from analytical focus to synthetic perception. The clarity of the parts, of course, must not be lost as breadth of field is increased.

My focus here has, as the title indicates, been upon the Old Testament Pseudepigrapha. This stance is logical and necessary. I have been preoccupied with that corpus of literature, and no scholar today can claim to be a master of more than one ancient collection. Moreover, I tend to doubt whether any of us can really digest all that is in the Pseudepigrapha. It is, after all, more complex, disparate, and replete and at the same time, less understood and studied than the other collections, including Philo, Josephus, the Dead Sea Scrolls, and even the Mishnah. Yet limiting oneself to one collection is a fatal flaw; I therefore try to include, wherever pertinent, a discussion of these other collections, with the guidance of experts in the related fields.

The emphasis on Jewish sources in the present work indicates that I contend that the origins of Christianity are inextricably rooted in Early Judaism. It does not, however, suggest that the non-Jewish cultures were insignificant for the development of Christianity. Obviously the contention that Judaism was influenced by foreign cultures (see chapter 2) at least mirrors the importance of these other cultures for Early Christianity. The non-Jewish dimension of the development of Early Christianity is indicated, *inter alia*, by three quite different scholars. C.H. Talbert in *Literary Patterns, Theological Themes and the Genre of Luke-Acts* (SBLMS 20; Missoula, Mont., 1974) claims that Luke-Acts is 'organized both as a whole and in its parts' just as Vergil's *Aeneid* (p. 68), and that the Lucan writings are modelled after Aristotle's *Poetics* 17:5–10, Suetonius' *Life of Vergil* 22–3, Lucian's *How to Write History* 48, and Pliny's *Letters* 9:36 (p. 141). Subsequently, in *What is a Gospel? The Genre of the Canonical Gospels* (Philadelphia, 1977), Talbert argues that the Gospels are somewhat similar to the Greco-Roman biographies. H.D. Betz is famous for his knowledge of classical antiquity and his attempts to reveal the non-Jewish elements in Early Christianity; in *Galatians: A Commentary on Paul's Letter to the Churches in Galatia* (Hermeneia; Philadelphia, 1979), his most recent work, he contends that Paul's letter to the Galatians should be examined in the light of Greco-Roman rhetoric and epistolography (esp. see pp. 14–25). In numerous publications P. W. van der Horst points out some similarities between the writings in the New Testament and the early or contemporaneous Greek and Latin works. In his most recent article, 'Hellenistic Parallels to the Acts of the Apostles: *1* 1–26' (*ZNW* 74 (1983), 17–26) he presents a list of significant parallels to Acts. He collected most of these parallels personally or obtained them from a project in Utrecht, the Corpus Hellenisticum Novi Testamenti.

The footnotes to the following work attempt to guide the reader to other explorations; they also express my indebtedness to those who have preceded me in this area of research and those who are breaking new paths in our search for understanding. Some notes are intended for the student, others for the specialist. In order not to detract from the flow of an argument I have footnoted some insights that are very precious to me. All exotic scripts are transliterated; all translations are my own, unless otherwise noted.

The major part of the present work took shape as I read proofs for the new edition of the Old Testament Pseudepigrapha; it goes to press after the first volume arrived and while I double-check the galleys for the second (and final) volume. This related work has shown me how greatly indebted I am to many scholars throughout the world. I fear it would be unfair to express appreciation to only a select few. The team that helped produce the new edition deserves credit for many of the insights shared in the present book.

I am grateful to the officers of the Southeast Section of the American Academy of Religion and the Committee of the *Studiorum Novi Testamenti Societas* for invitations that encouraged me to organize my thoughts on some major and central questions. A grant from the Alexander von Humboldt Stiftung in Bonn-Bad Godesberg enabled me to complete this monograph. Professor M. Hengel graciously provided me with an *Arbeitszimmer* and access to reference works in the Institutum Judaicum. H. Lichtenberger's helpful criticisms are greatly appreciated. M. J. H. Charlesworth compiled the excellent indexes; I am significantly indebted to her. I am very pleased that the *SNTS* Editorial Board and the editor of the *SNTS* Monograph Series urged me to publish the present work in their distinguished series. I am especially grateful to Professor Graham Stanton and the editors at Cambridge University Press for helping me polish the presentation.

October 1983
J.H.C.
Princeton Theological Seminary and
Institutum Judaicum,
Eberhard-Karls-Universität
Tübingen

Dedicated to My Mentors,
Too Numerous to Mention,
But Especially

Hugh Anderson
W. D. Davies
Martin Hengel
and
Ed Sanders

and in memory of
the Rt Rev. John Robinson
(15 June 1919−5 December 1983)
who introduced me to the
collegiality of the *SNTS*

ABBREVIATIONS

1. Modern Publications

AAR	American Academy of Religion
AB	Analecta Biblica
AcOr	*Acta orientalia*
AGAJU	Arbeiten zur Geschichte des antiken Judentums und des Urchristentums
AK	Arbeiten zur Kirchengeschichte
ALBO	Analecta lovaniensia biblica et orientalia
ALGHJ	Arbeiten zur Literatur und Geschichte des hellenistischen Judentums
ALUOS	*Annual of the Leeds University Oriental Society*
ALW	*Archiv für Liturgie-Wissenschaft*
ANET	Pritchard, J. B., ed., *Ancient Near Eastern Texts* (Princeton, 1969³)
ANRW	Haase, W., and H. Temporini, eds., *Aufstieg und Niedergang der römischen Welt* (Berlin, New York, 1979–)
ANT	James, M. R., *The Apocryphal New Testament* (Oxford, 1924; corrected ed., 1955)
APAT	Kautzsch, E., ed., *Die Apokryphen und Pseudepigraphen des Alten Testaments* (2 vols., Tübingen, 1900)
Apoc. Lit.	Torrey, C. C., *The Apocryphal Literature: A Brief Introduction* (New Haven, Conn., 1945; repr. Hamden, Conn., 1963)
APOT	Charles. R. H., ed., *The Apocrypha and Pseudepigrapha of the Old Testament in English* (2 vols., Oxford, 1913)
ArOr	*Archiv orientální*
ASOR	American Schools of Oriental Research
ASTI	*Annual of the Swedish Theological Institute*
ATANT	Abhandlungen zur Theologie des Alten und Neuen Testaments
ATR	*Anglican Theological Review*
AUPHR	Acta Universitatis Upsaliensis Historia Religionum
AusBR	*Australian Biblical Review*
BAR	Biblical Archaeology Review
BASOR	*Bulletin of the American Schools of Oriental Research*
BEvT	Beiträge zur evangelischen Theologie
BHH	Reicke, B., and L. Rost, eds. *Biblisch-historisches Handwörterbuch* (3 vols., Göttingen, 1962–6)
BHM	Jellinek, A. *Bet ha-Midrasch* (2 vols., Jerusalem, 1967³)
Bib	*Biblica*
Biblia Sacra	Weber, R., *et al.*, eds., *Biblia Sacra: Iuxta Vulgatam Versionem* (2 vols. Stuttgart, 1969)
Bibliographie	Delling, G., *Bibliographie zur jüdisch-hellenistischen und*

	intertestamentarischen Literatur 1900–1970 (TU 106^2, Berlin, 1975^2)
BibO	Biblica et Orientalia
BibSt	Biblische Studien
BIFAO	*Bulletin de l'institut français d'archéologie orientale*
BiKi	*Bibel und Kirche*
BIOSCS	*Bulletin of the International Organization for Septuagint and Cognate Studies*
BJRL, BJRULM	*Bulletin of the John Rylands Library, Bulletin of the John Rylands University Library of Manchester*
BJS	Brown Judaic Studies
B-L^2	Haag, H., ed., *Bibel-Lexikon* (Zurich, 1968^2)
BLE	*Bulletin de littérature ecclésiastique*
BO	*Bibliotheca orientalis*
BSOAS	*Bulletin of the School of Oriental and African Studies*
BZ	*Biblische Zeitschrift*
BZAW	Beihefte zur Zeitschrift für die alttestamentliche Wissenschaft
BZNW	Beihefte zur Zeitschrift für die neutestamentliche Wissenschaft und die Kunde der älteren Kirche
CB	*Cultura bíblica*
CBQ	*Catholic Biblical Quarterly*
CCSL	Corpus Christianorum, Series Latina
CETEDOC	Centre de traitement électronique des documents
CG	Cairensis Gnosticus
CSCO	Corpus scriptorum christianorum orientalium
CTM	*Concordia Theological Monthly*
DB	Vigouroux, F., ed., *Dictionnaire de la Bible* (5 vols. Paris, 1895–1912)
DBSup	Pirot, L., *et al.*, eds., *Dictionnaire de la Bible, Suppléments* (Paris, 1928–)
DJD	Discoveries in the Judaean Desert
DTT	*Dansk teologisk Tidsskrift*
EB	*Estudios Bíblicos*
EF	Erträge der Forschung
Enciclopedia de la Biblia	Gutiérrez-Larraya, J. A., ed., *Enciclopedia de la Biblia* (5 vols., Barcelona, 1963)
Encyclopedia of Christianity	Palmer, E. H., *et al.*, eds., *The Encyclopedia of Christianity* (Wilmington, Del., 1964–)
EncyJud	Roth. C., *et al.*, eds., *Encyclopedia Judaica* (16 vols., New York, 1971–2)
EOS	*Eos. Commentarii Societatis Philologae Polonorum*
EtB	Études Bibliques
ETL	*Ephemerides theologicae lovanienses*
EvT	*Evangelische Theologie*
ExpT	*Expository Times*
EPROER	Études Préliminaires aux Religions Orientales dans L'Empire Romain
Falasha Anthology	Leslau, W., *Falasha Anthology* (Yale Judaica Series 6; New Haven, 1951)
FGH	Jacoby, F., ed., *Fragmente der griechischen Historiker* (3 vols., Leiden, 1923–)
FRLANT	Forschungen zur Religion und Literatur des Alten und Neuen Testaments

GamPseud	Hammershaimb, E., *et al.*, eds., *De Gammeltestamentlige Pseudepigrapher* (2 vols. Copenhagen, 1953–76)
GCS	Die griechischen christlichen Schriftsteller der ersten drei Jahrhunderte
GDBL	Nielsen, E., and B. Noack, eds., *Gads Danske Bibel Leksikon* (2 vols., Copenhagen, 1965–6)
GLAJJ	Stern, M., ed., *Greek and Latin Authors on Jews and Judaism*, vol. 1: *From Herodotus to Plutarch* (Jerusalem, 1974)
GNS	Good News Studies
GNT	Grundrisse zum Neuen Testament
Goodenough Festschrift	Neusner, J., ed., *Religions in Antiquity: Essays in Memory of Erwin Ramsdell Goodenough* (Sup *Numen* 14; Leiden, 1968)
Gunkel Festschrift	Schmidt, H., ed., *Eucharistērion: Studien zur Religion des Alten und Neuen Testaments. H. Gunkel Festschrift*, Part II: *Zur Religion und Literatur des Neuen Testaments* (Göttingen, 1923)
Hastings' *DB*	Hastings, J., ed., *Dictionary of the Bible*, rev. ed. by F. C. Grant and H. H. Rowley (New York, 1963)
HAW	Handbuch der Altertumswissenschaft
HeyJ	*Heythrop Journal*
History [Pfeiffer]	Pfeiffer, R. H., *History of the New Testament Times with an Introduction to the Apocrypha* (New York, 1949)
History [Schürer]	Schürer, E., *A History of the Jewish People in the Time of Jesus Christ* (5 vols., plus index, trans. J. MacPherson *et al.* Edinburgh 1897–8)
History ... The Time of the Apostles	Hausrath, A., *A History of New Testament Times: The Time of the Apostles* (4 vols., trans. L. Huxley, London, 1895)
HNT	Handbuch zum Neuen Testament
HR	*History of Religion*
HSM	Harvard Semitic Monographs
HSW	Hennecke, E., W. Schneemelcher and R. McL. Wilson, eds., *New Testament Apocrypha* (2 vols., London, 1963–5)
HTKNT	Herders theologischer Kommentar zum Neuen Testament
HTR	*Harvard Theological Review*
HTS	Harvard Theological Studies
HUCA	*Hebrew Union College Annual*
IB	Buttrick, G. A., *et al.*, eds., *The Interpreter's Bible* (12 vols., New York, 1952–7)
ICC	International Critical Commentary
IDB	Buttrick, G. A., *et al.*, eds., *The Interpreter's Dictionary of the Bible* (4 vols., New York, 1962)
IDBS	Crim, K., *et al.*, eds., *The Interpreter's Dictionary of the Bible, Supplementary Volume* (Nashville, Tenn., 1976)
IEJ	*Israel Exploration Journal*
Int	*Interpretation*
Introduction	Denis, A.-M. *Introduction aux pseudépigraphes grecs d'Ancien Testament* (SVTP 1; Leiden, 1970)
ITQ	*Irish Theological Quarterly*
JA	*Journal asiatique*
JAAR	*Journal of the American Academy of Religion*
JAC	*Jahrbuch für Antike und Christentum*
JAL	Jewish Apocryphal Literature
JAOS	*Journal of the American Oriental Society*

JBC	Brown, R.E., J.A. Fitzmyer and R.E. Murphy, eds., *The Jerome Biblical Commentary* (Englewood Cliffs, N.J., 1968)
JBL	*Journal of Biblical Literature*
JBLMS	Journal of Biblical Literature Monograph Series
JE	Singer, I., *et al.*, eds., *The Jewish Encyclopedia* (12 vols., New York, London, 1901–6)
Jewish Symbols	Goodenough, E.R., *Jewish Symbols in the Greco-Roman Period* (13 vols., New York, 1953–68)
JJS	*Journal of Jewish Studies*
JNES	*Journal of Near Eastern Studies*
JPOS	*Journal of the Palestine Oriental Society*
JQR	*Jewish Quarterly Review*
JR	*Journal of Religion*
JRAS	*Journal of the Royal Asiatic Society*
JSHRZ	Kümmel, W.G., *et al.*, eds., Jüdische Schriften aus hellenistisch-römischer Zeit (Gütersloh, 1973–)
JSJ	*Journal for the Study of Judaism*
JSS	*Journal of Semitic Studies*
JThC	Journal for Theology and the Church
JTS	*Journal of Theological Studies*
Kommentar	Strack, H.L., and P. Billerbeck, *Kommentar zum Neuen Testament aus Talmud und Midrasch* (5 vols., Munich, 1922–56)
KS	*Kirjath Sepher*
Kuhn Festschrift	Jeremias, G., H.-W. Kuhn and H. Stegemann, eds., *Tradition und Glaube: Das frühe Christentum in seiner Umwelt. Festgabe für Karl Georg Kuhn zum 65. Geburtstag* (Göttingen, 1971)
Lampe	Lampe, G.W.H., ed., *A Patristic Greek Lexicon* (Oxford, 1961–8)
LAOT	James, M.R., *The Lost Apocrypha of the Old Testament* (TED; London, New York, 1920)
LCL	Loeb Classical Library
Legends	Ginzberg, L., *The Legends of the Jews* (7 vols., trans. H. Szold, Philadelphia, 1909–38; repr. 1937–66)
LSJM	Liddell, H.G., and R. Scott, *A Greek-English Lexicon*, rev. by H.S. Jones and R. McKenzie (Oxford, 1940)
*LTK*²	Buchberger, M., J. Höfer and K. Rahner, eds., *Lexikon für Theologie und Kirche* (11 vols., Freiburg, 1957–67²)
LUOS MS	Leeds University Oriental Society Monograph Series
MBPAR	Münchener Beiträge zur Papyrusforschung und Antiken Rechtsgeschichte
McCQ	*McCormack Quarterly*
MGWJ	*Monatsschrift für Geschichte und Wissenschaft des Judentums*
Missionsliteratur	Dalbert, P. *Die Theologie der hellenistisch-jüdischen Missionsliteratur unter Ausschluss von Philo und Josephus* (Hamburg-Volksdorf, 1954)
M. Smith Festschrift	Neusner, J., ed. *Christianity, Judaism and Other Greco-Roman Cults: Studies for Morton Smith at Sixty* (SJLA 12; Leiden, 1975)
NCE	McDonald, W.J., *et al.*, eds., *New Catholic Encyclopedia* (15 vols., New York, 1967–)
NHC	Nag Hammadi Codex
NHL	Nag Hammadi Library
NHS	Nag Hammadi Studies
NovT	*Novum Testamentum*

*NovT*Sup	*Novum Testamentum,* Supplements
NTA	*New Testament Abstracts*
NTAP	New Testament Apocrypha and Pseudepigrapha
NTS	*New Testament Studies*
NTTS	New Testament Tools and Studies
OCA	*Orientalia Christiana Analecta*
Or	*Orientalia*
OrChr	*Orientalia Christiana*
OrSyr	*L'Orient syrien*
OTM	Oxford Theological Monographs
OTS	Oudtestamentische Studiën
Pauly-Wissowa	Wissowa, G., *et al.,* eds., *Paulys Real-Encyclopädie der classischen Altertumswissenschaft,* new ed. (Stuttgart, Munich, 1893–1972)
PCB	Peake, A. S., M. Black and H. H. Rowley, eds., *Peake's Commentary on the Bible* (London, New York, 1962)
PEQ	*Palestine Exploration Quarterly*
PETSE	Papers of the Estonian Theological Society in Exile
Peshitta	*The Old Testament in Syriac According to the Peshitta Version* (Leiden, 1966–)
PG	Patrologiae graecae, ed. J. Migne
PIOL	Publications de l'institut orientaliste de Louvain
PL	Patrologiae latinae, ed. J. Migne
Pseud 1	Fritz, K. von ed., *Pseudepigrapha I: Pseudopythagorica, lettres de Platon, littérature pseudépigraphe juive* (Entretiens sur l'antiquité classique 18; Geneva, 1972)
PTS	Patristische Texte und Studien
PVTG	Pseudepigrapha Veteris Testamenti Graece
RAC	Klauser, T., *et al.,* eds., *Reallexikon für Antike und Christentum: Sachwörterbuch zur Auseinandersetzung des Christentums mit der antiken Welt* (Stuttgart, 1950–)
RB	*Revue biblique*
RBen	*Revue bénédictine*
RechBib	Recherches bibliques
REJ	*Revue des études juives*
RESl	*Revue des études slaves*
RevistB	*Revista bíblica*
RevSem	*Revue sémitique*
RevSR	*Revue des Sciences Religieuses*
*RGG*³	Galling, K., *et al.,* eds., *Die Religion in Geschichte und Gegenwart* (6 vols., plus index, Tübingen, 1957–65³)
RHPR	*Revue d'histoire et de philosophie religieuse*
RHR	*Revue de l'histoire des religions*
Riessler	Riessler, P., *Altjüdisches Schrifttum ausserhalb der Bibel* (Heidelberg, 1927; repr. 1966)
RivB	*Rivista biblica*
ROC	*Revue de l'orient chrétien*
RQ	*Revue de Qumran*
RSR	*Religious Studies Review*
RTP	*Revue de théologie et de philosophie*
SBFLA	*Studii biblici franciscani liber annuus*
SBLSBS	Society of Biblical Literature Sources for Biblical Study
SBLDS	Society of Biblical Literature Dissertation Series
SBLMS	Society of Biblical Literature Monograph Series
SBT	Studies in Biblical Theology

SC	Sources chrétiennes
SCS	Septuagint and Cognate Studies
ScEs	*Science et esprit*
SEA	*Svensk exegetisk Årsbok*
Sem	*Semitica*
Septuaginta	Rahlfs, A., ed., *Septuaginta: Id est Vetus Testamentum graece iuxta LXX interpretes* (2 vols., Stuttgart, 1935, repr. 1965)
SH	Scripta Hierosolymitana
SHR	Studies in the History of Religions
SJ	Studia Judaica
SJLA	Studies in Judaism in Late Antiquity
SJT	*Scottish Journal of Theology*
SNTS MS	*Studiorum Novi Testamenti Societas* Monograph Series
SOR	Studies in Oriental Religions
SPB	Studia postbiblica
ST	*Studia Theologica*
StANT	Studien zum Alten und Neuen Testament
Studien	Eltester, W., ed., *Studien zu den Testamenten der zwölf Patriarchen (BZNW 36; Berlin, 1969)*
SUNT	*Studien zur Umwelt des Neuen Testaments*
Sup *Numen*	Supplements to *Numen*
SVTP	Studia in Veteris Testamenti Pseudepigrapha
T&S	Texts and Studies
T&T	Texts and Translations
TBT	*The Bible Today*
TD	*Theology Digest*
TDNT	Kittel, G., ed., *Theological Dictionary of the New Testament* (10 vols., trans. G. W. Bromiley, Grand Rapids, Mich., London, 1964–76)
TED	Translations of Early Documents
TEH	Theologische Existenz Heute
THNT	Theologischer Handkommentar zum Neuen Testament
ThRu	*Theologische Rundschau*
THS	Textes pour l'histoire sacrée
TLZ	*Theologische Literaturzeitung*
TQ	*Theologische Quartalschrift*
TS	*Theological Studies*
TSJTSA	Texts and Studies of the Jewish Theological Seminary of America
TU	Texte und Untersuchungen
TWAT	Botterweck, G. J., and H. Ringgren, eds., *Theologisches Wörterbuch zum Alten Testament* (Stuttgart, 1970–)
TZ	*Theologische Zeitschrift*
USQR	*Union Seminary Quarterly Review*
VC	*Vigiliae christianae*
VT	*Vetus Testamentum*
WBC	Word Biblical Commentary
WF	Wege der Forschung
WUNT	Wissenschaftliche Untersuchungen zum Neuen Testament
WZHalle	*Wissenschaftliche Zeitschrift der Martin-Luther-Universität, Halle-Wittenberg, Gesellschafts- und Sprachwissenschaftliche Reihe*
WZJena	*Wissenschaftliche Zeitschrift der Friedrich-Schiller-Universität, Jena. Gesellschafts- und Sprachwissenschaftliche Reihe*
WZKM	*Wiener Zeitschrift für die Kunde des Morgenlandes*
ZAW	*Zeitschrift für die alttestamentliche Wissenschaft*

ZDMG	*Zeitschrift der deutschen morgenländischen Gesellschaft*
ZKG	*Zeitschrift für Kirchengeschichte*
ZNW	*Zeitschrift für die neutestamentliche Wissenschaft und die Kunde der älteren Kirche*
ZPEB	Tenney, M. C., ed., *The Zondervan Pictorial Encyclopedia of the Bible* (5 vols., Grand Rapids, Mich., 1975)
ZRGG	*Zeitschrift für Religions- und Geistesgeschichte*
ZTK	*Zeitschrift für Theologie und Kirche*
ZWT	*Zeitschrift für wissenschaftliche Theologie*

Additional Abbreviations

aor.	aorist
AB	Anchor Bible
Ar	Arabic
Aram	Aramaic
Arm	Armenian
BH	Biblia Hebraica
BT	Babylonian Talmud
c.	circa
ch(s).	chapter(s)
col(s).	column(s)
Cop	Coptic
ET	English translation
Eth	Ethiopic
fol(s).	folio(s)
Gk	Greek
Heb	Hebrew
inf.	infinitive
JB	Jerusalem Bible
Kar	Karshuni
KJV	King James Version
l. ll.	line(s)
Lat	Latin
lit.	literally
LXX	Septuagint
MS(S)	Manuscript(s)
MT	Masoretic Text
n. nn.	note(s)
Ni	Niphael
NAB	New American Bible
Russ	Russian
SBL	Society of Biblical Literature
Slav	Slavic
SNTS	*Studiorum Novi Testamenti Societas*
SV	Standard Version
Syr	Syriac
Vat.	Vatican

II. Ancient Documents

Bible and Apocrypha

Gen	Genesis
Ex	Exodus
Lev	Leviticus

Num	Numbers
Deut	Deuteronomy
Josh	Joshua
Judg	Judges
Ruth	Ruth
1 Sam	1 Samuel
2 Sam	2 Samuel
1 Kgs	1 Kings
2 Kgs	2 Kings
1 Chr	1 Chronicles
2 Chr	2 Chronicles
Ezra	Ezra
Neh	Nehemiah
Esth	Esther
Job	Job
Ps(s)	Psalms
Prov	Proverbs
Eccl (Qoh)	Ecclesiastes
Song	Song of Songs
Isa	Isaiah
Jer	Jeremiah
Lam	Lamentations
Ezek	Ezekiel
Dan	Daniel
Hos	Hosea
Joel	Joel
Amos	Amos
Obad	Obadiah
Jonah	Jonah
Micah	Micah
Nah	Nahum
Hab	Habakkuk
Zeph	Zephaniah
Hag	Haggai
Zech	Zechariah
Mal	Malachi
2 Ezra	2 Ezra
Tob	Tobit
Jdt	Judith
AddEsth	Additions to Esther
WisSol	Wisdom of Solomon
Sir	Sirach
1 Bar	1 Baruch
LetJer	Letter of Jeremiah
PrAzar	Prayer of Azariah
Sus	Susanna
Bel	Bel and the Dragon
1 Mac	1 Maccabees
2 Mac	2 Maccabees
Mt	Matthew
Mk	Mark
Lk	Luke
Jn	John
Acts	Acts

Rom	Romans
1 Cor	1 Corinthians
2 Cor	2 Corinthians
Gal	Galatians
Eph	Ephesians
Phil	Philippians
Col	Colossians
1 Thes	1 Thessalonians
2 Thes	2 Thessalonians
1 Tim	1 Timothy
2 Tim	2 Timothy
Tit	Titus
Phlm	Philemon
Heb	Hebrews
Jas	James
1 Pet	1 Peter
2 Pet	2 Peter
1 Jn	1 John
2 Jn	2 John
3 Jn	3 John
Jude	Jude
Rev	Revelation

Pseudepigrapha

ApAb	Apocalypse of Abraham
TAb	Testament of Abraham
ApAdam	Apocalypse of Adam
TAdam	Testament of Adam
LAE	Life of Adam and Eve
Ah	Ahiqar
AnonSam	An Anonymous Samaritan Text
LetAris	Letter of Aristeas
ArisEx	Aristeas the Exegete
Aristob	Aristobulus
Art	Artapanus
2 Bar	2 (Syriac Apocalypse of) Baruch
3 Bar	3 (Greek Apocalypse of) Baruch
4 Bar	4 Baruch
CavTr	Cave of Treasures
ClMal	Cleodemus Malchus
ApDan	Apocalypse of Daniel
Dem	Demetrius
ElMod	Eldad and Modad
ApEl	Apocalypse of Elijah
HebApEl	Hebrew Apocalypse of Elijah
1 En	1 (Ethiopic Apocalypse of) Enoch
2 En	2 (Slavonic Apocalypse of) Enoch
3 En	3 (Hebrew Apocalypse of) Enoch
Eup	Eupolemus
Ps-Eup	Pseudo-Eupolemus
ApocEzek	Apocryphon of Ezekiel
ApEzek	Apocalypse of Ezekiel
EzekTrag	Ezekiel the Tragedian
4 Ezra	4 Ezra

GkApEzra	Greek Apocalypse of Ezra
QuesEzra	Questions of Ezra
RevEzra	Revelation of Ezra
VisEzra	Vision of Ezra
HecAb	Hecataeus of Abdera
Ps-Hec	Pseudo-Hecataeus
HelSynPr	Hellenistic Synagogal Prayers
THez	Testament of Hezekiah
FrgsHistWrks	Fragments of Historical Works
TIsaac	Testament of Isaac
AscenIs	Ascension of Isaiah
MartIs	Martyrdom of Isaiah
VisIs	Vision of Isaiah
LadJac	Ladder of Jacob
PrJac	Prayer of Jacob
TJac	Testament of Jacob
JanJam	Jannes and Jambres
TJob	Testament of Job
JosAsen	Joseph and Aseneth
HistJos	History of Joseph
PrJos	Prayer of Joseph
Jub	Jubilees
LAB	*Liber Antiquitatum Biblicarum*
LosTr	The Lost Tribes
3 Mac	3 Maccabees
4 Mac	4 Maccabees
5 Mac	5 Maccabees
PrMan	Prayer of Manasseh
SyrMen	Syriac Menander
ApMos	Apocalypse of Moses
AsMos	Assumption of Moses
PrMos	Prayer of Moses
TMos	Testament of Moses
BkNoah	Book of Noah
Ps-Orph	Pseudo-Orpheus
PJ	*Paraleipomena Jeremiou*
PhEPoet	Philo the Epic Poet
Ps-Philo	Pseudo-Philo
Ps-Phoc	Pseudo-Phocylides
FrgsPoetWrks	Fragments of Poetical Works
LivPro	Lives of the Prophets
HistRech	History of the Rechabites
ApSedr	Apocalypse of Sedrach
TrShem	Treatise of Shem
SibOr	Sibylline Oracles
OdesSol	Odes of Solomon
PssSol	Psalms of Solomon
TSol	Testament of Solomon
5 ApocSyrPss	Five Apocryphal Syriac Psalms
Thal	Thallus
Theod	Theodotus
T12P	Testaments of the Twelve Patriarchs
TReu	Testament of Reuben
TSim	Testament of Simeon

TLevi	Testament of Levi
TJud	Testament of Judah
TIss	Testament of Issachar
TZeb	Testament of Zebulun
TDan	Testament of Dan
TNaph	Testament of Naphtali
TGad	Testament of Gad
TAsh	Testament of Asher
TJos	Testament of Joseph
TBenj	Testament of Benjamin
Vita	*Vita Adae et Evae*
ApZeph	Apocalypse of Zephaniah
ApZos	Apocalypse of Zosimus

Dead Sea Scrolls

Abbreviations are according to J. A. Fitzmyer, S. J. *The Dead Sea Scrolls: Major Publications and Tools for Study* (SBLSBS 8; Missoula, Mont., 1975, 1977^2)

CD	Cairo Damascus Document
1QS	The Rule of the Community
1QSa	The Rule of the Congregation
1QapGen	A Genesis Apocryphon
1QM	The War Scroll
1QpHab	The Habakkuk Commentary
2Q24, 5Q15, 4QJN, 11QJN	Description of the New Jerusalem
2QapMoses	Apocryphon of Moses
3Q15	The Copper Scroll
4QpIs	The Isaiah Commentary
4QJer^b	Jeremiah
4QWiles	Wiles of the Wicked Woman
4QAgesCreat	Ages of Creation
4QCryptic	An Astrological Cryptic Document
4QPrNab	Prayer of Nabonidus
4Q 'Amram^{b-e}	Visions of 'Amram or 'Testament' of 'Amram
4QŠirŠabb	Angelic Liturgy
11QPs^{a,b}	The Psalms Scroll
11QPsAp	The Apocryphal Psalms in the Psalms Scroll
11QTgJob	A Targum of Job
11QMelch	The Melkisedek Scroll
11QTemple	The Temple Scroll

'Dead Sea Scroll' Pseudepigrapha

Jubilees (see chapter 2, n. 35)

1QJub^{a,b}	Jubilees
2Q19 (2QJub^a)	Jubilees
2Q20 (2QJub^a)	Jubilees
3Q5 (3QJub)	Jubilees
4QJub^{e,f}	Jubilees
11QJub 1–5	Jubilees
11QJub M 2	Jubilees
11QJub M 3	Jubilees

Testaments of the Twelve Patriarchs (see chapter 2, nn. 25, 26, 28)

1QTLevi ar	A Testament of Levi
4QTLevi ar[a]	A Testament of Levi
Aramaic Enoch	(not yet clearly arranged with acknowledged sigla; see chapter 2, nn. 22, 25)
4QHenAstr[a-d]	1 (Aramaic) Enoch
4QEn[c,e]	1 (Aramaic) Enoch
4QHenGiants[a-f]	Book of the Giants

Philo

All abbreviations are according to *Studia Philonica*

Josephus

Ant	*Jewish Antiquities*
Apion	*Against Apion*
Life	*Life of Josephus*
War	*Jewish Wars*

New Testament Apocrypha and Pseudepigrapha

EBar	Epistle of Barnabas
GBart	Gospel of Bartholomew
QuesBart	Questions of Bartholomew
1 Clem	1 Clement
2 Clem	2 Clement
PseudClemRec	Pseudo-Clementine Recognitions
Did	Didache
GEbion	Gospel of the Ebionites
GEgyp	Gospel of the Egyptians
GHeb	Gospel of the Hebrews
ShepHerm	Shepherd of Hermes
ApIoan	*Apokalypsis tou hagiou Ioannou*
ProtJames	Protoevangelium of James
ActsJn	Acts of John
GMatthias	Gospel of Matthias
GNic	Gospel of Nicodemus
ActsPaul	Acts of Paul
ApPaul	Apocalypse of Paul
ApPet	Apocalypse of Peter
GPet	Gospel of Peter
PrPet	Preaching of Peter
ActsPhil	Acts of Philip
GPhil	Gospel of Philip
ActPil	Acts of Pilate
RevSteph	Revelation of Stephen
ActsThom	Acts of Thomas
ApThom	Apocalypse of Thomas
GThom	Gospel of Thomas
GTr	Gospel of Truth
ApVirg	Apocalypse of the Virgin

Early Fathers

AdvHaer	Epiphanius, *Adversus haereses*
AposCon	Apostolic Constitutions
CommGen	Procopius of Gaza, *Commentary on Genesis*, Part I

CommIsa	Basil Caesar, *Commentary on Isaiah*
CommJn	Origen, *Commentary on the Gospel of St. John*
DialTrypho	Justin, *Dialogue with Trypho*
DivInst	Lactantius, *Divine Institutes*
EpJE	Didymas the Blind, *In Ep. Judae Enarratio*
ExcerPss	Origen, *Excerpta in Psalmos*
HE	Eusebius, *Historia ecclesiastica*
HebQuaestinLib-Gen	Jerome, *Hebrew Questions on the Book of Genesis*
Hom	Macarius, *Spiritual Homilies*
Paid	Clement of Alexandria, *The Tutor (Paidagōgos)*
Philoc	Origen, *Philocalia*
PrEv	Eusebius, *Praeparatio evangelica*
Princ	Origen, *De principiis*
Ref	Hippolytus, *Refutation of All Heresies*
Strom	Clement of Alexandria, *Stromata*

Rabbinics

Ab	Abot
ARN	Abot de-Rabbi Nathan
AZ	'Abodah Zarah
b. (before a rabbinic text)	Babylonian Talmud
BB	Baba Batra
Bek	Bekorot
Ber	Berakot
BHM	Bet ha-Midrasch
Bikk	Bikkurim
BM	Batei Midrashot
BMes	Baba Meṣi'a (Talmudic tractate)
DeutR	Debarim Rabbah
EcclR	Qohelet Rabbah
'Eduy	'Eduyyot
'Erub	'Erubin
ExR	Šemot Rabbah
GedMos	Gedulah Moshe
GenR	Bere'šit Rabbah
Giṭṭ	Giṭṭin
Ḥag	Ḥagigah
Ḥall	Ḥallah
Ḥull	Ḥullin
Ker	Keritot
Ket	Ketubot
Kid	Kiddushin
LamR	Ekah Rabbah
LevR	Wayyiqra Rabbah
m (before a rabbinic text)	Mishnah
Makk	Makkot
Meg	Megillah
Men	Menaḥot
Mik	Mikwa'ot
MK	Mo'ed Katan
Naz	Nazir

Ned	Nedarim
Nidd	Niddah
NumR	Bemidbar Rabbah
OM	Ozar Midrashim
Pes	Pesaḥim
PetMos	Petiroth Moshe
PR	Pesikta Rabbati
PRE	Pirke de-Rabbi Eliezer
RH	Rosh Hashanah
RuthR	Rut Rabbah
Sanh	Sanhedrin
SER	Seder Eliyahu Rabbah
Shab	Shabbat
SifDeut	Sifre Deuteronomy
SongR	Šir Hašširim Rabbah
Soṭ	Sotah
Sukk	Sukkah
t. (before a rabbinic text)	Tosephta
Ta 'an	Ta 'anit
TargOnk	Targum Onkelos
TargYer	Targum Yerushalmi
TarJon	Targum Jonathan
Ter	Terumot
y. (before a rabbinic text)	Jerusalem Talmud
Yad	Yadayim
Yeb	Yebamot
Zeb	Zebahim

INTRODUCTION

The present monograph contains my attempts to assess the significance of the documents in the Old Testament Pseudepigrapha for a
better understanding of Early Judaism, Christian Origins, and especially the writings in the New Testament. Chapter 1 is a revision
of a plenary lecture delivered at Atlanta, Georgia, in the Spring of
1983 to the Southeast Section of the American Academy of Religion.
Chapters 2 and 3 are expanded versions of a plenary address presented
at Canterbury, England, in the Summer of 1983 to the *SNTS*. In order
to reach not only specialists but also students I have deleted much
of the technical language, lengthened some discussions, provided a
Glossary, and added a Bibliography (with subheadings to guide
further research and study).

As we attempt to apprehend the *essentia* dynamically poured into
the documents in the Pseudepigrapha, let us remember that the
historia (cf. LSJM, p. 842) — both 'histories' and 'stories' so pregnant
in the Greek — were often first circulating for centuries within the
familiar circle round the evening fire. Warmth poured from the
incandescent light of the hearth and from vibrant legends in their
living oral form (cf. Chapter 3, 'Comparing One Document with
Many Others', pp. 78–80). The need to tell stories animated the con-
versations in the varied Palestinian settings; despite oppressions by
foreign overlords, the innate need resounded. R. Price, thinking on
'The Origins and Life of Narrative' pens thoughts germane to our
endeavour:

> A need to tell and hear stories is essential to the species *Homo*
> *sapiens* — second in necessity apparently after nourishment
> and before love and shelter. Millions survive without love
> or home, almost none in silence; the opposite of silence leads
> quickly to narrative, and the sound of story is the dominant
> sound of our lives.[1]

Some of the stories cherished by Jews lived on because of their religious dimension, or because of their subsequent association with religious fervour, perhaps due to their significance for the *shebe'al peh* as well as the *Torah shebikhtabh*; the memorized moved towards the written. Any thoughts on the comparisons between the Pseudepigrapha documents and the New Testament writings must be prefaced by the attempt to perceive what it would have been like to hear a charismatic person tell· *historia*, not only on the hillside with the multitudes but also around the fire in the evening.

Eventually, for reasons historians cannot explain satisfactorily, the stories grew and some were recorded for us to read. But once written, the context and setting is not preserved. The non-transferable linguistic dimensions of the eye,[2] the spontaneous gesture, and the echoing laughter were left behind as the traditions became formalized on leather skins. Once written, the stories can fall into the hands of others; the sacred can be touched by the profane. Perhaps this fear is partly responsible for the idea of the *hidden* seventy books (4 Ezra 14:44–7; cf. 1 En 9:61), and the belief that the evil angel Pinem'e taught mankind how to write:

> Furthermore he caused the people to penetrate (the secret of) writing and (the use of) ink and paper, on account of this matter, there are many who have erred from eternity to eternity, until this very day. For human beings are not created for such purposes to take up their beliefs with pen and ink.
>
> (1 En 69:9–10)[3]

There is evidence, therefore, to suggest an oral stage for many stories (and songs) in the Pseudepigrapha. To camouflage this insight with interjections that some pseudepigrapha come from very erudite scholars is to miss the mark: some pseudepigrapha do reflect the Jewish joy of telling stories and reciting history, others mirror the refined setting of scholarly circles, yet even the wise inherited traditions that had been shaped by many factors, including the love of and the need to recite *historia* and engage each other in narratives. The emphasis on narrative and the need to narrate is related to the injunction to write found in some apocalypses (cf. e.g. 1 En 89:62–4, 104: 7–13).

If mankind is over three million years old, and the earliest evidence of real writing is barely five thousand years old, then it took us an incredibly long time to learn to write and to record *historia*. As quickly as we ask, 'Why did it take so long?' we are impeded from answering by another question: 'Why did we do it at all?' With the 'invention' of writing, even before alphabetic script,[4] we are known to have been fascinated by stories. Some of the significant early ones affected the *Geschichte* that unfolds in the Old Testament, others are lost forever; a very few early Jewish ones affected and perhaps were incorporated into the writings brought together in *The Old Testament Pseudepigrapha* (2 vols., Garden City, N.Y., 1983–5). These ancient and fluid traditions swirled around, even buoyed up the authors, compilers and redactors of the Jewish writings from 200 B.C.E. to 200 C.E. It is this living world of traditions, this *Zeitgeist* and *Lebenswelt*, that helped produce and relate those documents that became separated and are now collected into the Old Testament Pseudepigrapha and the Greek New Testament. To remove two or more books from their present place in an artificial collection is not to sever them from an umbilical cord; it may be to move them closer together and ideally back into a thought-world that reflects the attempt to appropriate what can never be recovered. That task is our journey, if not our goal. It is the presupposition for any trustworthy and truthful comparison. It is the whole, and not abstracted selections, that must be sought.

Realizing that attempts at such comparisons as ours will undoubtedly be judged harshly – we are trained for years to criticize and to debate – I confess my frustrations and self-doubts. Little do I know, and much must I yet learn. I apologize for the infelicities at the moment unseen, but soon to be revealed by critics. Nevertheless, I have attempted to initiate a better way of performing our craft. In this small work I am trying to accomplish numerous purposes, namely I am attempting:

(1) to sketch the history of research on the Old Testament Pseudepigrapha, especially from Fabricius to the present, in order to clarify major methodological and perceptual developments, and to reveal how social histories and ideologies have excited or deflated research;

(2) to draw attention to a vast area for fruitful research in our ongoing search for the meaning of the writings in the New Testament, and the Jewish origins of Christianity;

(3) to instil in New Testament specialists an appreciation for the erudition and sophistication in early Jewish literature;

(4) to polemicize against any attempt to celebrate Christian truths at the expense of Judaism, and to point to a lingering tendency among some scholars, even some brilliant ones (and cherished

friends), to treat as inferior the Jewish literature that much later was declared 'uncanonical';

(5) to show that Jewish literature, like the writings in the New Testament, must be read *thoroughly, sympathetically* and *reflectively* before any attempt is made to compare them with so-called Christian documents, and that any comparison between two very similar 'religions' — such as Early Judaism and Early Christianity — must compare ideas, symbols and words in their full living context;

(6) to point to the inadequacies of such terms as 'sectarian', 'normative', 'orthodox' and 'heretical';

(7) to expose a shared error among New Testament scholars in their approach to 1 Enoch and the Testaments of the Twelve Patriarchs;

(8) to suggest a methodology for studying and assessing parallels between two documents;

(9) to illustrate briefly some of the significance of the Old Testament Pseudepigrapha for understanding and dating some New Testament writings;

(10) to encourage more New Testament scholars through the publication of the proceedings of the *SNTS* Pseudepigrapha seminars and through personal observations to join with the specialists who have demonstrated clearly the significance of the Pseudepigrapha for Christian origins and for the New Testament documents;

(11) to contend that earliest Christian thought was intellectually sophisticated and that high Christology does not indicate late chronology;

(12) to call for a reassessment of what we mean by canonical and apocryphal, divine inspiration and perspicacious speculation.

In the attempt to move closer to the ancient authors and to grasp their needs and dreams it is essential to be ever self-critical of who we are and from where we are coming, and to struggle for a sensitive *indwelling* of their world.[5] While we are primarily occupied with their bequeathed *words* we must always endeavour to supplement the received words with other non-literary artefacts and archaeological discoveries, and to define words broadly, *inter alia*, in terms of their essence, their content, their function, and their social setting. I presume that they, like we, struggled towards an intended meaning, not scouring around in search of words, but by flowing through perception and intentionality to communication.[6] Words, after all, come somewhat mysteriously as we shuttle between worlds of silence. Since most words in the Pseudepigrapha have not yet influenced our lexicons, and since most of the ancient Semitic words disappeared when Hebrew and Aramaic died out,[7] it is unwise to support arguments or develop ideas by myopically citing lexicographical data. It is the living word, not the dead record of how it was employed in a few surviving texts, that alone can open our eyes to that world two thousand or so years ago when the documents in the Pseudepigrapha and in the New Testament were being composed and read aloud.

1

THE PSEUDEPIGRAPHA: NEW OPPORTUNITIES AND CHALLENGES FOR THE BIBLICAL SCHOLAR

Introduction

After eleven years of research, writing and co-operation by an international team of experts the two-volumed *Old Testament Pseudepigrapha* will appear in 1983 and 1985.[1] This event provides us with the opportunity to scan the modern study of these early Jewish documents, and to evaluate their significance for biblical scholars.

The Modern Study of the Pseudepigrapha

Prior to the eighteenth century some of the works in the Pseudepigrapha received considerable attention, primarily because they were perceived as authentically attributed to the eponymous author who was also seen to have advocated truths in harmony with the Bible. Pseudo-Phocylides was used as a textbook in many medieval schools; the *editio princeps* appeared in 1495 (Venice), and many editions were published in the sixteenth century. Similarly, editions of the Sibylline Oracles were published by Betuleius in 1545, by Opsopoeus in 1599, and by Servatius from 1687 to 1689.

The Period of the Precursor (1722–1820)

(1) *Prelude: Pre-Eighteenth-Century Interest (Erasmus, Luther and the Polyglots)*

Erasmus showed considerable interest in 4 Maccabees, perhaps because he had been fearing his own martyrdom. He completed an edition of the Greek text in 1517 and published it in 1524. Two years later Cephalaeus published another Greek text of 4 Maccabees; his edition is often called the *editio princeps* of this document. Martin Luther was very pleased with the Prayer of Manasseh (in the new edition of the Pseudepigrapha and also in collections of the Apocrypha), which he could not put into the canon, preferring it to the Epistle of

James, which he could not excise from the canon. He translated this pseudepigraphon into German, and utilized it in his polemic against the Duke of Braunschweig. Luther urged him to repent, and to beseech God 'with words such as those that appear in the Prayer of Manasseh'.[2]

During the fifteenth and sixteenth centuries, however, scholars' interest was not really in the Pseudepigrapha; it was only in some individual writings now assembled under that title. For example, the Latin Bible of Johannez Brenz, published at Tübingen in 1564, contained 3 Maccabees, as B.M. Metzger has recently pointed out.[3] Further examples of this interest in a few individual pseudepigrapha is represented in the great Polyglot Bibles of the sixteenth and seventeenth centuries; these tomes incorporated only a few of the writings in the Pseudepigrapha. This work on some early Jewish writings preceded the modern study of the Pseudepigrapha, which I have divided into five periods.

(2) *The Precursor: J.A. Fabricius*

The first period was from the early eighteenth century until the early nineteenth century. The European Enlightenment of the seventeenth and eighteenth centuries ushered in a vigorous awareness of the penetrating powers of human reason and an appreciation of the importance of man's intellectual accomplishments in antiquity. A product of this intense vitality is the publication in Greek and Latin of some early Jewish documents by J.A. Fabricius. He published the first major collection of the Pseudepigrapha, a two-volumed work, which was entitled *Codex pseudepigraphus Veteris Testamenti*, and which appeared in 1722 and 1723. Fabricius bequeathed to us two legacies: the concept of a collection in two volumes, and the ponderous − unfortunately misrepresentative − term 'Pseudepigrapha'. This first phase in modern research on the Pseudepigrapha should be called the period of the precursor.

Fabricius was a forerunner of modern research on the Pseudepigrapha; but his work did not immediately spawn numerous and significant studies on the Pseudepigrapha, and it predates the explosion of new discoveries of ancient manuscripts. It would be one century before his pioneering insights would be followed by a phalanx of scholars. In the interval there were only a few enlightened followers, notably Sabatier who, in 1749, published a Latin edition of 4 Ezra, and Mai who, in 1817, issued a Greek text of the Sibylline Oracles.

The Nineteenth-Century Awakening (1821–1913)

(1) *The Near East is Rediscovered*

The explosion of interest began shortly after the crushing defeat of Napolean at Waterloo (18 June 1815). It followed the rediscovery of the fascinating aspects of the Near East, new appetites and realizations brought home by Napolean's conquests in Africa, and then Britain's involvement in Egypt and the Levant.

In the first half of the nineteenth century large crates full of manuscripts arrived at the major European libraries, notably the Bibliothèque Nationale in Paris and the British Museum in London. Certainly one of the most sensational discoveries was the recovery of the Book of Enoch in the Ethiopic language. The Book of Enoch was known in antiquity and even quoted in one of the New Testament writings, the Epistle of Jude; but it was lamented in the West as a lost book.

(2) *J. Bruce, R. Laurence and 1 Enoch*

Three manuscripts of the Book Enoch were discovered in Abyssinia by James Bruce who brought them to Europe in 1773; but it was not until 1821 that R. Laurence published an English translation of so-called 1 Enoch. In 1833 A. G. Hoffmann published a German translation based partly on Laurence's English and partly on the Ethiopic. In 1838 Laurence issued an Ethiopic text, based on only one manuscript; in 1851 A. Dillmann issued a text based on five Ethiopic manuscripts; two years later he published a German translation.

While the best scholars thought that Ethiopic Enoch was a medieval version of a lost early Jewish document, it was not possible to disprove the lingering claims by Lücke (1832), Hofmann (1852), Weisse (1856), and Philippi (1868) that a Christian scribe had composed the Book of Enoch. It was not until the second half of the twentieth century that this claim was decisively put to rest; again the proof came with another momentous discovery. Pre-Christian Aramaic fragments of 1 Enoch were recovered among the Dead Sea Scrolls; one of the fragments contains the passage quoted by Jude (see Chapter 3).

(3) *L'Abbé Migne*

The period of great awakening soon saw the publication of the second major collection of the Pseudepigrapha, it is L'Abbé Migne's two-volumed *Dictionnaire des apocryphes, ou collection de tous les livres apocryphes relatifs à l'ancien et au nouveau testament*. Migne's work, which appeared in 1856 and 1858, did not contain the term 'Pseudepigrapha', because he was a Roman Catholic who affirmed that the Protestant's Apocrypha were deuterocanonical works, hence the so-called Pseudepigrapha were to him Apocrypha. This confused nomenclature unfortunately still lingers to mislead the cursory reader.

Migne's work was followed by a cascade of publications, most notable among these were editions of the pseudepigraphical books. Texts were produced by prominent scholars in Austria, Italy, Russia, France, Britain, and especially in Germany. From 1850 to 1900 more than fifty editions of the documents in the Pseudepigrapha were published and, as reprints witness and translators affirm, many of these editions are still considered reliable, even at times indispensable. The quantity of these editions is impressive; from 1850 to 1900 at least one edition on average appeared each year.

(4) *R. H. Charles and E. Kautzsch*

This scholarly activity on the continent attracted the interest of a brilliant Irish scholar, who in 1889 went to Germany to study the apocalyptic thought preserved in the Pseudepigrapha. In Germany he studied in Weimar, Dresden, Leipzig and Berlin; he discussed the Jewish apocalypses with the German scholars, notably T. Zahn and the luminary of that time, Dillmann. Upon his return to England, this scholar, R. H. Charles,[4] published within five years reliable editions on the Greek of 1 Enoch (1893), the Ethiopic of 1 Enoch (1893), Jubilees (1895), 2 Baruch (1896), and the Testament of Moses (1897).

The need grew for a collection of the Pseudepigrapha in translation. It was partly met in 1900 by E. Kautzsch's two-volumed work, titled *Die Apocryphen und Pseudepigraphen des Alten Testaments* (Tübingen). This work is the third great collection. The fourth, an English version, was not long in coming. It was published in 1913 by Charles himself, and is the two-volumed work on the shelves of almost every distinguished English-speaking biblical scholar. The work is the monumental *The Apocrypha and Pseudepigrapha of the Old Testament in English*.

The German and English versions of the Pseudepigrapha tended to be conceived as the definitive collections of the Pseudepigrapha. This tendency was unfortunate, and is partly the fault of Kautzsch and Charles who, in comparison with Fabricius and Migne, were far too selective, especially in light of the abundance of pseudepigrapha edited in the nineteenth century. In fairness to them, however, it is wise to call their selections the last two major collections of the Pseudepigrapha. As Paul never intended his letters to become part of sacred scripture, so Kautzsch and Charles never attempted to delimit the works in the Pseudepigrapha, or intended their collections to dominate the scholarly community as they certainly have for the last seven decades. An attempt to explain this monopoly leads us into the next period of modern research on the Pseudepigrapha.

Dark Clouds over 'Intertestamental' Judaism (1914–1949)

(1) *The World-Wide Psychosis*

One year after the publication of Charles' collection the Victorian dream came crashing down; the impossible occurred. Charles completed his 'Preface' in Oxford in March 1913; Francis Ferdinand was assassinated in Sarajevo in June 1914. For the first time in the history of man almost all nations on earth were entwined in a global war, eventually and unfortunately to be labelled the First World War. A great cloud not only obscured any research on the Pseudepigrapha, it threatened to obliterate civilization. The Syriac Apocalypse of Baruch vividly depicted the Jewish crises of the late first century in language disturbingly appropriate to the Great War:

> And it happened at the end of the cloud that, behold, it poured black water and it was much darker than all the water that had been before. And fire was mingled with it. And where that water descended, it brought about devastation and destruction.   (2 Bar 53:7)[5]

The Great War directly or ultimately produced enduring problems, most significant among these were the establishment of communism in Russia, the world-wide depression, the appearance of 'einem der größten Demagogen aller Zeiten',[6] the Nazi scourge, and finally the Second World War. Hence, I have labelled the period from 1914 to 1949 as the period of dark clouds over 'intertestamental' Judaism.

(2) *Orthodox Bias Against the Pseudepigrapha*

Only one black cloud has been mentioned briefly, namely the world-wide psychosis. Another equally acid cloud preventing the growth of pseudepigrapha research was the orthodox bias rampant in seminaries, universities, and even academies. Interest in the Pseudepigrapha was very much the by-product of the preoccupation with the theology of the Bible. These documents were important only because of the bridge they tended to provide, no matter how obscurely, between 'the two sacred and canonical collections of God's holy word'. It is obvious why the favourite term for these early Jewish works became 'the intertestamental writings'. The Pseudepigrapha was categorized and relegated, to be brought forward only to illustrate a theme, like the messianic kingdom and its banquet, a term, like the Son of Man, or a concept, like the belief in the bodily resurrection of the individual after death. The Pseudepigrapha contained writings not to be understood, but to be mined (or to put it perhaps too harshly, not to be loved but to be used as Dinah was by Shechem; cf. Gen 34:2, Levi 6:5–8).

(3) *Denigration, Relegation and Compartmentalization*

Three facets of the lack of work on the Pseudepigrapha during this period, 1914 to 1949, are represented by three words: denigration, relegation and compartmentalization. First, the documents in the Pseudepigrapha were subjected to denigration; they were conceived as sectarian writings on the fringes of a ruling orthodoxy that was centralized in Jerusalem and would evolve into normative, rabbinic Judaism. And for Jewish scholars there was no impetus to look at books branded by the Tannaim as *sepharim ḥiẓonim*, that is, as G. Vermes states, to use 'books beyond the pale of religious influence and not meriting to be preserved'.[7]

Second, the Pseudepigrapha suffered relegation. The preoccupation of biblical scholars was now with theology and many flirted with existentialism. Certainly this attitude was true of the most influential New Testament scholar, Rudolph Bultmann, and his school. The proper study of the New Testament specialist was the kerygma; the appropriate perception was that the gospels were post-Easter confessions produced by the *Sitz im Glauben* of the early communities. Hindsight discloses the insight that scholars had been more faithful to Kähler[8] than to kerygma, and more sensitive to ideological forms than to historical norms.

Third, the Pseudepigrapha endured compartmentalization. They were categorized behind the label 'intertestamental stuff' and judged minuscule beneath the canon. As the Synagogue and the Church rejected them from the canon, so the learned elite tended to remove them from their central files.

It is abundantly clear why Kautzsch's and Charles' collections were not rivalled. There were neither financial resources nor mental energies available to accomplish the task. There was a marked waning of interest in sacrificing so much on so little.[9] Hence, we also grasp why a second edition never appeared of either Kautzsch or Charles; moreover, a Charles *redivivus* became virtually unthinkable.

The Twentieth-Century Re-Awakening (1950–1982)

(1) *New Beginnings*

With the end of the Second World War there were many new beginnings in Europe, Asia, and elsewhere; most notably the establishment of apartheid in South Africa, the creation of Israel, and the appearance of Pakistan. Winds of change were felt blowing almost everywhere, especially by those prominent and scholarly enough to sense the climactic changes emanating from Nag Hammadi and Qumran. All of these heterogeneous forces effectively mark a new period in the modern study of the Pseudepigrapha; from 1950 to 1982 is the period of the twentieth-century re-awakening.

(2) *The Remarkable Discovery of the Dead Sea Scrolls*

The reason for the renewed interest in the Pseudepigrapha during this period is usually explained by the discovery of hitherto unknown ancient Jewish documents in the caves to the west of the Dead Sea. Certainly there is much that can be said for this explanation;[10] some Pseudepigrapha, namely 1 Enoch, Jubilees, and an earlier version perhaps of the Testaments of the Twelve Patriarchs, were found in fragments among the Dead Sea Scrolls (see Chapter 2). In 1950 M. Burrows, J. C. Trever and W. H. Brownlee launched the first edition of the scrolls; the series was entitled 'The Dead Sea Scrolls of St. Mark's Monastery'. The importance of the discovery of the scrolls for a rejuvenated interest in the Pseudepigrapha should not be minimalized; but at times it has been the only explanation offered. I can think of another major reason.

(3) *An Acknowledged Bankruptcy in Biblical Theology and the Perception of* Geschichte.

An equally important cause of the renewed interest in the study of the Pseudepigrapha is the perception of the vast problems involved in any attempt to define, or even describe, biblical theology, and this recognition demands much more than merely improving on past methods and presuppositions. Two factors are most significant: First, the pure theological and ideological approach to the Bible had run its course and was found wanting. In the late 40s and early 50s quite independently and without apparent knowledge of the others' position P. Benoit, N. Dahl and E. Käsemann suggested that there is history in the gospels, that there is tradition in the kerygma, and that it is possible and theologically legitimate to search for *bruta facta* in Jesus' life and for *ipsissima verba Jesu*.[11]

Second, the incisive discovery of biblical theologians was that Israel, unlike the other nations, confessed a relationship between God and history. At first the major recognition was only that *Heilsgeschichte* meant that Israel's history was sacred; eventually it also included a recognition of *Geschichte* as also the sphere of God's action. History was the proper study for biblical scholars; and this entailed a return to the history of Early Judaism which included her literature, especially the Pseudepigrapha. As earlier, we can see three significant emphases in this renewed interest: the appearance of the term 'Christian Origins', a broader perspective, and a fresh appreciation.

(4) *'Christian Origins', Perspective and Appreciation*

The renewed interest in the Pseudepigrapha coincided with the appearance of the term 'Christian Origins'. The older terms, 'intertestamental period', became more and more inappropriate to denote the period from 200 B.C.E. to 200 C.E. It was simply inaccurate; the youngest book in the Old Testament is Daniel, which dates from around 165 B.C.E., and the oldest writing in the New Testament is 1 Thessalonians, which dates from near 50 C.E. Hence, 'intertestamental' had been used to denote both the decades before Daniel and the century in which the New Testament writings were composed. The term is also demeaning; it suggests that the Jewish literature in these centuries is inferior to that in the canon, and important only because of the documents' meaning for other writings, namely those that were later eventually claimed to be scriptural. Finally, the term 'intertestamental' belies a Christian bias and confessional belief in two testaments. After 1950 many institutions of higher learning began to use a new title for their resident scholars in this field. Those who had been titled professors of intertestamental Judaism were often now called professors of Christian Origins, or professors of Early Judaism, or a similar title. Martin Hengel, for example, is Professor of New Testament and Early Judaism in the Eberhard-Karls-Universität, Tübingen.

The second emphasis is a broader conception of sources. The feverish activity and preoccupation with the Dead Sea Scrolls was followed by a similar focus upon the fifty-two Nag Hammadi treatises, and upon the fifty-two documents in the Old Testament Pseudepigrapha. This shift by biblical scholars demanded a concomitant commitment to Coptic, Syriac, Latin, Ethiopic, Old Church Slavonic and Armenian, as well as to the more traditional languages, Hebrew, Aramaic and Greek. Now almost all biblical scholars recognize that a study of the New Testament must include the sources contemporaneous with it.

The third emphasis is a fresh appreciation of the Jewish writings in the Pseudepigrapha. These works represented the cherished traditions and beliefs of many early Jews. The documents were not to be branded as sectarian, since it now becomes very clear that Early Judaism was not defined by a controlling, centralized, normative and orthodox Judaism (see chapter 2).

Especially significant for an understanding of Early Judaism and Christian Origins is the recognition of Jewish apocalyptic thought and the apocalypses themselves. H.H. Rowley's *The Relevance of Apocalyptic*, first published in 1944, with new editions in 1947 and 1963, was a forerunner of this new approach and appreciation. Soon to follow were the major works by S.B. Frost in 1952, D.S. Russell in 1964, J. Schreiner in 1969, J.M. Schmidt in 1969 and 1976, K. Koch in 1970 and 1972 (ET), W. Schmithals in 1973 and 1975, and P.D. Hanson in 1975 and 1979. From Bultmann's own school we even hear the claim by E. Käsemann that apocalyptic thought is the mother of all Christian theology.[12] As Charles' edition was inspired by a keen interest in eschatology, certainly stressed in the brilliant publications by A. Schweitzer, so the new English edition of the Pseudepigrapha has been buoyed up by a phenomenal interest in Jewish apocalyptic claims and perspectives, palpably highlighted in the striking claim by E. Käsemann.

The western Christian canon contains only two apocalypses, Daniel and Revelation; the new edition of the Pseudepigrapha contains in its first section, 'Apocalyptic Literature and Related Works', the following nineteen documents: 1 Enoch, 2 Enoch, 3 Enoch, Sibylline Oracles, Treatise of Shem, Apocryphon of Ezekiel, Apocalypse of Zephaniah, The Fourth Book of Ezra, Greek Apocalypse of Ezra, Vision of Ezra, Questions of Ezra, Revelation of Ezra, Apocalypse of Sedrach, 2 Baruch, 3 Baruch, Apocalypse of Abraham, Apocalypse of Adam, Apocalypse of Elijah, and Apocalypse of Daniel.

(5) *A Need for Texts, Translations and Collections*

During the period 1950 to 1982 scholars felt the need for reliable texts and translations of the Pseudepigrapha. In 1953 J. Bonsirven published *La Bible Apocryphe* (THS; Paris, 1953; repr. 1975). This French collection is not as inclusive as Migne's work, but it does contain extracts of nine pseudepigrapha. Also in 1953 E. Hammershaimb launched in Denmark the fascicles on the Pseudepigrapha that appeared periodically under the title *De Gammeltestamentlige Pseudepigrafer*. These are now bound in two volumes (Kopenhagen, 1953–63; 1970–6). A new German translation was organized under the direction of W. G. Kümmel and the first two fascicles of *Jüdische Schriften aus hellenistisch-römischer Zeit* appeared in 1973. The same year saw the first collection of translations into modern Greek by S. Agourides. It is titled *Ta Apokryphen tēs Palaias Diathēkēs* (Athens, 1973). A.-M. Denis and M. de Jonge in 1970 launched two major series *Pseudepigrapha Veteris Testamenti Graece*, and *Studia in Veteris Testamenti Pseudepigrapha*. The first volume in the latter series contained the first introduction to the Pseudepigrapha, namely Denis' *Introduction*.

Specialists in America launched the SBL Pseudepigrapha Newsletter, and two series in 1972, namely the Texts and Translations: Pseudepigrapha Series, and the Septuagint and Cognate Studies. The seventh volume in the latter series in 1976 contained *The Pseudepigrapha and Modern Research*, and then five years later in 1981 *The Pseudepigrapha and Modern Research with a Supplement*. The year 1981 also saw the appearance of the first volume of translations into Italian. It was edited by P. Sacchi and titled *Apocrifi dell'antico Testamento* (Turin, 1981). Finally, it is also symptomatic of the renewed interest in the Pseudepigrapha that the RSV committee on the Apocrypha, chaired by B. M. Metzger, has now included in their collection works contained in the new English version of the Pseudepigrapha, namely 4 Ezra, the Prayer of Manasseh, 3 Maccabees, 4 Maccabees, and Psalm 151.

While recognizing the major accomplishment by Charles in 1913, and lauding his distinguished and pioneering publications, there yet appeared a recognition that his collection could be improved and must be supplemented. It was difficult to explain why he had not included more documents, especially Joseph and Aseneth, the Lives of the Prophets, The Testament of Job, The Apocalypse of Abraham, and many other works.[13] It was disturbing how cavalier he and his colleagues had been with the ancient manuscripts, emending them far too frequently. Moreover, his view of Judaism was now outdated, as is clearly displayed in his view that the author of Jubilees 'was unquestionably a Pharisee of the strictest sect' (*APOT*, vol. 2, p. 8).

The preparation of the new English edition of the Pseudepigrapha began in earnest in 1972, eleven years ago. The appearance of volume 1 in 1983 marks the beginning of a new period. In contrast to the other translations being prepared by local teams in various countries, the new English version is the product of an international team of translators in ten countries, and the co-operation and assistance of scholars in other countries, especially those in Ireland, France, Czechoslovakia, Russia, Italy and Egypt.

A New English Edition Opens Vast Frontiers (1983–)

The appearance of *The Old Testament Pseudepigrapha* in 1983 and 1985 coincides with the preparation of other translations. We have already mentioned the appearance of the Danish, modern Greek, Italian, and German versions. Collections of translations are also in preparation by teams of scholars in France under the direction of M. Philonenko and A. Dupont-Sommer, in Spain under the guidance of A. Díez Macho, and in Japan under the editorship of M. Sekine and S. Arai.[14]

(1) *An Astounding Increase of Sources*

The appearance of a second English edition of the Pseudepigrapha seventy years after the first one prompts a question regarding the major differences between them. Perhaps the first significant difference is the huge increase in the number of documents included; certainly this factor has already been anticipated from the previous judgment that Charles' version was a reductional collection.

Volume 1 of Charles' collection contained two documents that are now included within the Pseudepigrapha; they are 3 Maccabees and the Prayer of Manasseh. Volume 2 contained seventeen documents, but two of them, Pirkē Aboth and the Zadokite Document, do not belong in the Pseudepigrapha; hence Charles' two-volumed collection contained seventeen pseudepigrapha. Each of these seventeen are included in the new edition, along with thirty-five additional documents. Moreover, the large supplement contains the fragments of Jewish writings known primarily from quotations by Eusebius, who in his *Preparation for the Gospel*, book 9, borrowed from Alexander Polyhistor's *On the Jews*, which was written in the first century B.C.E.

and cited these Jewish writings. The new edition contains more than three times as many pseudepigrapha as in Charles' collection; and in addition the supplement contains translations of thirteen extracts from otherwise lost early Jewish writings.

(2) *International Co-operation*

The second significant difference between the two English versions is that the first one was translated by a British group and the second one by an international team. The 1913 collection was produced by a local team of fifteen British scholars from Oxford, Cambridge and London. The 1983 and 1985 version is translated by fifty-two scholars, white and black, male and female, Christian and Jewish, and even a Falasha. They are specialists who work in the United States, Canada, England, Scotland, Holland, Germany, Poland, Greece, Israel and Australia. The contemporary acknowledgement that work on the Pseudepigrapha demands international co-operation and its obvious success in this and other enterprises indicates how much progress we have made. The point is driven home by reflections on a quaint comment in the review of the first edition. It appeared in *The Expository Times* (24 (1912–13), p. 513): this work 'surpasses all other complete editions of the Apocrypha or Pseudepigrapha in any language. It is just such a work as our own great Universities, alone perhaps of the educational centres of the world, could have produced, and our own University presses published.'

(3) *Refined Methodologies*

The third significant difference pertains to method. The new edition shows a marked advancement in precision, especially in working on manuscripts and understanding the syntax and subtleties of ancient languages. It also reflects an awareness that a translator must not improve a text by emending it or rendering it in flowing prose; sometimes a literal, even inelegant, rendering is best if faithfulness to the base manuscript demands it. An increased awareness of the rich variety of traditions in Early Judaism has led to the vast reduction of marginal references to Old Testament passages. Since allusions can be misleading, only dependency should be noted. Of course, the vast increase in manuscripts available for a base text and the recovery of manuscripts far less contaminated and much earlier than those available in 1900 have produced translations that may not be recognizable to specialists who have nearly memorized portions of Charles' work.

New Opportunities and Challenges

Enoch is the Son of Man

(1) *Charles' Emendation of 1 Enoch 71*

The new methodology and the increased philological and historical sensitivity may be indicated by three brief examples, and each of these mirrors some new opportunities and challenges before us. Charles emended the climax of 1 Enoch 37−71 so that in 71:14 Enoch is told, 'This is the Son of Man who is born unto righteousness' (*APOT*, vol. 2, p. 237). The whole thrust of this section of the document is lost by the emendation.

The text is now accurately represented in E. Isaac's fresh translation: 'You, son of man, who art born in righteousness and upon whom righteousness has dwelt, the righteousness of the Antecedent of Time will not forsake you' (1 En 71:14).[15] In his 1978 edition of Ethiopic Enoch M. A. Knibb likewise correctly connects the phrase 'Son of Man' with Enoch, and not someone else; but he follows Charles' lead and takes this phrase as a *terminus technicus*: 'And that angel came to me, and greeted me with his voice, and said to me: "You are the Son of Man who was born to righteousness".'[16]

(2) *Returning to the Manuscripts*

Charles' emendation misled scholars, prompting them to look for the identity of the 'Son of Man'. The Ethiopic either, according to Isaac's translation, has no title 'Son of Man', or, according to Knibb, rewards Enoch himself with the title 'Son of Man'. The implications of this actual reading has profound ramifications for both the theology of Early Judaism and early Christian Christology − and perhaps even for Jesus himself if the Parables of Enoch, 1 Enoch 37−71, are Jewish and predate seventy as most specialists are now contending.[17] The meticulous editing and translating of Ethiopic Enoch − the passage, of course, has not been found in Aramaic or Greek − helps to disprove Milik's claim that this section of 1 Enoch is Christian.[18] One problem may be solved but others loom large: is this passage pre-Christian and Jewish; if so, does it elevate Enoch as 'the Son of Man'? Or, is the passage a post-Christian Jewish polemic against Jesus as the 'Son of Man', stating that not he but Enoch is the 'Son of Man'? These and other related questions will now occupy our skills for some time, or until other momentous discoveries are made.

Hillel and Jesus are Contemporaneous with Ḥanina and Banus

A Non-Sectarian Approach

The second example reflects the increased perception of the complexities in Early Judaism and the corresponding hesitation to attribute any early Jewish document to one of the four great sects. In Charles' collection Jubilees, as we saw earlier, was attributed to the Pharisees. Likewise, G. B. Gray assigned the Psalms of Solomon to the Pharisees. He argued, 'we need not hesitate to see in the "righteous" of the Psalms the Pharisees, and in the "sinners" the Sadducees (cf. iv. 2ff.); and in the Psalms themselves the work of one or more of the Pharisees' (*APOT*, vol. 2, p. 630). Similarly, Charles argued that the author of the Testament (or Assumption) of Moses 'was a Pharisee of a fast-disappearing type' (*APOT*, vol. 2, p. 411). In the new English version not one document is assigned to the Pharisees or to any other sect.

We know far too little about the sects. The only sources for the Pharisees are the new Testament writings, Josephus, and a few paragraphs in the Mishnah; and certainly we all agree that these are tendentious and heavily edited. The Pharisees were far more latitudinarian than either our publications portray or the debates between Hillel and Shammai convey. A legalistically oriented Pharisee, for example, may have been closer in many ways to a Sadducee than to an apocalyptically-inspired fellow Pharisee. The Essenes likewise were subdivided into separate groups: some were celibate and monastic, others married and raised families. The Zealots, the last sect to appear of the popularly conceived 'four sects', may have arisen only around 66 C.E. and they need to be distinguished from the brigands and the *sicarii*.[19]

Multifaceted Varieties

Seeing Early Judaism through four sectarian windows is myopic and unperceptive. A sensitive investigation of Early Judaism leads to the discernment of other groups; we must include in our description (at least) also the Ḥasidim, the Hellenists, the Nazarenes, the Samaritans, the Boethusians, the Herodians, the Hemerobaptists, the Masbothei, the Galileans, the mystics, the apocalyptic groups, the baptist movements led by John the Baptist, and others, perhaps including Jesus of Nazareth at the beginning of his public ministry (if we can trust the Gospel of John, and I think we should), and the early followers of Jesus (members of 'the Way' according to Acts 24:14

and *Nazōraiōn* and *Iessaioi* according to Epiphanius in *AdvHaer* 29:1, 29:4, 29:5).[20] Older groups or 'sects' continued to be active; for example, our evidence is growing especially on the continuing presence of the Rechabites.[21]

The priestly groups do *not* represent a well-defined sociological unit; they often differed violently among themselves, as we know from studying the history of the Qumran Essenes. The prominence given to Levi in the Testament of the Twelve Patriarchs, the preferential treatment of the Levites in the Temple Scroll, the significance of the Zadokites for the exiled community at Qumran (cf. 1QSa) and elsewhere (CD), the obvious struggles among the priests reflected in the late Old Testament writings,[22] and the rift among the priests in the second century that produced the Qumran phenomenon allow us now to penetrate deeply into the struggles among the priests in Early Judaism. The greatest nineteenth-century historian of Early Judaism, E. Schürer, did not have the complex and revealing data we possess; he claimed incorrectly that the 'Zadokites formed the kernel and chief element of the priesthood in the postexilic period.'[23] Moreover, by the time of Early Judaism the priests and scribes had split into two separate groups; and these were often related polemically.

The 'am ha-aretz

Equally as important as the abundance of divergent groups is the fact that both Josephus and Philo reported that the vast majority of the Jews belonged to *no sect*. Certainly calling this majority the *'am ha-aretz* is far from satisfactory. The meaning of the term is not clear and has been variously understood by scholars during this century. In 1906 A. Büchler argued (*contra* A. Harnack who is probably 'der protestantischen Forscher' p. 3) that it held two different meanings.[24] In Early Judaism the *'am ha-aretz 'la-Torah'* designated the Jew who was ignorant of the Torah; the *'am ha-aretz 'le-mitzwot'* specified the Galilean who after Usha (140–170 C.E.) was disparaged by the Sages because he did not observe the commandments. Later S. Zeitlin contended that the *'am ha-aretz* in Early Judaism was a peasant farmer who was not an ignoramus but knew the Torah.[25] The farmer, Zeitlin argued, simply did not have leisure time in which to study the Torah. The social dimensions to this insight are significant and need full exploration.[26]

Recently A. Oppenheimer has carefully examined the term in rabbinic literature.[27] There are five aspects to his conclusion: (1) Jews in Galilee and Judea bore the same 'halakhic-Pharisaic stamp'

(p. 7). (2) The *Halakoth* contrasting the *'am ha-aretz 'le-mitzwot'* with the *Ḥaberim* are similar to the laws of the Qumran community (esp. 1QS); hence they predate 70 C.E. (3) In Early Judaism, that is from 200 B.C.E. to shortly after 200 C.E., the term 'signified alike an active social concept and an element in the social stratification of the people of Israel' (p. 12). (4) The term has two meanings. The *'am ha-aretz 'le-mitzwot'* − in contrast to the *ḥaber* − was disparaged because of his failure to observe 'either the commandments associated with the produce of the land in Eretz Israel or the precepts relating to ritual purity' (p. 12). The *'am ha-aretz 'la-Torah'* − in contrast to the *Talmid ḥakham* − was stigmatized as one ignorant of the Torah. (5) The *'am ha-aretz*, because of his ignorance of the Torah, the *Halakoth*, and civil laws, was in the lowest sociological rank.

Oppenheimer's conclusions are somewhat distorted by his un-critical adherence to the model of a normative Judaism, and he may have tended to export from post-70 statements a too disparaging view of the *'am ha-aretz*;[28] nevertheless it is now beyond any doubt that the *'am ha-aretz* represents a complex and significant sociological group.[29] The term is almost always used in rabbinic literature to point to (without clear definition) the Jew who is 'unclean'; it is a term that *defines the other*. It is used in contradistinction to the pious in pre-70 Jewish society. We must admit considerable ignorance regarding the *'am ha-aretz* (as well as the *ḥaber*[30]) and the pre-70 judgments concerning them; the earliest preserved rulings are post-70 and are associated with Yavneans (c. 70−140 C.E.).[31]

These brief comments indicate why I am convinced that our cus-tomary sectarian approach to Early Judaism is inappropriate, and that reference to four major sects is no longer adequate if we want to portray sensitively religion and daily life in Early Judaism. We also need to seek to understand how the largest number of Jews, namely the Jews of the Diaspora, affected the Palestinian Jews through com-merce, debates, pilgrimages, and the yearly half-shekel Temple tax.[32]

It should now be clear that a sectarian approach to Early Judaism is anachronistic. That approach represents the time when scholars could talk about a normative Judaism; and it tends to warp a portrayal of the varieties of responses to Torah in Early Judaism. Sometimes it is not clear what is meant by the noun 'Judaism' or by the adjective 'Jewish'. The contemporary search for the essence of Early Judaism (see chapter 2) and for the Jews' own self-definition is represented in many publications, and by the MacMaster University Project on Jewish and Christian Self-Definition.

We have portions of one Essene library;[33] but not one document clearly by the Pharisees, Sadducees, or Zealots has come down to us. To discern the pulse of Early Judaism we turn not to a discussion of sects; we turn to the thirteen documents in the Apocrypha, the early traditions in the rabbinic corpus, and especially to the fifty-two documents and thirteen fragmentary quotations from lost works now collected together in the new version of the *Old Testament Pseudepigrapha*.[34]

The Need for a Social History of Early Palestinian Judaism
These reflections demonstrate that far too often our depictions of early Jews are actually caricatures of religious Jews. A sociological description must now be much more careful, refined and precise. We must explore, *inter alia*, the relationships between the 'sects' (I think we should cease using this term; see the Glossary p. 190), groups, classes, and parties; and we must attempt to discern when social or theological *functions*, such as being a scribe or a priest, impinge upon our understandings of the terms (or concepts) given to the numerous groups.

In a deeper sense, in our search for a social understanding of Early Judaism, we must acknowledge the multi-dimensional role of linguistic phenomena. We have been preoccupied with the meaning of the language in the texts, yet there is another extremely important dimension to them, namely the function of the language of the text for the early Jew who was embodying in his or her own contemporary world the functional meaning of the text. As W. A. Meeks, a New Testament scholar and a social historian who is a moderate functionalist, writes, 'The comprehensive question concerning the texts that are our primary sources is not merely what each one says, but what it does' (p. 7).[35]

I take 'what it does' not in a unilateral but in a multi-phenomenal sense: the function of the words when written or copied, when heard, when read, when memorized, when remembered, when acted upon volitionally and consciously (and when involitionally and subconsciously), when used to hide behind, when employed aggressively, when digested contemplatively or meditatively, and when inculcated intellectually and creatively. In other words the functional identity of a passage in the Torah may well have produced an identity between Pharisee and Sadducee, especially when both in a spirit of solidarity simultaneously functioned as priests in the Temple cult. Yet, an intense preoccupation with the meaning of a text (or document) would result in a conclusion that sects denote differences and hence Pharisee and Sadducee represented different strands in a system. It is a sensitivity to the social dimension behind (and somehow within) our texts that should guard us from repeating distortions, caricatures and false portrayals.

In short, we need to ensure that our students and colleagues in other disciplines realize that Hillel and Jesus are roughly contemporaneous with Ḥanina ben Dosa, the Galilean miracle worker, and with Banus, the Palestinian ascetic with whom Josephus claims he lived from when he was 16 to when he was 19 (cf. Josephus, *Life* 1); and that would be from circa 53 to 56 C.E., or at the same time as Paul was writing the Epistle to the Romans.

Melkisedek is Born Miraculously

The Original Ending of 2 Enoch

The third example of a new methodology bringing about scholarly reappraisal entails the vast increase in the awareness of the problems encountered while working on the pseudepigrapha preserved only in Slavonic. Using manuscripts of both the long and the short recension of 2 Enoch discovered recently in Russian libraries, F. Andersen demonstrates that the careful scholar must use both recensions, and be sensitive to the possibility of early Jewish traditions in both of them. A surprising result of Andersen's research is the fact that Charles and Forbes truncated the text of 2 Enoch , ending with chapter 68. They omitted the conclusion, namely chapters 69 to 73, which contains a fascinating account of Melkisedek's miraculous birth. Chapter 71 contains the following account:

> And Sothonim ... conceived in her womb, but Nir the priest had not slept with her, ... Sothonim was ashamed, and she hid herself ... And Sothonim came to Nir, her husband; ⟨and⟩ , behold, she was pregnant, and at the time for giving birth. And Nir saw her, and he became very ashamed about her. And he said to her, 'What is this that you have done, O wife?' ... And it came to pass, when Nir had spoken to his wife, that Sothonim fell down at Nir's feet and died. Nir was extremely distressed; ... And the archangel Gabriel appeared to Nir, and said to him: '... this child which is to be born of her is a righteous fruit, ...' ... And Noe (and Nir) ... placed Sothonim on the bed ... And when they had gone

out toward the sepulcher, a child came out from the dead
Sothonim. And he sat on the bed ... And behold, the badge
of priesthood was on his chest, and it was glorious in appear-
ance. ... And Noe and Nir ... called his name Melkisedek.
... And the LORD ... said to him: '... don't be anxious, Nir;
because I, in a short while I shall send my archangel Gabriel.
And he will take the child, and put him in the paradise of
Edem.' (2 En 71:2−28[A])[36]

I would like to find someone who can help me understand this
tradition and its importance for the theology of Early Judaism and
the earliest Christologies. What is the relationship, if any, between
this description of the miraculous birth of Melkisedek and the description of Noah's spectacular birth according to the fragment from a
Book of Noah preserved in 1 Enoch 106:10−12 (*et surrexit inter
manus obstetricis suae eadem hora, qua procidit de utero matris
suae*)?[37] Does either story provide a background to the Christian
concept of the virginal conception of Jesus by Mary? Is it a key to
unlocking some mysteries in the theology of Hebrews (see chapter 3)?
Or, is it a post-Christian Jewish expansion of 2 Enoch? Or, is it a
medieval fabrication by the Bogomils? I am afraid we are confronted
by more questions than answers.

The examples given above have been selected from the documents
in both the 1913 and 1983−5 English editions. Other documents
included in both editions appear now in their full extant form. The
Sibylline Oracles are in their complete form, all the so-numbered
sixteen books found in the two disparate manuscript collections;
earlier only the opening fragments, and books 3, 4 and 5 were
included. The Fourth Book of Ezra is represented with all sixteen
chapters; earlier only books 3 to 14 were selected. The Ascension of
Isaiah is presented in its full form, chapters 1 to 11; earlier only
chapters 1 to 3, and 5 were chosen.

There is certainly no space here to suggest the significance of the
additional thirty-five documents and of the thirteen writings in the
Supplement. The following documents will probably be challenging
to most biblical scholars: The History of the Rechabites describes the
present abode and living conditions of the Rechabites, who disappeared from history after they fled to Jerusalem in the days of
Jeremiah (cf. Jer 35). The Treatise of Shem explains the characteristics
of each year according to the sign of the zodiac in which it begins.
Joseph and Aseneth describes the conversion of Aseneth to Judaism,

the resulting cosmological and phenomenological ramifications, and the sacred meal and honeycomb that have utterly defied our attempts to explain them. The Hellenistic Synagogal Prayers are alleged to be early Jewish prayers that have been redacted by Christians. Pseudo-Phocylides and Syriac Menander both appear to be Jewish wisdom and ethical writings. The Apocryphon of Ezekiel contains a full-blown parable with an eschatological message and warning. The Testament of Job greatly expands on the Book of Job, sprinkling the narrative with impressive psalms, and introducing on centre stage his wife, Sitidos, who finally exchanges her hair for three loaves to feed her husband and herself; then she dies in a manger, but not before she sees her children wearing crowns in heaven. Pseudo-Philo expands the Old Testament narrative, and is a haggadic midrash on Genesis to 2 Samuel; especially moving is the lament of Seila, Jephthah's daughter (cf. Judg 11:30−40), who is shocked to learn that her father's vow demands her death. Finally, a section on 'Prayers, Psalms, and Odes' brings together the extra-canonical poetic collections in Early Judaism, including the expansions to the Psalter, the so-called 'More Psalms of David'.

The Canon, Inspiration and the Pseudepigrapha

One final issue must suffice for the present. What are the ramifications of this collection of early Jewish writings for our theories of inspiration, the composition and compilation of the biblical books, and the judgment that the Bible alone is our canon?

As is well known, B. S. Childs, with impressive erudition, claims that the task of the Old Testament scholar is to examine the canonical text, 'the final form of the biblical text', which 'alone bears witness to the full history of revelation'.[38] Does 'the canonical method' Childs describes not undermine any sensitivity to the Pseudepigrapha, and the claim of many pseudepigrapha to record God's inviolate word, a claim also found in the Dead Sea Scrolls, especially in the Temple Scroll? If Childs is correct, then how can we understand the canonical Epistle of Jude? This epistle not only quotes from 1 Enoch but prefaces the quotation by the statement that these words were 'prophesied' by Enoch (see chapter 3). As we wrestle with the canonical dimension of our traditions we shall have more problems with these questions than do the Ethiopian Falashas; for they have 'canonized' 1 Enoch.

Conclusion

The above comments indicate some opportunities and challenges that now confront those of us who are biblical scholars. It is difficult today to perceive what could be the ultimate significance of these Jewish documents, now collected under the title the Old Testament Pseudepigrapha. One insight is now vividly brought home: Early Judaism, like hellenistic culture generally,[39] was literary. The Pseudepigrapha are significant — we have all been acknowledging that fact — but I am not yet sure how significant they may prove to be. Certainly the team of translators has had *Sitzfleisch*, and has done well to put these works before scholars for their judgment.

2

THE PSEUDEPIGRAPHA, EARLY JUDAISM AND CHRISTIAN ORIGINS

Introduction

As a scholar who has spent the last twelve years preparing a new edition of the Old Testament Pseudepigrapha, I shall now try to assess what this large corpus of writings, from *basically* 200 B.C.E. to 200 C.E., is telling us about Early Judaism. In the next chapter I shall attempt to explain the possible ramifications these documents may have for a better understanding of the New Testament writings. This chapter flows on into the next. It is only honest to admit that I cannot explain these documents as a Jew. I can only be what I have become: a New Testament scholar trained in Christian Origins.

If I am a pioneer in the recent study of the Pseudepigrapha, then to a certain extent I have been fortunate to move a little ahead with work on a few documents and can look back on how these and other writings are now being used and have been used by New Testament specialists. My impression is twofold: on the one hand, it is evident that some writings in the Old Testament Pseudepigrapha have been fairly well known by the best New Testament scholars and have often played a prominent role in their publications. On the other hand, I note a tendency to conceive of the Old Testament Pseudepigrapha as a relatively limited number of writings, amounting to approximately fifteen or seventeen documents. This impression certainly has been inherited from the collections published at the beginning of this century by Kautzsch and Charles.

This perspective is erroneous; it must be widened immediately or Early Judaism will be miscast. New Testament scholars should not read only the new translations of the pseudepigrapha which were included in Kautzsch' and Charles' collection – certainly Pirkē Aboth and the Cairo Damascus Document belong not in the Pseudepigrapha collection but respectively in the rabbinic corpus and in the Dead Sea Scroll collection – they should also peruse the other writings now contained in the new editions of the Pseudepigrapha (see chapter 1).

The increase in the quantity of literature is extensive, as we saw in chapter 1.

The *whole* Pseudepigrapha is to be digested and assessed for its possible assistance in clarifying the characteristics of Early Judaism. That should mean a careful evaluation of all the fifty-two documents and all the excerpts in the Supplement in the light of all the other Jewish writings we have from the period, including especially the Dead Sea Scrolls, Philo, Josephus, the Mishnah, and many other writings too numerous to mention, and then an attempt to portray the main features of Early Judaism. This task certainly cannot be completed in one book, and I am not convinced it can be accomplished adequately today. Yet, it is necessary for us to attempt now to grasp the importance of the Pseudepigrapha for a better understanding of Early Judaism, which, as I shall try to show, is the matrix in which and out of which *Early* Christianity arose.

The Enormous Growth of Literary Data

Hundreds of Primary Sources

Today New Testament specialists are confronted by hundreds of documents that demand attention. Besides the 27 New Testament documents, there are the dozens of so-called Dead Sea Scroll manuscripts and fragments of manuscripts, the 13 Old Testament Apocrypha, the volumes of Philo and Josephus, the Hermetica, the Jewish Magical Papyri, the rabbinic writings, the Talmudim, the Targumim, and the 52 Nag Hammadi treatises. Now we must try to master the 52 documents in the new English edition of the *Old Testament Pseudepigrapha*, as well as the 13 fragmentary quotations in the Supplement.

The Boldness of Our Historical Dialogue

With the explosion of publications on each verse in the New Testament it is tempting to slip behind one New Testament document, or even one of its chapters, and to defend one's ground against the charge of not being abreast of the latest publications in dozens of periodicals and in many modern languages. Given this inhuman pressure upon each of us, it is salutary to observe that we boldly demonstrate through our best efforts that the New Testament documents are influenced by historical and sociological situations, and that they can be understood only by a continuing dialogue on the relationships between these twenty-seven writings and the documents roughly contemporaneous with or anterior to them. The purpose of the next two chapters, therefore, is to seek to discern how and in what ways the Old Testament Pseudepigrapha is important for the study of Early Judaism and of the New Testament documents. The questions that I am most sensitive to from my colleagues are the following: to what extent can I really ignore the Pseudepigrapha? How can I use these documents? How can I be certain that a document, or a passage in a composite work, is earlier than, or roughly contemporaneous with Hillel or Jesus?

The continuing success of the *SNTS* Pseudepigrapha seminars and the SBL Pseudepigrapha group illustrates that biblical scholars are keenly interested in the Pseudepigrapha. And − it is necessary to emphasize − we are studying them not only as documents important for an understanding of the sixty-six biblical books, but also because they are fascinating and important for a perception of Early Judaism, and are literary works intrinsically worthy of careful scrutiny. Our examinations of these ancient writings related to the Bible have opened up a new approach to a more representative assessment of them; one reason for this progress has been an avoidance of two extremes.

Two Extremes to Avoid

First, members of the *SNTS* and SBL seminars have avoided the tendency, found in many publications, to treat the ancient documents in the Old Testament Pseudepigrapha as if they were spurious and inferior. Yet, there is a large group of scholars who denigrate the Pseudepigrapha. It is certainly true that these documents have been misunderstood and too often discussed emotionally rather than with the detachment of the critical scholar or historian. Misleading and uninformed is the following definition published in the distinguished *Encyclopaedia Judaica*: 'The Apocrypha, for the most part, are anonymous historical and ethical works, and the Pseudepigrapha, visionary books attributed to the ancients, characterized by a stringent asceticism and dealing with the mysteries of creation and the working out of good and evil from a gnostic standpoint.'[1]

Some of the works in the Pseudepigrapha are 'visionary books attributed to the ancients', but at least twenty-five of them are expansions of the biblical narrative, wisdom tracts, or poetic compositions. The rest of the definition is surprising; it has little or nothing to do with the Pseudepigrapha. It is not a collection of gnostic documents.

While such a pejorative stance is anachronistic and distorted, we need to be cognizant and wary of another distortion which exaggerates the positive aspect of the Pseudepigrapha. Neither typical of the best scholarship, nor characteristic of their own careful pioneering work, is the following statement by Charles and Oesterley:

> When we pass from Jewish literature to that of the New Testament we enter into a new and larger atmosphere at once recalling and transcending what had been best in the prophetic periods of the past ... But though Christianity was in spirit the descendant of ancient Jewish prophecy, it was no less truly the child of that type of Judaism which had expressed its highest aspirations and ideals in pseudepigraphic and Apocalyptic literature.[2]

These words sound forth from a side of scholarship that is influenced by Christian confessionalism and an unattractive triumphalism. It is hard to resist the impression that Christianity proceeds out of decadence, and alone preserves the 'highest aspirations and ideals' of Judaism. Yet, just this very strain of thought is developed not by amateurs, but by Charles and Oesterley, and not in a sermon but in the *Encyclopaedia Britannica*. After the above-quoted paragraph the next words are as follows:

> Early Christianity had a special fondness for this class of litera-ture. It was Christianity that preserved Jewish Apocalyptic, when it was abandoned by Judaism as it sank into Rabbinism, and gave it a Christian character either by a forcible exegesis or by a systematic process of interpretation.

A similar denigration of Judaism – typical of the Victorian era and unfortunately exploited by some, notably the Nazis – is found in the classical tomes by Schürer. In 'Life Under the Law' Schürer claimed that Jewish prayer 'was bound in the fetters of a rigid mechanism, vital piety could scarcely be any longer spoken of'.[3] Fortunately, in the new version of this work these words are excised and replaced by the representative statement that a 'preoccupation with ritual is apparent in the Mishnaic treatment of formal prayer'.[4] A similar sensitivity to Early Judaism is necessary for a proper assess-ment of the importance of the Pseudepigrapha for New Testament studies. Certainly G.F. Moore,[5] early in this century, and E.P. Sanders,[6] more recently, have shown how our view of Early Judaism has been less shaped by a sensitive and first-hand knowledge of the Jewish sources than by a second-hand acquaintance with these sources, read with prejudices, even polemics, inherited by many earlier writers, notably F. Weber,[7] E. Schürer, P. Billerbeck,[8] W. Bousset,[9] and R. Bultmann.[10]

Too often our interpretations of Early Judaism have been from an intimate knowledge of a distinguished scholar's position and perception. What is needed now is a full and sensitive understanding of *all* facets of Early Judaism, including far more than those we now conveniently separate and label as literary, archaeological and sociological. For the present our gaze will be focused upon only one modern[11] collection of Jewish documents, the Old Testament Pseudepigrapha.

Dating The Evidence

The Question

In these introductory remarks I must confront immediately the major fear expressed by New Testament specialists when they consider using the Old Testament Pseudepigrapha to enlighten a study of Early Christianity. 'How can I be certain that the Pseudepigrapha is earlier than the New Testament?' This question, of course, is fraught with imprecisions. The Pseudepigrapha is a collection of writings that covers at least four centuries, or from 200 B.C.E. to 200 C.E., and the New Testament covers approximately one century, or from circa 50 to 150 C.E.

The question is subsequently rephrased: 'Is 1 Enoch earlier than the Gospel of John so that I can use it in interpreting John?' Here again we confront much confusion. 1 Enoch is composite; it is an edited version of sources dating from at least four centuries. And John is a gospel that may have as many as five editorial layers.[12]

Before frustration turns to despair the question comes out something like the following: 'Can I be certain that some passages in the Pseudepigrapha may be used to portray a reliable portion of Early Judaism, and can I use these passages to help me understand the world view, symbols, metaphors, and concepts in the New Testament documents?' The answer is a simple 'Yes'. Let me elaborate on this straightforward answer.

Clarifying the Answer: Problematic Documents

(1) *Too late*

Some clarification is necessary because the question contained the qualifying phrase 'some passages in the Pseudepigrapha'. Not only does that phrase warn that some passages must *not* be used in the study of the New Testament, but it also proscribes the use of some books. A few documents now collected in the Old Testament Pseudepigrapha are far *too late* for New Testament research. To be excluded, for example, are the late writings titled 3 Enoch, the Apocalypse of Ezra, the Vision of Ezra, the Questions of Ezra, the Revelation of Ezra, the Apocalypse of Sedrach, the Apocalypse of Daniel, the Testament of Isaac, the Testament of Jacob, the Testament of Solomon, the Testament of Adam, the History of Joseph, and Syriac Menander.[13]

(2) *Slavic Pseudepigrapha*

Another special group that should not yet be used (without the guidance of experts) in the study of the New Testament is the Slavic Pseudepigrapha — the Old Testament Pseudepigrapha preserved only in Slavonic. This group includes 2 Enoch, the Apocalypse of Abraham, and the Ladder of Jacob. These documents, in their earliest forms, certainly have a strong claim to being both Jewish and from the late first century C.E., but the phrases and passages most interesting for New Testament scholars are almost always the ones in which there are reasons to suspect that medieval dualists, especially the Bogomils, have heavily redacted the document.[14] The Bogomils were not only shaped by Jewish Pseudepigrapha; they *shaped — even composed — pseudepigrapha*. A portrayal of Early Judaism or Early Christianity based upon medieval redactions and late compositions would seriously undermine our entire work. These documents need to be studied jointly by a team of well-trained New Testament specialists and Slavic experts. At present I know of no New Testament scholar who is trained for this task; in other words we New Testament scholars have not mastered Slavonic and Old Church Slavonic, and conversely Slavic experts are lost in New Testament research.

This point is so important that it should be illustrated. In the Russian Primary Chronicle[15] there is reflected a dualism between God and the Antichrist. Yan, the representative of the good, struggles against two magicians, pawns of the devil. The magicians gain power and a following by purporting to explain the causes of a devastating famine. The salvific knowledge they offer is that 'the handsomest women' have caused the famine. The magicians proclaim that these women 'prevent plenty, and if we remove them, abundance will return'. The beautiful women are killed.

Yan turns the swelling tide of support for the magicians, and the dualism develops according to a pattern: God, who 'dwells in heaven', is opposed by the Antichrist, who 'dwells in the abyss'. A group called 'the faithful' belongs to God, another segment of humanity labelled 'the ignorant' are seduced by the devil (the Antichrist). The struggle focuses upon Yan and his twelve followers, who eventually conquer and kill the two magicians and their forces.

Of primary importance in this metaphysical and cosmic dualism is an epistemological dualism,[16] which stresses two opposing understandings of reality. Yan proclaims that 'God made man out of earth'; hence, mankind 'knows nothing, and it is God alone who possesses knowledge'. The magicians retort that 'Satan quarrelled with God as to which of them should create man'. They proudly confess that 'the devil made man, and God set a soul in him'. The magicians affirm that they, thence, believe in Antichrist. After Yan dispatches the magicians, demonstrating the profligate nature of their predictions — they did not 'really know the future' — the excerpt concludes on a hortatory and clearly epistemological dualistic note: 'But of such a nature is the instigation of devils; for devils do not perceive man's thought, though they often inspire thought in man without knowing his secrets. (179) God alone knows the mind of man, but devils know nothing, for they are weak and evil to look upon.'

For us the essential issue is not to trace the origin of these traditions; on that issue we would concur that surely some of them — such as the passage that the 'Antichrist was cast out [of heaven] from the number of those angels and expelled from heaven for his presumption' — remind us of many biblical and extracanonical traditions and documents, most notably Genesis 6, 1 Enoch and the Revelation of John. Our task is not even to compare this dualism with that in the Dead Sea Scrolls, especially 1QS 3.13–4.26; and, of course, there are parallels between Yan with his twelve followers and the *Môrēh haṣ-Ṣedek* with his (twelve special?) followers, both of whom represent an ontological and terrestrial dimension to a metaphysical and cosmic dualism. The real question for us is not the development of traditions. What we are confronted with here are not shared traditions but ideological similarities. Dualism, we must recall, is the most logical philosophical explanation for the existence of evil in a universe created by *or somehow related to* an ostensibly benevolent God.

The essential issue for us to perceive is that the dualism we find in the middle ages, as for example in the fourteenth-century Russian Primary Chronicle,[18] could have caused expansions to Jewish apocryphal documents that are similar to the paradigms and concepts typical of Jewish thought from circa 200 B.C.E. to 135 C.E. We would all agree that to use such medieval passages to clarify analogous phenomena thousands of years earlier is an egregious error.

The references to Yan and other obvious medieval names, phrases and concepts demonstrate that the above-quoted passage in the Russian Primary Chronicle is neither early nor Jewish. But what about other sections in the Slavic Pseudepigrapha? Medieval passages almost identical with much earlier Jewish literary production could have been caused by numerous factors: first, independent reflections on the causes of misfortunes and evil in the world; second, the separate development in similar ways of much older literature, such as the books in the Old Testament; third, the influence of Jewish extra-canonical traditions or passages in a document, either the same one or another separate one; fourth, the cumulative reciprocal phenomenon of creating medieval works based upon earlier Jewish writings and then the reshaping of the latter in terms of the former as they were copied, reshaped, and distributed.

All of these reflections lead to two methodological insights. First, it is not the appearance of Jewish-looking phrases and concepts in Slavic works that indicate they are pre-Christian or even Jewish. Second, it is only — or at least for the present solely — the recognition of ideas or metaphors typical of Early Judaism and concurrently atypical of medieval dualistic thought that indicates the probable discovery of an early Jewish stratum or passage. Meshchersky has been the first to discover one of these early Jewish peculiarities.[19] The appearance of apologetics for a solar calendar and polemics against a lunar calendar placard sections of the short recension of 2 Enoch as not only pre-medieval but also pre-Christian and Jewish.

These observations leave me both sad and optimistic. It is sad we cannot now assess the significance of 2 Enoch for Christian Origins and for the New Testament writings. We can be optimistic, however, that we are much closer to unravelling the mysteries that surround this most fascinating document. Perhaps some day we shall know whether passages in 2 Enoch (or in the Apocalypse of Abraham and the Ladder of Jacob) influenced the early Christians (and perhaps even Jesus of Nazareth), whether they were influenced by or interpolated by them (or even later Christians), whether they were influenced perhaps by Jesus himself, or whether they were polemical anti-Christian creations by apocalyptically-inspired Jews who wrote between 70 and 135 C.E.

Some of the passages in 2 Enoch will prove most striking to New Testament scholars. Note, for example, only two: 2 Enoch 49:1 states that an answer should be simply 'yes, yes' or 'no, no'. This exhortation is reminiscent of Jesus' words, according to Matthew, delivered in the Sermon on the Mount (Mt 5:33–7). Likewise, 2 Enoch 61:2 promises that in the future there are 'many mansions' (or shelters) prepared for the righteous. This concept is one we have long labelled, perhaps incorrectly, as Johannine; for in John 14:2 Jesus is reputed to have said, 'In my Father's house are many mansions: if it were not so, I would have told you. I go to prepare a place for you' (KJV).

When work on the Pseudepigrapha is more advanced, and when New Testament experts have read *thoroughly, carefully* and *sympathetically* the new translations now readily available in English, German, Italian, French, Danish, Spanish, Dutch, modern Greek and Japanese, then many of our scholarly conclusions will need to be discarded. Certainly we need to be more careful in the use of such adjectives as 'Matthean', 'Johannine', and 'Pauline', and, of course, the terms 'Jewish' and 'Christian'. Even more likely, however, is the probability that our detailed, careful and self-critical publications will be categorically distinct from other publications, such as C. F. Potter's *Did Jesus Write This Book* (New York, 1965), which contains, incredibly, the suggestion that Jesus composed 2 Enoch ('it may well be that he wrote it, or part of it' (p. 27)).

To scrutinize the learned introductions to the Slavic Pseudepigrapha, and to read through the translations, and even through the Slavic texts – as some of us can, albeit with some difficulty – scarcely will suffice to resolve the problems. We are in the end only reading uncritically through texts which contain early traditions and later redactions: as of the present, no one has been able to devise a methodology that will help us separate tradition from redaction in the Slavic Pseudepigrapha.

We must use these documents, of course; it is unwise to ignore what is now so conveniently before us. But we must be cautious in the use of the apocryphal works preserved only in medieval Slavic manuscripts, admitting frequently that we do not possess the underlying Old Church Slavonic *Untertext*, nor the presumed Greek, Hebrew or Aramaic Jewish *Urtext*; and, moreover, we acknowledge the possibility that early Jewish sections may be contaminated by interpolations and redactions by medieval dualists.

(3) *Pseudepigrapha now Christian Through Expansions*
The documents too late for our work as New Testament scholars and also the Slavic Pseudepigrapha are two categories that resonate with warnings for us to be cautious. There is a third category of pseudepigraphical works which should also be used with great circumspection. These documents are originally Jewish but have received both Christian interpolations and extensive and occasionally imperceptible Christian redaction. Caution is necessary because we *must not* use Christian redactions that postdate 150 C.E. to portray the intellectual world of Early Judaism or first-century Christianity. Foremost among these documents is the Testaments of the Twelve Patriarchs (see the following discussion), followed closely by the History of the Rechabites, the Martyrdom and Ascension of Isaiah, and the Hellenistic Synagogal Prayers. Of a different type are the relatively clear Christian expansions to 4 Ezra (so-called 5 and 6 Ezra) and to the Sibylline Oracles.

Further Elaboration: Proof of Pre-Christian Jewish Compositions

Many of the documents in the Pseudepigrapha can be invaluable for assisting us in describing Early Judaism, and in perceiving the indebtedness of early Christianity to Jewish phenomena. For at least three main reasons we can be relatively certain that many documents in the Pseudepigrapha are not medieval works but pre-Christian Jewish compositions.

(1) *Quotations*
Many early Church Fathers quoted documents in the Pseudepigrapha, and considered them ancient and Jewish, and sometimes even inspired. The list of these early scholars is impressive: Justin Martyr (c. 100–c. 165), Clement of Alexandria (c. 150–c. 215), Hippolytus (c. 170–c. 236), Origen (c. 185–c. 254), Lactantius (c. 240–c. 320), Eusebius (c. 260–c. 340), and Epiphanius (c. 315–c. 403). Similarly, the Apostolic Fathers quoted one or more documents in the Pseudepigrapha: Hermas preserves a quotation from Eldad and Modad, 1 Clement has a citation from the Apocryphon of Ezekiel, and the Epistle of Barnabas contains a passage from an anonymous apocryphal work.[20] Most importantly, Jude not only quotes 1 Enoch; it also alludes to an apocryphal story about Moses' death that

may have been described in the now lost ending of the Testament of Moses (see chapter 3, pp. 75–7).

(2) *Papyri*

Some documents and fragments of others are extant in early collections of papyri, signifying that at least the portion of the document preserved in them is not a medieval 'forgery' but must predate the papyrus. Some of the documents in the Pseudepigrapha are preserved in third-, fourth- and fifth-century papyri as illustrated in the chart of some of them given below.

Century	Language	Document	Papyrus	City
III	Gk	OdesSol	P. Bod. XI	Geneva
IV/V	Gk	PrMan	P. Vindob. G. 330	Vienna
V	Cop	ApEl	PSI 7 (Aschmunên)	Florence
IV/V	Gk	2Bar	P. Oxy. 403	New York
IV/V	Gk	TSol	P. Vindob. G. 330	Vienna
IV	Gk	1En	P. Oxy. 2069	Oxford
IV	Gk	1En	C. Beatty Bib. Pap. XII	Dublin
IV	Gk	1En	P. Mich. Inv. 5552	Ann Arbor
IV	Gk	PrJac	P. gr. 13895	Berlin, DDR
V/VI	Gk	AscenIs	Amherst Gk. Pap. 1	New York
IV	Gk	ApocEzek	C. Beatty Bib. Pap. XII	Dublin
IV	Gk	4Ezra	P. Oxy. 1010 [MS. Gr. Bibl. g. 3 (P)]	Oxford

(3) *Qumran Fragments*

Fragments of some documents in the Pseudepigrapha were found among the Dead Sea Scrolls; since these are in Semitic scripts that predate Christianity by a century or more, it is obvious that the *portion* of the work represented is early enough to provide data for reconstructing Early Judaism and the matrix of Early Christianity. As Vermes states, the discovery of these fragments demonstrates, 'not just hypothetically', that the Pseudepigrapha are early Jewish literature. He continues: 'Together with the Qumran Community's own compositions, they have suddenly appeared, not as a secondary and negligible phenomenon, but as clear evidence of Palestinian Jewry's rich intellectual creativity in the multi-party system of the pre-Destruction era.'[21]

1 Enoch. Even here at our strongest point chronologically we must be keenly aware of what is and what is not proved. We dare not conclude too quickly that because portions of 1 Enoch are extant in pre-Christian Semitic manuscript fragments,[22] that all of 1 Enoch is pre-Christian, or even Jewish. The document we call 1 Enoch is certainly composite; it may contain six separate works and one of these may come from a lost Book of Noah.[23] Similarly, the discovery of Aramaic fragments of *a* Testament of Levi does not prove the pre-Christian origin of all of *the* Testament of Levi, let alone the thoroughly redacted Testaments of the Twelve Patriarchs.

The results of labours by scholars throughout the world, however, have moved us far away from a level of exasperation or frustration when working with 1 Enoch and the Testaments of the Twelve Patriarchs. Thanks to the papers read in and the proceedings of the *SNTS* Pseudepigrapha Seminars in Tübingen and Paris,[24] it is now clear that specialists on 1 Enoch at present affirm not only its Jewish character but also its pre-Christian, or pre-70 date; and that judgment pertains to all segments of this composite work, as we shall see when we turn to this pseudepigraphon and assess its significance for New Testament scholars in chapter 3.

The Testaments of the Twelve Patriarchs. The issues regarding the character and date of the Testaments of the Twelve Patriarchs are somewhat analogous to 1 Enoch. Fifty-nine fragments from a work some scholars call '*a*' Testament of Levi were found in caves 1 and 4 (1QTLevi ar, 4QTLevi ar[a]), and these are related to the late, redacted and abbreviated Greek pseudepigraphon entitled 'The Testament of Levi'. It is indeed conceivable that two independent testaments could have been attributed to Levi, one of the historical figures paradigmatically important for the thoughts of Early Judaism (as we all know even more clearly thanks to the recovery and publication of the Temple Scroll). But facts very significant for assessing the character and date of the Testament of Levi, and, therefore, at least to a certain extent, the Testaments of the Twelve Patriarchs, are the similarities and the undeniable organic relation between the Qumran Aramaic fragment and the Greek text of the so-called 'Testament of Levi'. The Testament of Levi is related to the Qumran fragment, it is an edited and abbreviated version of it. 1QTestament of Levi and 4QTestament of Levi[a] share not only words but also phrases with the Greek of the Testament of Levi, enabling J. A. Fitzmyer and D. J. Harrington[25] to restore lacunae from the Greek recension or recensions[26] and from the Aramaic Cairo Geniza fragments. Even M. de Jonge, the scholar famous for arguing that the Testaments of the Twelve Patriarchs should be seen as a *Christian composition* that has reshaped some earlier Jewish traditions, claims that the 'Testament of Levi presupposes a source which was much nearer to the stage of tradition reflected in the various fragments than the Testament itself, and in many cases the fragments can help us to determine how the author of the Test.XII Patr. used and redacted his source'.[27]

Indeed, the Testaments of the Twelve Patriarchs in its present and final form is a Christian document. It is, however, not a *Christian composition*, but a *Christian redaction* of earlier Jewish testaments. Not only were fragments of a Testament of Levi found among the Dead Sea Scrolls, but also fragments of a Testament of Naphtali; and these are in Hebrew. Although they were identified and announced by J.T. Milik almost thirty years ago,[28] they have not yet been published. If they are related in any way to the Testament of Naphtali in the Testaments of the Twelve Patriarchs, then we certainly would be wrong to conclude that only two testaments were composed and attributed to two of the twelve sons of Jacob. If Naphtali was so honoured then surely others were too, especially Judah, Joseph and Benjamin. I have no qualms about stating boldly that it is highly probable that behind each one of the twelve testaments in the Testaments of the Twelve Patriarchs there is a Jewish substratum which can be reconstructed tentatively once the clearly Christian redactions and interpolations have been identified.[29]

The issue, to be precise, is not whether there are early Jewish elements in the Testaments of the Twelve Patriarchs, nor whether the Greek Testament of Levi has been translated and abbreviated from the (or a) version represented by the Aramaic Testament of Levi. We all tend to agree that both of these conclusions are warranted. The issue is whether, on the basis of these facts, we can conclude that the Testaments of the Twelve Patriarchs is a Christian composition that was influenced by Jewish traditions and even some testaments, or whether it is a Christian redaction of a Jewish document that honoured each of the twelve sons of Jacob. Again it is well to remember that almost all specialists who participated in the *SNTS* Pseudepigrapha seminar on the Testaments of the Twelve Patriarchs expressed the opinion that this document is certainly Christian in its present and final Greek form, but that beneath the final layer lies an early Jewish source, even a document that honoured the twelve sons of Jacob.[30]

In attempting to solve the issue of the essential character of the Testaments of the Twelve Patriarchs, I agree with H. C. Kee who, in the *Old Testament Pseudepigrapha*, concludes a discussion of the character of the Testaments of the Twelve Patriarchs as follows:

> ... we must reckon with an author who, in writing the Testaments, is drawing on a free tradition and creating from it his own distinctive literary product. The peculiarities of the document can be accounted for fully if we assume that it was written originally in Greek, with Hebrew and Aramaic testaments serving loosely as models and perhaps to a very limited extent as sources for details. The Christian interpolations, which number not more than twelve, and which occur in the latter part of those testaments that contain them, are conceptually peripheral to the main thrust of the document and are literarily incongruous, so that they may be readily differentiated from the original Greek text.[31]

These observations lead to the conclusion that New Testament scholars should – indeed must – use 1 Enoch and the Testaments of the Twelve Patriarchs in examining the literary evidence of Early Judaism and its importance for reconstructing Christian origins.[32] These documents demand our continued attention, we must not reject them as too controversial for inclusion in our work – and this tendency has almost become a scholars' fad.[33] It is now relatively certain that both 1 Enoch and the Testaments of the Twelve Patriarchs (in its original form) were documents used not only by Christian communities, but also by Palestinian pre-Christian Jewish groups. Again we must perceive that the Jewish source or sources behind the Testaments would have looked appreciably different from the extant Greek version; and that, of course, means that the Testaments of the Twelve Patriarchs is not to be read as a Jewish document, like Jubilees or 1 Enoch, that predates Early Christianity. The abundant and explicit references to the Messiah are unparalleled in Jewish documents, but these passages, I must emphasize, are not Jewish; they are certainly Christian.[34] The explicit christological phrases and passages are the result of Christian interpolation and redaction. They must not be used in describing the background of the New Testament. Yet, most specialists can perceive the relatively obvious, and at times quite clear, limits of the Christian addition to the Jewish document. Kee, rightly, therefore, seeks an understanding of the Jewish portion of the Testaments of the Twelve Patriarchs by focusing upon the ethical dimensions.[35]

Jubilees. Another document in the Pseudepigrapha has also been recognized among the Dead Sea Scrolls. It is Jubilees; fragments of this pseudepigraphon have been found in Caves 1, 2, 3 and 4 (1QJub[a,b], 2QJub[a], 2QJub[b], 3QJub, 4QJub[e], 4QJub[f], 11QJub 1, 11QJub M 2, 11QJub M 3, 11QJub 2, 11QJub 3, 11QJub 4, 11QJub 5).[36] With this pseudepigraphon we do not confront the storm clouds that have overshadowed 1 Enoch and the Testaments of the Twelve Patriarchs. This conservative writing is clearly Jewish, pre-Christian, and free from Christian interpolations and redactions.[37] It predates the establishment of the Essene-type community[38] at Qumran, and was composed probably before 152 B.C.E., as J.C. VanderKam[39] and O. Wintermute[40] have concluded.

There is no reason to doubt the judgment of R.H. Charles,[41] recently reaffirmed by Wintermute,[42] that many New Testament passages contain phrases and concepts that are also found in Jubilees. Paul, the authors of Luke–Acts, James, Hebrews and 2 Peter could well have been familiar with the traditions recorded in Jubilees.

Clearly Pre-Christian Jewish Documents: A List

We shall return to some of these possibilities later; but for the present it is clear that a few documents in the Pseudepigrapha antedate Jesus and his early followers, and by comparison with these documents and other writings of Early Judaism, such as the Dead Sea Scrolls, it becomes obvious that many documents in the Pseudepigrapha are pre-Christian Jewish compositions.

Apocalyptic Literature and Related Works

In the category of 'Apocalyptic Literature and Related Works'[43] are three documents that are Jewish and pre-Christian:[44]

(1) 1 Enoch
(2) The Jewish Sibyllines
(3) The Treatise of Shem (perhaps).[45]

Two are probably Jewish and pre-Christian:

(4) Apocryphon of Ezekiel
(5) Apocalypse of Zephaniah.

Three documents were composed from earlier Jewish traditions and in the decades that followed the destruction of the Temple in 70:

(6) 4 Ezra
(7) 2 Baruch
(8) 3 Baruch.

Two documents are more difficult to date:

(9) The Apocalypse of Adam in its present form is late and gnostic, but there are reasons to suspect the presence of Jewish traditions that may derive ultimately from the first century.
(10) The Apocalypse of Elijah is relatively unknown. It may date in its present form from the fourth century, but it certainly contains much older Jewish material.

Testaments

Among the documents considered 'Testaments' (often with Apocalyptic Sections) three seem to be Jewish and pre-Christian:

(1) The Testaments of the Twelve Patriarchs
(2) The Testament of Job
(3) The Testament of Moses.

Another testament, namely the Testament of Abraham, dates from the later part of the first century C.E. or the beginning of the second.

Expansions of 'The Old Testament'

In this category are five documents that are probably Jewish and pre-Christian:

(1) The Letter of Aristeas
(2) Jubilees
(3) Martyrdom of Isaiah
(4) The Life of Adam and Eve
(5) The Lives of the Prophets.

Four others are Jewish and roughly contemporaneous with the New Testament writings:

(6) Joseph and Aseneth
(7) Pseudo-Philo
(8) 4 Baruch
(9) Jannes and Jambres.

Two writings are difficult to assess:

(10) Eldad and Modad predate Hermas, which quotes from it; but the document is lost, except for Hermas' brief quotation.

(11) The History of the Rechabites may preserve in its earliest core a Jewish source, but the extant document is heavily redacted by a Christian. Until this document has been thoroughly discussed by experts it should not be used to elucidate New Testament passages. See chapter 1, note 21.

Wisdom and Philosophical Literature
Among these writings are two that are certainly pre-Christian:

(1) Ahiqar
(2) 3 Maccabees.

Two others seem to be roughly contemporaneous with the New Testament writings:

(3) Pseudo-Phocylides
(4) 4 Maccabees.

Prayers, Psalms and Odes
Three of these works are Jewish and pre-Christian:

(1) 5 More Psalms of David
(2) Prayer of Manasseh
(3) Psalms of Solomon.

Four other similar compositions are roughly contemporaneous with the writings in the New Testament:

(4) Hellenistic Synagogal Prayers[46]
(5) Prayer of Joseph
(6) Prayer of Jacob
(7) Odes of Solomon.

The Supplement
In the 'Supplement' are partial quotations from Jewish writings that clearly date from the third to the first century B.C.E.:

(1) Philo the Epic Poet
(2) Theodotus
(3) Ezekiel the Tragedian
(4) Fragments of Pseudo-Greek Poets
(5) Aristobulus
(6) Demetrius the Chronographer
(7) Aristeas the Exegete

(8) Eupolemus
(9) 'Pseudo-Eupolemus'
(10) Cleodemus Malchus
(11) Artapanus.

Two others are probably pre-Christian, but may be contemporaneous with the earliest writings in the New Testament:

(12) Orphica
(13) 'Pseudo-Hecataeus'.

Assessing the Facts

This long discussion of the writings in the Pseudepigrapha that are clearly, most likely, or possibly pre-Christian or roughly contemporaneous with the New Testament shows how vast and all-encompassing this area of research has become. We must now return to the question which we took as our starting point. 'Can I be certain that some passages in the Pseudepigrapha may be used to portray reliably a portion of Early Judaism, and can I use these passages to help me understand the world view, symbols, metaphors, and concepts in the New Testament documents?' The answer is 'yes'; but the New Testament scholar needs to be guided constantly by a specialist in this vast expanse of documents, sources, Jewish interpolations, Jewish redactions, later Christian interpolations, and Christian redactions.

(1) *The Pseudepigrapha and the Dead Sea Scrolls*

Some comparisons might help sharpen the full perspective received when attempting to see the potential significance of all these documents in the Pseudepigrapha for the study of the New Testament writings. For the last thirty years we have been preoccupied with assessing the significance of the Dead Sea Scrolls and the Nag Hammadi Codices for a better understanding of Christian Origins, and more specifically for a better exegesis of the documents collected into the New Testament. Similar work on the Pseudepigrapha has been more sporadic, less precise, and often unsophisticated. Let us now, therefore, set the Pseudepigrapha briefly alongside the Dead Sea Scrolls, and then the Nag Hammadi Codices.

Like the Dead Sea Scrolls some documents in the Pseudepigrapha, notably Jubilees, probably all of 1 Enoch, and the Psalms of Solomon are clearly pre-Christian Jewish compositions. Unlike the Dead Sea Scrolls some of the Pseudepigrapha are contemporaneous with the

New Testament.[47] All of these Pseudepigrapha are extremely important in searching for the characteristics of Early Judaism and the origins of Christianity, and in examining critically the New Testament writings.

Unlike the Dead Sea Scrolls some of the Pseudepigrapha are interpolated or redacted, sometimes both, by Christians; others are late Christian compositions that record and preserve early Jewish traditions. These post-second-century C.E. documents in the Pseudepigrapha are more important for Church historians than for New Testament scholars (but see the following discussion).

Also unlike the Dead Sea Scrolls, which may occasionally contain ideas and rules peculiar only to the monks living in the wilderness on the western shores of the Dead Sea, the early Jewish documents in the Pseudepigrapha represent ideas, hymns, exhortations, cosmic speculations, wisdom and apocalyptic reflections representative of Jews living in many parts of Palestine and even, with some documents like Aristeas and 3 Maccabees, in Egypt or other Jewish centres in the Diaspora.

This recognition brings forth a problem not found when working with the Dead Sea Scrolls, but it also reflects a major advantage the early Jewish Pseudepigrapha have over the Qumran Scrolls. The problem is the great difficulty we have in ascertaining the provenance of a document. We simply do not know what distinguishes Palestinian Judaism from Egyptian Judaism, or these two forms of Judaism, from the Judaism in the major centres such as Rome, Ostia Antica, Antioch, Damascus and Adiabene. Conversely, the advantage is that we do not have to wrestle with the problems encountered in seeking to see to what extent the ideas typical of the Qumran sect can also be projected to other Jews living elsewhere in Palestine, and − of course − the spin-off of this advantage of the early Jewish Pseudepigrapha is that they can provide us with avenues for moving Qumran ideas or perspectives into a wider arena. The peculiar and extremely important history of the Qumran sect provides us with clues that can protect us from exporting indigenous Qumran theology.

(2) *The Pseudepigrapha and the Nag Hammadi Codices*
Like the Nag Hammadi Codices − and to a certain extent like the Targums[48] − in their present form some of the Pseudepigrapha are from the second to fourth centuries C.E., and must be judged to be earlier and perhaps Jewish only on the basis of rigorous and refined methods. Both groups of documents are too late in their present forms

to serve as evidence for either Early Judaism or earliest Christianity; but both are important for us, and are not simply the vested domain of the Church historian. It should not be too surprising to note, therefore, that, as the Gospel of Thomas is the only Nag Hammadi document that finds a home in the New Testament Apocrypha and Pseudepigrapha,[49] so the Apocalypse of Adam is the only one situated among the Old Testament Pseudepigrapha. Both of these documents are gnostic in their present and final form, but both originated much earlier than the third or fourth century C.E., and have much to tell us, I am convinced, respectively about the early transmission of *ipsissima verba Jesu* and about early Jewish baptist groups.

Unlike the Nag Hammadi Codices many of the Pseudepigrapha are clearly anterior to or contemporaneous with the documents in the New Testament. Also, unlike almost all of the Nag Hammadi Codices only one of the Pseudepigrapha – the Apocalypse of Adam – is clearly gnostic; almost all are Jewish, while a few are Christian.

(3) *Ancient and Modern Collections*

Unlike either the Qumran Scrolls or the so-called Nag Hammadi Codices, the Pseudepigrapha is not an ancient collection of documents; the former two groups of writings bear the name of the geographical area[50] near which they were found.[51] The Pseudepigrapha is a modern collection of documents brought together by teams of international specialists who judged, in the light of two hundred years of work on them,[52] and from decades of experience with them, that they belong together under the rubric Old Testament Pseudepigrapha.[53]

The Pseudepigrapha is a modern collection of some documents that have been well known, and others that have been available but little known. One must not have the impression, therefore, that with the translations of these documents in collections easily accessible to each of us something unprecedented has happened. We must not support an enthusiastic exclamation that sounds like the late J. Daniélou's justified comment on the discovery of the Dead Sea Scrolls: 'Hence one can say that this discovery is one of the most sensational that has ever been made.'[54]

Methodology: A Search for the Essence of Early Judaism

Appreciation and Critique of E. P. Sanders' Methodology

(1) *Appreciation*

E. P. Sanders has critically assailed the methods, presuppositions and attitudes of New Testament scholars as they compare Early Judaism with Early Christianity;[55] hence, it is fitting to reflect now on the strengths and weaknesses of his methodology. First, Sanders correctly disparages any comparison of Early Judaism with Early Christianity that is unsympathetic to Early Judaism. Far too often, as we saw above (pp. 30–1), scholars have assessed Early Judaism pejoratively, letting a triumphalism or Christian bias of prophetic fulfillment over a putative Pharisaic legalism besmear the obvious authentic piety and joy in the Torah, 'Simḥat Torah', characteristic of many segments of Early Judaism. A loud proclamatory approach to the religious data has deafened ears to the plaintive plea for grace and forgiveness in many early Jewish prayers, notably in the Prayer of Manasseh.

When references are made by New Testament scholars to the Eighteen Benedictions it is almost always only to the twelfth benediction, and there to the *Birkath hām-Mînîm*,[56] and almost never to the sixth benediction, which reads as follows:

> Forgive us, our Father, for we have sinned against thee.
> Erase and blot out our transgressions from before thine eyes,
> For thou art abundantly compassionate.
> Blessed art thou, O Lord, who forgives readily.[57]

This concept of God and this plea for forgiveness shatters Weber's systematic categorization of Judaism, and any projection of Early Judaism as a system of rigid legalistic subservience through a binding system of works-righteousness to a *deus ex machina*.[58] And this confessed *need for forgiveness*, probably typical of an introspective devotee of the Torah, is found echoing throughout the Pseudepigrapha. I think readily of the Prayer of Manasseh ('I have sinned, O Lord, I have sinned; And I certainly know my sins ... Forgive me, O Lord, forgive me! ... For you are the God of those who repent.' My idiomatic translation of the Syriac) and Joseph and Aseneth 12:5 ('I have sinned [*hēmarton*], O Lord, before you I have greatly sinned') and 12:12 ('Rescue [*rusai*] me, O Lord ... Rescue me, O Lord ...'). How Paul could have missed this concept of repentance so typical of Judaism is, as G. F. Moore stated, 'inexplicable'.[59]

Far too often New Testament scholars have claimed to have painted an accurate picture of Early Judaism, when in fact they have read back into the period before 70 much of the tension and the distasteful anti-Jewish polemic that we have all, perhaps reluctantly, come to admit is characteristic of Paul's polemical utterances,[60] and of the *Tendenzen* in Matthew and John. If a New Testament scholar wishes to understand Early Judaism he or she must listen sensitively to *all* of the extant literature.

To accomplish that task, and it is a *sine qua non* for any comparisons, years of concentration are required. It simply will not suffice to read carefully a good translation, nor to try not to confuse the chronological layers of a document, nor to consider whether one is reading a late Jewish or Christian interpolation or redaction. It takes more than all of these attempts together.

Far too often I hear about a young 'scholar', who after studying the New Testament in Greek for ten years expresses confidence that he or she is well-equipped and prepared to compare, for example, the Apocalypse of John with 4 Ezra. In answer to my question how well he or she knows 4 Ezra the answer comes back rather proudly that last week, all of it, had been spent reading 4 Ezra. The false pride of knowledge acquired is due almost solely to the fact that the student has read a document competitive peers have only heard about or scanned cursorily. The student never contemplated reading the document in the extant Syriac or Latin, or searching for the theological threads that unite yet disrupt this pseudepigraphon. He or she never really wanted to know that much about 4 Ezra! He or she never began to search for the sociological *Sitz im Leben* and chronological period in Early Judaism represented by the tortured entelechy behind 4 Ezra. Without empathy for the loss and frustration experienced by the author of 4 Ezra, any comparison is not only unwarranted; it is a massive miscomparison.

This lengthy discussion is necessary because it isolates and clarifies a major problem in our comparisons of Early Judaism and Early Christianity. We all tend to have contempt for the individual who simply picks up a translation of the New Testament, reads through it, and feels confident to defend an opinion. Each of us attempts to explain to this person the necessity of perceiving the historical matrix of the documents, the possible layers of tradition, and the alterations of traditions evident thanks to years of form critical analysis and redaction criticism. We should now turn this judgment back upon ourselves to see to what extent we have tended to read documents of Early Judaism as if they were this morning's newspaper.

In the light of these criticisms, it is appropriate to recall an old American Indian piece of folk-wisdom: 'Do not criticize your brother until you have walked a mile in his moccasins.'

We turn now to a second weakness of some current New Testament scholarship which Sanders has rightly criticized. Often comparisons are made without even reading the document to be cited. Even Strack and Billerbeck's list of parallels of important concepts shared by the rabbinic corpus and the New Testament writings (p. 31, n. 8), and indexes in collections of translations of Jewish documents, concordances, and other reference aids serve us badly if we use them to replace a quest for understanding by scrutinizing the document itself. What great disservice the computer will do to our combined search for understanding if we let it do the collecting of data for us. Concordances and other aids to research are, of course, invaluable; but they should be used as guides, and not as a replacement for the time-consuming study of the document itself, and then of the other writings cognate with it.

The extrapolation of a term, phrase or concept from a living document tends to kill both the term and even the document. As words in a dictionary have no life, and hence many meanings which are sometimes almost contradictory, so excised words can be manipulated to mean what we would like or dislike. Not only must the context of a word or phrase be observed, and not forgotten, but also the organic living relationships between it and other words and phrases webbed together by an author in narrative or poetry or in other ways must be considered. For example, all of us know where the term for the divine *logos* appears in the New Testament, and that in the Gospel of John it does not appear after 1:14. We also know that there is a categorical difference between *logos* and *rēma*. Some of us know, moreover, that in Syriac literature the former is always represented by *mell^ethâ* and the latter by *pethghāmâ*. How many recognize, however, that there is an exception? In the Odes of Solomon they are both used to represent the divine *logos*, and not as in John only in the opening verses but throughout the collection. When perceptions such as these are before us we may proceed with fruitful comparisons between documents.

It is disheartening to pick up book after book, published by New Testament scholars, and find neatly separated out for scrutiny the use of a pertinent theme in 'The Apocrypha and Pseudepigrapha'. Tables of contents disclose that these sections customarily appear in the beginning of books and cover less than four pages. These documents, now numbering seventy-eight,[61] are not only treated cavalierly, but they are also isolated and not integrated into the discussion. Certainly, in future our work must be more objective, inclusive and sophisticated.

There is certainly a canonical bias and myopia operative in much work that proposes to compare Early Judaism and Early Christianity. The Old Testament often fares much better in such comparisons than do the documents of Early Judaism. Perhaps this unbalanced methodology is because of one or more of the following attitudes or presuppositions: the Old Testament is inspired but those other books are not; the Old Testament is canon but the other writings are both extracanonical and apocryphal; the Old Testament was normative for early Jews but the Pseudepigrapha is a collection of esoterica that influenced only a few; the Old Testament is a treasure house of precious truths but the 'discarded' documents are characterized by wild and fanciful speculations; the Old Testament is a selection of books deliberately chosen by the intelligent leaders of Early Judaism but the other second-rate works were carefully assessed and deliberately rejected as inferior writings. Some theologians may still be able to survive while subscribing to one or two of these positions. But no critical historian – and therefore no New Testament scholar interested in Christian Origins – will advocate any of them. These opinions, briefly summarized, pervert Judaism and doom the launching of any comparative analysis. My comments here may have at times seemed too polemical; but with Sanders I am endeavouring to implant a better understanding of Early Judaism, and one which will let it speak on its own terms and in its own words.[62]

The third and final point of major agreement with Sanders[63] in developing a reliable methodology for comparing Judaism and Christianity is that each religion must be understood holistically and compared as a whole with the other also understood as a whole.[64] Both religions must be treated in precisely the same way, with the same justice and empathy. Each is to be understood on its own terms. Motif research and the study of parallels between Judaism and Christianity must not be abandoned for fear of the charge of parallelomania; but these comparisons must take careful cognizance of the whole and the function and context of the words excised.

(2) *Critique*

The major difficulty I have with Sanders' methodology is his insistence that we must compare Judaism and Christianity (Paul), each 'an entire religion', as 'two wholes' (p. 16). While Sanders rightly criticizes comparisons based on 'reduced essences', his quest to compare 'essential elements' (pp. 9–10) and 'two wholes' is often tantamount to the comparison of two 'essences' and does not allow for the fundamental diversities in Early Judaism. Sanders' claim that 'it is not necessary to say much about the comparison of essence' (p. 13), elicits considerable reflections.[65] First, what is an 'essence'? What signifies the boundaries between what is an essence and what is not an essence? Is an 'essence' tantamount to that which is essential? If so, how do you move from 'the essential' to 'the essence'? If not, how do you go about searching for or speaking about 'essence'? This whole enterprise has filled tomes with philosophical debate. The search for *essentia* is an elusive and very theoretical, indeed subjective enterprise. As D. Bonhoeffer stated in *Akt und Sein* (Munich, 1956; ET by B. Noble, New York, 1961), his most brilliant philosophical work, which was his inaugural dissertation in 1931, a *via* must be 'found at once through theory to the pre-theoretic givenness. The simple givenness is marred by all interpretation, and anything real already represents interpretation, for reality is constituted by consciousness, and so everything real must be absolutely "ruled out of bounds"' (pp. 52f). This quotation, which contains critical reflections on Husserl's phenomenology, indicates the problems involved in searching for the 'essence' of a thing, reveals the thinker's proclivities for distorting the essence, and suggests to us that at best 'Early Judaism' is our scholarly construct from numerous elusive and ill-defined essences.

The search for an essence involves, *inter alia*, an appreciation of the need for both the panoramic and the particular, as I have learned from reflecting on Bonhoeffer's words and subsequently reading L. Baeck's *Das Wesen des Judentums* (Wiesbaden, 1960[6]). To obtain an approximation of a description of the essence of a 'religion' − and a straight-forward definition often tends to obscure the phenomenon or subjectively discard what is deemed unessential − means both to have a panoramic view of all manifestations of it, and thereby to blur almost all particulars, and subsequently also to focus upon one facet, and hence to leave the totality less clear and perhaps unperceived. Our human eye cannot see all at once, and so our attention must fluctuate between panoramic perception and clear focus. Along such lines of thought Baeck was led to the insight that the one who wishes to perceive the essence must see each entity in terms of the totality (p. ix). Yet, even this methodology only serves to open up a very difficult task.

I know how to go about trying to discern the essence of an homogenous document written by one author. But when I conclude, through introspective debates with myself, what is probably the essence, I know full well that my interpretation will cause not immediate agreement from scholars, but waves of disagreements. The conclusion, if not intensely personal, was at least partially subjective and the result of numerous successive choices. Now, if this is indeed a fact, how much more difficult it would be for anyone then to proceed from one document to the sixty-five works in the Pseudepigrapha and conclude what is the essence of this type of writing — or even what seems to be essential to it. And if we could all agree upon an articulation of what is the essence of the Pseudepigrapha that would still be at least several steps away from comparing the essences of other types of Jewish literature to that elusive quantum called far too facilely by Sanders 'the *essence* of Judaism' (p. 9, his italics).

It is instructive to ask how anyone, let alone a scholar as brilliant and well read in Jewish literature as Sanders, can talk, not about a confessional core, but about 'the essence' of Judaism. To search for an essence is to assume or presuppose that there is one there to be found. In all of my discussions with specialists of Early Judaism either privately or in seminars none of us has ever mentioned the word 'essence' or sought for what is 'essential' in Judaism. I take that fact to be significant; it does not indicate that our discussions were myopic or too inductive. It may indicate that one should not assume an essence.

Let us leave aside for the moment whether it is possible that there was an essence to Early Judaism, and consider how Sanders seeks to identify this essence or whole. First, Sanders does admit at the outset that there is a problem:

> What is difficult is to focus on *what* is to be compared. (p. 12)
> The problem is how to discover two wholes, both of which are considered and defined on their own merits and in their own terms, to be compared with each other. (p. 16)

It is indicative of the problems involved that Sanders italicizes 'what' in the statement '*what* is to be compared'. Sanders rightly sees the problem in comparing *reduced* essences; but does he not perhaps avoid the issue when he states that we must compare "essential elements" or "two wholes". How do we find that 'essence or whole'? It must come from somewhere; it must frankly be *posited*, not *observed*.

Secondly, Sanders posits the essence of Judaism from a reputed essence in *rabbinic* Judaism. It is singularly significant that Sanders tends to equate the two very different terms 'Palestinian Judaism' and 'rabbinic Judaism' (see esp. pp. 2—5). Sanders, to be sure, has invested his time in reading the rabbinic corpus, and that assuredly under a master, the late Dr Mordechai Kamrat (p. xv). It is through rabbinics that he entered the arena of Early Judaism. Sanders reveals more than he may realize when he claims that 'early Rabbinic (Tannaitic) literature ... deserves pride of place' (pp. 24f).[66] It is obvious, therefore, why he spent 1963 and the year I first met him, 1968–9, studying 'rabbinic Hebrew' (p. xv). He was becoming a master of rabbinics.[67] He has not shown any similar interest in studying the Ethiopic of Enoch, the Syriac of 2 Baruch, the Coptic of the Apocalypse of Zephaniah, the Latin and Syriac of 4 Ezra, or the Slavonic of 2 Enoch. This disparity in his interests and training, is now manifest in his methodology.

I can see how one can be tantalized about searching for the essence of Judaism when one is immersed in rabbinics. That corpus, while containing diverse documents,[68] has been carefully edited by masters, who as Neusner states, included what they thought essential, and excluded what they thought unimportant.[69] Likewise, rabbinic literature reflects the vicissitudes of history, most notably the burning of the Temple in 70, the razing of Jerusalem in 135, and the raising of Aelia Capitolina in the second century.

By excluding exceptions to the rule one can write grammatical laws, by ignoring inconsistencies and odd factors one can develop a philosophical system, and by excluding many divergent early phenomena one can arrive at an edited body of literature; perhaps to a certain extent this is characteristic of rabbinic literature. Sanders himself admits that the 'Tannaitic literature offers a better opportunity of describing a pattern of religion than much of the literature which is presumably much older, such as Jubilees and the various portions of 1 Enoch' (p. 25).[70] But, if our quest is not for the essence of Tannaitic literature but of Early Judaism, or of Palestinian Judaism before 70, we have more, much more, to consider.

Sanders now moves toward a creative unifying tool, namely the definition of a 'pattern of religion' (p. 17), which he thinks solves the problems he sees in a holistic comparison of Judaism and Christianity (p. 16). The definition of a pattern of religion as 'the description of how a religion is perceived by its adherents to *function*', entails primarily how its adherents sense '*getting in and staying in are understood*: the way in which a religion is understood to admit and retain members is considered to be the way it "functions"' (p. 17, italics his).

All these words, which are accompanied by an unusual number of disclaimers, exclusions and qualifications, sound strange and so far removed from the documents I have been studying for a quarter of a century; indeed it is not a description related to documents, but a *highly philosophical abstraction*. It is a theoretical position.[71] As Nils Dahl stated, Sanders' approach is 'ahistorical. Sanders pays little attention to social conditions and historical change.'[72]

Only one brief further reaction is possible here. I am struck by how strange Sanders' words would sound to an early Jew. In my opinion the Jew who wrote one of the Dead Sea Scrolls, one of the Apocrypha or Pseudepigrapha, or a Jew we know by name such as Hillel, Philo, Josephus, or Johanan ben Zakkai, would have responded to this prescription for approaching Judaism with a dumbfounded and glazed stare. Perhaps one of them would stutter, 'but a Jew does not get in or get out of this abstraction you call a religion. We were born into Judaism and our fathers circumcised us on the eighth day, to signify our families' devotion to tradition, covenant and Torah, and we were called *bar-mitzwah*, "son of the covenant", at the age of twelve'. (Compare Paul's comments in Phil 3:5.) 'We are what we are, not because of any paradigm of "getting in" or "staying in", but because of our forefathers, almost infinite in number, and their response to Yahweh. We are not even agreed among ourselves that epispasm can make a Jew a non-Jew. Even punishing, such as the stoning of Achan the son of Zerah [cf. Josh 7:16−26], does not remove one from Israel, but ensures, perhaps, their presence among the sons of Israel in the age to come.' What tends to bother me is that all that I have just written and imagined seems irrefutable[73] and diminishes the usefulness of Sanders' pattern-of-religion approach to Early Judaism;[74] but if any one scholar should agree with me it would be Sanders, who was so impressed by the search for a definition of what makes one a 'Jew' or a 'Christian' that he launched the significant project that has now given us three volumes entitled *Jewish and Christian Self-Definition*.

The present comments do not intend to do justice to the erudition and answers Sanders has been giving to us on some major questions. For the present I am attempting to understand how to compare justly and faithfully the documents in the Pseudepigrapha with those in the New Testament. Sanders' work has come before us only because he has defined a methodology, and did promise to 'cover the great bulk of the surviving Palestinian material dating from the period 200 B.C.E. to 200 C.E., so that it will be possible ... to draw some conclusions about Judaism in Palestine in the first century' (p. 18). Regarding this quotation, it is perplexing how he can be certain which of the extant documents are Palestinian. And to refer to the first century is to refer to two distinct periods in the history of Judaism, specifically pre- and post-70 Judaism.

The major judgment is clear: Sanders did not include in his examination 'the great bulk of the surviving Palestinian material'. He admits, later on, that his work on the Dead Sea Scrolls 'will be primarily limited to the major Scrolls from Cave I and the Covenant of Damascus' (p. 25). He will deal only 'with a selection of works from the Apocryphal and Pseudepigraphical writings' (p. 25). Moreover, several 'works which probably come from Palestine and which can be dated to the period under consideration have been omitted' (p. 25). He admits he will not consider in his comparisons the Testaments of the Twelve Patriarchs and 2 Baruch. He will also leave 'out of consideration the Aramaic Targums' (p. 25). It is clear that Sanders, by his own admission does not 'cover the great bulk of the surviving Palestinian material'. What is not clear is how Sanders can omit so many documents which he does not even mention.[75] It is clear also that by omitting so much he not only presents a partial approach, but he also shapes a religion that never existed; a random selection of documents from any norm gives contours and shapes to a phenomenon which is thus created by the norm and selection.

I have no doubt that Sanders has been far more successful in demolishing Weber's system of Early Judaism and in pinpointing the egregious errors in the presuppositions and methodologies of many publications than he has been in grasping Early Judaism or carrying off a comparison of religions. We are all indebted to him for encouraging us to face some major questions, to wrestle with primary sources, and to rise above our minute analytical, often textual and linguistic studies, narrow concentration on only one or two documents, or collections of documents, and to ponder with some synthesis in mind what all of this is *really about*. I shall always be grateful to him for his work, and agree with Meeks[76] and Hooker[77] that it is a 'monumental' work. Because Sanders' book is 'one of the very great works of New Testament scholarship of our time',[78] as Sandmel stated, I have felt free to clarify my personal disagreements with the methodology he adopted.

The Elusiveness of the Search

Should we search for 'the essence' of Early Judaism? Should we acknowledge problems with present methods and try either to patch them up or to construct new ways of searching for 'the essence'? If 'essence' is the invariable nature of a phenomenon or thing or the significant constant feature of it, then we are not justified in searching for that which never existed according to *all* the literary evidence of Early Judaism. We must not assume there is an essence to Early Judaism, and then in a heavy-handed way construct models and techniques for helping us find what we think is there.

It is important to clarify two points. First, 'essence' is an abstract term, influenced by Greek logic and abstraction. The early Jews characteristically did not write abstract philosophy. They were pre-occupied with God-centred and liturgically influenced expressions and confessions, and praised not abstract principles but a living God who had moved towards them repeatedly in history and tradition (Deut 7:6–11; cf. 4 Ezra 4:27).[79]

Second, each segment of this gigantic complex we call Early Judaism (I am not persuaded 'religion' is a helpful term) would have had different answers to the main questions we raise, and that is because the Jews formed non-doctrinal dynamic responses to God and formatively important traditions. Early Judaism was not a philosophy, a theology, or a doctrinal system; it rather reflected myriad faithful (and unfaithful) responses to a Creator, to a dynamically active God, who was confessed in one universally binding prayerful affirmation, the *Shema*, which was recited by religious Jews at least twice daily on the week days (*'ar^ebhîth w^eshah^arîth*). *Liturgy*, based upon shared traditions and history, memories and hope, kept the differences, so essential to a lively faithfulness, from exploding apart the living reality we call Judaism. Perhaps the theologian and not the pure historian knows best − as any careful student of 1 Baruch, 2 Baruch, or 4 Ezra readily concludes − that what has kept the Hebrews, Israel and Judaism together is not the *b^enei Israel*, but Yahweh.

These points raised against any attempt to posit an essence in Early Judaism by failing to observe all *essentia* need to be emphasized and repeated. Despite the distinguished efforts of scholars, like W. D. Davies,[80] the idea of a normative Judaism seems unfortunately to be entrenched among New Testament scholars, and others. The arguments against a normative Judaism are not diminished by the recognition that pre-revolt (pre-66) Palestinian Judaism was neither a chaos nor in anarchistic disarray; they are not altered by the obvious fact that the Romans tended to recognize one ruling body of Jews in Jerusalem. The Great Sanhedrin (*snhdryn gdwlh*; mSanh 1:6) in the first century represented the political and legal body to the Romans and was perhaps the supreme court of the people (cf. Josephus, *Ant* 20.10.5);[81] but an *establishment* must be distinguished from a normative theological system. Recognition of a group by a conquering nation and the acknowledgement of a high-priestly aristocracy is not to be construed as an internal essence.

Without any doubt, the cult in Jerusalem was dominant (cf. Tob 1:4), and only to a relatively minor extent rivalled by the Samaritan temple which was destroyed by John Hyrcanus in 107 B.C.E.[82] Jews throughout Judea and Galilee tended to acknowledge the central religious significance of Jerusalem (cf. Sir 36:13, the Eighteen Benedictions 14) and the cultic importance of the Temple, 'the holy dwelling of the Most High' (Ps 46:5).[83] But to acknowledge the Temple as the national sanctuary[84] is not to forget the anti-Temple rhetoric found at Qumran, and in many writings in Early Judaism, especially the apocalypses (1 En 89:73, 74; cf. 2 Bar 68:6−7). The recognition of the centripetal significance of the Temple (cf. 2 En 51:4) can and did go hand in glove with a rejection of the priestly ruling class (cf. Mal 1:6−8) − considered by some religious Jews to be illegitimate − and the deep and ancient traditions that the present Temple is but an imperfect model of the future earthly, heavenly, or eschatological (perhaps messianic; cf. PssSol 17:32−6) Temple (cf. SibOr 5.414−33).[85] The genius and antiquity of such reflections has been proved by the discovery of the Dead Sea Scrolls and especially by the publication of the Temple Scroll. To acknowledge the centripetal force of the Temple is not to confess that the Temple was the norm for a monolithic Judaism.[86] Jews could and apparently did frequent the Temple in a spirit of disgust for the desecration of the sacred spot.[87] The cult not only proved to be a unifying force in Judaism, it also tended to spawn differences, as the struggles for control, as well as the corruption within the priesthood, produced opposition. Rabbinic texts tend to idolize what had existed earlier;[88] some apocrypha and pseudepigrapha, most of the Dead Sea Scrolls, as well as some late Old Testament books, as Hanson has demonstrated,[89] reflect tremendous tensions among rival priestly groups who struggled for control of the cultus.

Hence the Temple cult was dominant and central, the ruling priestly class was the establishment;[90] but this ideal unity was torn by rival factions − as the terrifying actions in Jerusalem from 66 to 70 show clearly. An acknowledged *axis mundi* with a living cult is not to be confused with a theological system or a normative Judaism. If we recognize that the Temple cult was controlled by Sadducees and a few prestigious Pharisees, we also need to note carefully that some 'priests' were aligned with the social group so abhorrent and unclean to the pious in Early Judaism: before 70 there were *'am ha-aretz* priests (cf. *khn 'm h'rṢ* in tAZ III.10; bSanh 90*b*; Masseket Derek Erez I.14 (ed. M. Higger, vol. 1, p. 64); bNed 20*a*; ARN Version A, xli (ed. S. Schechter, p. 132)).[91]

Perceptions of Early Judaism and Christian Origins

The preceding comments clarify my position, or at least methodology. It should be clear that I stand resolutely against any abstract attempt to extract from the extant documents a systematic theology of Early Judaism.[92] These documents, and, of course, the Bible also, are not to be viewed as deposits of revealed truths from which a theology of doctrine can be systematically constructed.

These books have been produced out of crises.[93] The search for the intent of the human author must be accompanied by a study of the social, historical and intellectual aspects of the writer's (or writers') own time. This process in no way suggests that the critical historian can adequately assess the revelatory claims or experiences of the author. Revelation represents a concept that frustrates and finally embarrasses any critic who attempts to examine it critically from the stance of the historian. The historian *qua* historian will be overcome by the demands of the present collection of Pseudepigrapha, and will find sanity in the wisdom that the revelatory claims of the authors are not perspectives he, or she, must assess theologically. The historian is called on to describe not to prescribe; it should be obvious that I have been attempting to reduce the pressures upon me by acknowledging the limitations and responsibilities of the historian.

Let me warn, therefore, that we should not tacitly assume that there is a theology of the Pseudepigrapha. There are far too many *theologies* in these writings. Some documents are very conservative, among these are Jubilees and the Psalms of Solomon which tend to argue that no gentile will enter the kingdom. Other documents are liberal, among these are the Testaments of the Twelve Patriarchs and the Odes of Solomon, which suggest that the gentiles will turn to God. Some works, like 4 Ezra, are pessimistic; others, like 2 Baruch, are optimistic. *A collection* of documents to be called the Pseudepigrapha is *not* to be confused with *a canon* of ancient texts.

Nomenclature: New Definitions and Discarded Terms

Great misrepresentations have been caused and precious insights lost due to imprecise nomenclature. The imprecisions in our language and the chaotic state of our terms has led R. Murray to call for precise definitions and new terminologies.[94] This is certainly not the place to digress into a long debate with him,[95] I shall set out only the areas in which I am in agreement with him. At the outset, of course, is the shared recognition that our special area of research is fraught with imprecise definitions and confused, even contradictory, terms. He is also correct to stress that the recognition of the diversity in Early Judaism discloses the inappropriateness of the terms 'Jews', 'Jewish', and 'Judaism'. Frequently I have felt compelled to put these nouns within inverted commas or (less frequently) to use qualifying adjectives, such as 'apparent' or 'so-called'. He is understandably discontented with the term 'sectarian Judaism' (p. 198), and correctly argues that the false distinction between 'Hellenistic and Palestinian Judaism' founders on the perception that 'the whole spectrum' of Jewish phenomena was shaped 'by factors other than the impact of hellenistic culture'.[96]

Without full elaboration or discussion the major terms – I believe – should be defined as follows:

Early Judaism – certainly not 'Late Judaism' or 'Spätjudentum'[97] – should be the term used to refer to the phenomena in Judaism dating from around the end of the third century B.C.E. until the end of the second century C.E. As 'Early Christianity' signifies the origins of Christianity so 'Early Judaism' denotes the beginnings of synagogal (modern) Judaism. Unlike such terms as 'Late Judaism', *Early* Judaism has the connotation of being alive with refreshing new insights: we find here highly-developed and sophisticated metaphysical speculations, and introspective perceptions into the psychological complexities of being human. As Stone observes, from his intimate knowledge of the Pseudepigrapha, the earliest portions of Aramaic Enoch provide us with a surprising, 'picture of a rather sophisticated and rich realm of speculation and "sacred science" within Judaism, the highly developed ascent vision and the broad interest in "scientific" matters are totally unexpected'.[98] Early Jews were brilliantly alive with penetrating speculations into almost every facet of our world and universe. For this, and many other reasons, I prefer to use the term 'Early Judaism', and not others that (may or definitely do) reflect a distorted view of Jewish phenomena.

Since the term *hellenistic* must no longer be used in a geographical sense, I think we should use it to denote only aspects of a chronological period.[99] The hellenistic period, which has different chronological limits at divergent archaeological sites, should denote the time period when hellenistic (Greek and then Roman) influences penetrated emphatically and deeply into Palestinian Judaism; in the Diaspora it should specify the time following Alexander the Great's mastery over one geographical area after another. By this definition, hellenistic influence is possible before the hellenistic period; this flexibility allows us, for example, to speak about the hellenistic influence on the Samaritan papyri before the conquest of Alexander. Discussions will obviously be spawned on the *terminus a quo* and *terminus ad quem* of the hellenistic period; but if so, then we have moved away from the confusion that now reigns. Some scholars use this term correctly, others cause unfortunate confusion by referring to Diasporic Jews as hellenistic Jews.

Using 'hellenistic' as an adjective for a chronological period clarifies our comparative analyses; for example, we can with lucidity compare the exilic Jews with hellenistic Jews and those two with early Byzantine Jews. Since we shall now need an adjective to refer to Jews living outside Palestine I propose that we refer to them as *Diasporic Jews*, or perhaps more precisely as *Roman Jews, Egyptian Jews, Palestinian Jews*, or other clearly meaningful and precise terms.

Some terms, while inappropriate etymologically or in a strict sense, probably should − at least for a while − be retained because of their popular coinage. We dare not retreat into a nomenclature that smacks of opaque scholarly jargon. Hence, while 'Old Testament' is often not as appropriate as Hebrew Scriptures, or *Biblia Hebraica*, or Tanach, it is not offensive to modern Jews and is well recognized by the public; it refers to sacred scriptures cherished by Jews and Christians, and promises, hopefully, a future in which Jews and Christians may recognize shared *sacra scriptura*.

The term 'New Testament' is more problematic than the term 'Old Testament'. Here, Christians will draw a line, refusing to rename the twenty-seven books so important for their faith. The term shall be retained with two caveats: first, it should never be used to indicate that the 'Old Testament' is old, archaic, and out-of-date. Fortunately, the authors of the New Testament documents can be cited against such preposterous thoughts, and happily (or providentially) the Church that gave us the canon denounced Marcion who espoused such thoughts. Second, we must acknowledge that it is very difficult to decide whether the New Testament documents should be studied within the history of Judaism or the history of the Church.[100] The caveat, therefore, is that New Testament scholars do not work on the New Testament; that is the domain of the Church historian of the late fourth and subsequent centuries. New Testament scholars devote their lives to the study of the *documents* in the New Testament, or passages in these writings. It is for this reason that I have been referring to a comparison of the documents in the Pseudepigrapha and those in the New Testament, and stressing that the former is a modern collection and the latter an ancient one.

Many terms should now be discarded as no longer appropriate. In such a list should be at least the following: *intertestamental*, because it is misrepresentative and offensive (see chapter 1); *normative Judaism*, since this concept is a product of nineteenth-century scholars who pounded early Jewish literature into a desired shape by means of reading back into pre-70 Judaism what was perceived by some as 'normative' in post-70 rabbinic Judaism (see the following discussion); *heresy* and *orthodoxy*, because if there was no monolithic Judaism, then there was no one to rule before all Jews that an idea was not acceptable[101] – Judaism was not doctrinally based and debates over the meaning of Torah reflect a living tradition and a tolerance of informed opinions; *sectarian Judaism* without careful qualifications,[102] because if there is no normative, orthodox and monolithic Judaism then sects cannot be seen as hostile to and outside a non-existent core, because there were many different types of Jews (there were far more than four sects), and because not one document among the sixty-five in the Pseudepigrapha is now assigned with any confidence to a known sect (see chapter 1, 'A Non-Sectarian Approach' p. 19); *primitive Christianity*,[103] because Christianity did not evolve out of a dying mother, but out of a highly sophisticated, and phenomenologically complex Jewish 'religion' and culture. Christianity was the heir of over a thousand years of traditions, both written (edited, expanded, and debated upon as we know so well thanks to two-hundred-years research on and study of Isaiah) and oral. Christianity arose in a cosmopolitan Jewish culture which was impregnated after the exile repeatedly by influences from Babylon, Egypt, Persia, Syria, Greece, Parthia and Rome.

Since many of these influences came through wars and economic relationships, especially the caravan routes, we dare not assume that a Jew is a 'religious' Jew. Many Jews were religious only for convenience, social respectability, or because of the perennial need for an efficacious 'god'. It is easy to slip and think about Jews as 'religious' people because we are working — except with some papyri, like the Zeno papyri, the Samaritan papyri, and the Bar-Kokhba letters — almost always with religious texts. I can think of no book in the canon, in the Apocrypha, or in the Pseudepigrapha that was written by a non-religious Jew. Certainly that would be a rash judgment to make on the authors of Ecclesiastes and 4 Ezra, for a religious Jew can be thoroughly pessimistic.

Methodology and Sensitivity

From the beginning of this book we have been discussing the proper methodological approach to phenomena in Early Judaism. The major positive factors are the following: first, to let the authors of the documents speak on their own terms and with their own concepts, fears and dreams. Secondly, to be humble, sympathetic and non-apologetic in our approach. Not only Christians but also Jews have repeatedly failed to listen with sufficient sympathy. Thirdly, to focus upon a coherent whole document, or portion of a composite work, and to see terms, motifs, and possible parallels in their context and with their given functions; and then to step back and attempt to perceive additions to the document, and the document's relationships with other remnants of Early Judaism.

What augurs well for our present task and projects is to note that precisely this methodology and sensitivity is being practised throughout the world by international experts on the Pseudepigrapha to name *only a few* of them: by Stone and Flusser in Israel, by Agourides in Greece, by Dexinger in Austria, by Burchard, Kümmel, Hengel, Betz, and many others in Western Germany, by Walter in E. Germany, by Denis in Belgium, by Baarda, de Jonge, Klijn and van der Horst in Holland, by Philonenko in France, by Knibb, Shutt, Vermes and Alexander in England, by Anderson and Black in Scotland, by M. Smith, J. Z. Smith, Metzger, MacRae, Wintermute, Strugnell, Priest, Nickelsburg, Kee, Harrington, Collins, VanderKam, Sanders, Harrelson, Kraft, Attridge, and others in the United States, by Meshchersky in Russia, by de Villieurs in South Africa, by Anderson in Australia, by Hultgård in Sweden, and by Sanders, Pietersma, Lutz and Lindenberger in Canada.

Canon and *Sacra Scriptura*

It is disheartening to note that out of an anachronistic and confessional canonical stance some scholars continue to disparage those who focus their research on the so-called extracanonical works as if they are second class citizens in the academy. To a certain extent this attitude is fostered by names given to our endowed chairs and professorships. We are all professors of the New Testament or of Christian Origins,[104] none of us is a professor of the Pseudepigrapha, or a professor of the Dead Sea Scrolls. The importance of these other collections of texts is recognized only because they are perceived to be relevant for the Bible, in particular to the New Testament or to a recognized essential in the curriculum, 'Christian Origins'.

Perhaps it would be too optimistic to report that a refreshing breeze has begun to reshape the bureaucratic structures in our universities and seminaries. Perhaps someday a scholar can stand before us and state that in his or her institution the literary products of Early Judaism are accorded the same space in the curriculum and the same value as the Greek and Roman classics, and the other literary treasures of antiquity.

It is significant for the concept of the canon, which in terms of the New Testament canon clearly postdates the period of history we have endeavoured to master, that the librarians in the Vatican have been wise and perceptive. Charles' *APOT*, James' *ANT*, Kautzsch's *APAT*, the texts on 1 Enoch, 2 Enoch, 3 Enoch, the Testaments of the Twelve Patriarchs, and other so-called apocryphal documents, and studies upon them are shelved in the Biblioteca Apostolica Vaticana under *Sacra scriptura*, as I learned personally during some research after the *SNTS* Congress in Rome in 1981.

Synthesis: No Normative Judaism

While we have not yet been able to reconstruct a full portrait of Early Judaism, it is safe to say that the old portrait of a normative Judaism has been shattered by the vast amount of new literary evidence from Early Judaism, especially the documents gathered together in the *Old Testament Pseudepigrapha*. Against the whole idea of a normative Judaism many insights have been brought forward to demonstrate that the concept of a normative Judaism results primarily from a tendency to read back into pre-70 Judaism the 'religion' found in much later, heavily edited rabbinic texts, and secondarily from the impression that Paul somewhat inaccurately portrayed a Judaism with a normative system.[105] Most scholars have come to discard the concept of normative Judaism for pre-70 phenomena, but a few scholars linger on with this and other anachronistic models. One factor, perhaps the major one, has not yet been emphasized in our discussion of the total impossibility of any type of closed, systematic, normative Judaism; and, correlative to that model, an exoteric, insignificant aberrant phenomenon that would eventually be labelled 'Christian'.

During the post-exilic period, as von Rad so brilliantly pointed out, there was a major unparalleled shift in the perception of history and God's action for and on behalf of his chosen nation Israel. The old model of history as the arena in which God is moving his nation towards a perfect future has utterly collapsed. Now, after Ezra, and in the great apocalyptic literature, this model has been replaced; there is a 'complete alteration in the way of viewing history'.[106] History has been depleted soteriologically. Recent and contemporary events, namely the subjection of the sons of Israel to enslavement not to Yahweh but to foreign idolatrous nations, tended to falsify and to disprove the faithful recitation of confessions, recitals of history, and the Deuteronomic optimism in history. The salvation of the nation Israel, now assuredly seen as only a faithful remnant of it, must come from a cataclysmic event from the beyond, anticipated only through divine revelations obtained through apocalyptic trips to the heavens above, the world ahead, or in apocalyptic visions and dreams. The present is devoid of salvific movements; only the eschaton contains meaning, salvation, and the trifold unification of humanity with itself, humans with nature and animals, and created beings with the Creator. These characteristics permeated virtually all the writings of Early Judaism, whether they be apocalypses, testaments, wisdom tracts, or hymns and prayers.

What is so impressively clear is that this charged atmosphere in Early Judaism is precisely what is absent in later rabbinic Judaism. Rabbinic *Halakah* is designed for a people settled down in history, not living with one foot on earth and the other in the eschaton. In polishing these rules of conduct for daily life the Rabbis used much older traditions (originally preserved in oral form), which derived, sometimes with little modification, from pre-70 Judaism. What had been moved through the centuries to the Mishnah, Tosephta and Talmudim had been moved from a non-normative framework in which apocalyptic speculations and apocalypticism itself flourished into a more systematized, organized, so-called normative structure of Judaism in which *Halakoth* were pervasively paradigmatic for this life here and now. What is missing in the rabbinic writings and so pervasively characteristic in Early Judaism, is the thorough going, categorically eschatological form and function of thought and life. Granted, the belief in the bodily resurrection of the individual after death and the yearning for the sending of God's Messiah lingered on and were influential; but the role of these ideas and beliefs was totally different from what it had been, at least in many segments of Palestinian pre-70 Judaism. Neusner is entirely correct, therefore, in his magisterial work titled *Judaism: The Evidence of the Mishnah*, to argue forcefully against the classical treatment of Judaism so definitive for many New Testament scholars, namely Moore's *Judaism in the First Century of the Christian Era: The Age of the Tannaim*. Neusner is certainly right in his judgment: 'Moore describes many kinds of Judaism as if they formed a single, fully symmetrical construct. The claim of "normativity" for this Judaism is not merely wrong. It is confusing, for it specifies one "Judaism" where there are many.'[107] The new translations of the Pseudepigrapha amply illustrate the wide divergencies – each 'normative' in its own way and for its own group or circle – that were alive in Early Judaism.

The Cosmic Theology of Early Judaism

The Pseudepigrapha opens our eyes to a cosmos full of activity. Above the earth are the *heavens*; first it is simply 'heavens', then these are numbered: three, seven, and finally ten (cf. 2 En 1–22). The heavens are not silent, but replete with activity; often they are portrayed as full of singing angels (AscenIs, TAdam). The harmony in heaven is sometimes broken; sinners are sometimes seen being punished in one of the heavens. Yet, far from reflecting any harmonious astronomical system, the heavens are also portrayed as the site of Paradise. Visits to the heavens are possible by holy ones; first this visit was conceived of as taking place through a dream (Dan 7:1–2, 1 En 1:1–2), later it was claimed to be an actual physical ascent in the body (2 En 1:6–3:3). Angels fill the heavens and their names are introduced with a crescendoing force when the apocalypses are laid out in chronological order, from, for example, 1 Enoch – when it is broken down into its five sections – then 2 Enoch, and finally 3 Enoch.

Below the earth – conceived either subglobularly or subterraneanly – is the underworld, Sheol, the abode of the dead. The evil spirits are often seen as streaming forth from this arena; but such images are *not* characteristic of the Pseudepigrapha. The vision in the Pseudepigrapha is not of the region below; it is almost always of the realm above. Perhaps this cosmic focus results from an eschatology that is essentially utopian.

The earth is full of *demons*. Humanity is plagued by them. Almost all misfortunes are because of the demons: sickness, drought, death, and especially humanity's weaknesses about remaining faithful to the covenant. The region between heaven and earth seems to be almost cluttered with demons and angels; humanity is often seen as a pawn, helpless in the face of such cosmic forces, or already lost or saved, thanks to the determined nature of creation and the will of God. The head of the demons and evil angels is Satan, also called the Devil, Mastema and Belial. The leader of the good angels is Michael, assisted by Raphael, Sariel, and especially Gabriel. The misfortunes not caused by the demons are those sent by God, through intermediaries, to punish and to chastise his people.

Nor would it be representative of all the writings to say that *God* is *either* totally in heaven *or* fully present on earth. According to the apocalypses, if the one ascending is unusually holy he may approach close to God's throne; but the holy one never sees the face of God (cf. *idein gar opsin tēn emēn amēchanon*, EzekTrag *Exagoge* 101).[108] The holy one can only describe the contours around him: glory, purity, light, power, the throne, and especially the impenetrable brightness (cf. 1 En 14:8−25, esp. 21−5). God is, therefore, not far removed from mankind and unapproachable, or in an *Intermundia*, as Lucretius (c. 97−54 B.C.E.) thought; while he is no longer perceived as present in contemporary events, yet he is *always present to hear* the voice of the faithful ones. Angels are not the ones who separate humanity from God; they are the messengers who represent humanity's prayers, dreams, wishes, or needs to God, and conversely God's forceful presence to the recipient.

While God is not delimited to one locus in creation, he does tend to be portrayed, at least in the apocalypses, as residing above the highest heaven. And that language does not mean (as it did centuries earlier) that Yahweh is the most exalted god; it denotes the exalted holiness of the *only* God. Emanating from the court are concepts that become personified and eventually hypostatic. The earliest and best example of them is Wisdom, who can now be seen walking on earth. God's word is seen first as the word of God, then the word from God, and finally, perhaps in only a very few circles, 'the Word'. The voice of God, I am convinced, develops along analogous lines; but this possibility has not been observed or discussed in print (see Appendix).

Various means were found to articulate a covenantal relationship and bond between Yahweh and his people, Israel. In Judea many Jews would point to the *axis mundi* (cf. Jub 8:19), Jerusalem, and the Temple, with the high priest as central to the cult and this whole perception. In Galilee, some Jews turned to the itinerant miracle worker, like Ḥanina ben Dosa and Ḥoni. These were holy men, called 'Son of God', who could speak to God directly and influence him.

The Eschatological Anthropology of Early Judaism

Humanity is in a predicament (cf. 4 Ezra 3:20−7, the *cor malignum*). Almost all of the literature is anthropocentric in the sense that it evolves out of humanity's distress. Not only the prayers, but the narratives have a ringing sting of alienation about them. It is no wonder, therefore, that the author of Pseudo-Philo added a plaintive lament to the story of Sheila, Jeptha's daughter. It is out of this pathos, obviously generated by introspection as well as recognition of foreign domination that the religious Jew yearned more and more for the end of this age and the dawning of the age to come. In short the early Jew almost always thought in terms of eschatology.

All hope, all *dreams* were fired by recent *memories*, notably the Maccabean victories, which recalled the Davidic monarchy, which itself was seen through the Chronicler's rose-coloured glasses. Most especially germane was Yahweh's promise to David. Surely the Davidic Messiah will be revealed by God in our day, and speedily. Seldom has one nation been so vibrantly alive with so many religious dreams. In Early Judaism a quiet expectation billowed forth with excitement, caught the imagination of simple folk who tend to think with fists rather than with minds; the revolt against Rome became inevitable.[109]

The early Jews did not live in a world that was perceived according to an underlying philosophical or theological principle like the Stoic's *Logos*. Nor did they conceive of the world as cyclical and time as essentially unproductive and meaningless. Time was set in motion by God's chronological acts of creation; the Creator set in motion a linear history that was most of all *teleological*. The insightful and faithful Jews struggled to penetrate through secular history to the holy; the task became increasingly difficult, secular history darkened nearly everything. The view became almost opaque; but the vision was never lost.

The conviction — surfacing first (perhaps) in Essene and Samaritan traditions — that the Temple cult in Jerusalem was corrupt, and that sacred traditions had been accommodated to hellenistic practices ran through many segments of Early Judaism. True piety, and authentic commitment to the sacred was also felt in sectors of Early Judaism. And here the historian must pause to recall that the Knight of Faith, the truly pious one, as S. Kierkegaard perceived, may saunter unawares behind our literature and imperceptibly through the streets of first-century Jerusalem.

The individual's destiny was gradually explained by more and more Jews in terms of belief in the resurrection of the body after death. This idea or belief was not the sole possession of the Pharisees. It is found in many types of literature, notably in 2 Maccabees, the Psalms of Solomon,[110] and the common weekly prayer, the Eighteen Benedictions: O Lord, 'Thou art mighty ... sustaining the living, resurrecting the dead ... Blessed art thou, O Lord, who resurrects the dead.'[111] After one's death there is often a debate between the Devil and Michael over the fate of the individual, even if he is Moses, as we shall see in the examination of the relationship between Jude and the Testament of Moses (chapter 3, pp. 75–7). Other Jews thought of one's soul being weighed in the balance of good and evil works, or judged by Abel, the first one to die (TAb 13: *houtos estin huios Adam ... Abel ... kai kathētai hōde krinai pasan tēn ktisin kai elegchōn dikaious kai hamartōlous*).

Conclusion

All of these insights are possible because of the (chance) preservation of the Pseudepigrapha and other documents of Early Judaism. The understanding of the cosmos and humanity — the *Zeitgeist* of Early Judaism — is perhaps the single most important contribution the documents in the Pseudepigrapha can make to our research as New Testament scholars. When these documents are read reflectively and with empathy for hours without interruption, we come as close as we possibly can to the spirit and the vibrating pulse of Early Judaism, and the world in which the early Jews, including Jesus, Hillel and Shammai lived. And, when we *add* to this understanding the insights and feelings obtained from reading the *Halakoth*, especially the daily customs for prayer and piety, preserved in the Tannaitic literature, we draw even closer to the lively spirit which characterized the first-century Jew.

It should not diminish this insight to note that we have tended to see Early Judaism as characterized by religious people, because almost all the preserved literature is religious. Secular Jews probably did not write literature; they wrote legal and economic documents that almost always have not survived. And many of these 'secular' documents were most assuredly written by religious Jews. We can grasp some of the life of the early Jews not only because of the tortured words, struggles for survival, and intra-Jewish polemic in many of their documents, but also because we know the early Jews tended to share a common presupposition, namely that they were all chiselled out of the rock of a shared earthiness. We all are of the rocky dust, but all are not able to perceive footprints in the dust. — *Boy! Give me a break!*

3

THE PSEUDEPIGRAPHA AND THE
NEW TESTAMENT

Introduction

We have seen that some of the documents in the Pseudepigrapha are essential for any portrayal of Early Judaism. Some are earlier than the New Testament writings, others are contemporaneous with them. A few of these Jewish documents predate the New Testament works, but contain expansions or interpolations by Christians who lived after the last writings of the New Testament had been composed (if not themselves expanded and altered, as is the case especially with John 7:53–8:11). We turn now to an examination of the ways in which the Pseudepigrapha may help us better to understand the origins, life-setting, and meaning of the twenty-seven documents in the New Testament. The methodology for comparing documents must first be refined.

Scrutinizing the Literary Relationships Between the Pseudepigrapha and the New Testament

Comparing One Document with Another

In comparing two documents we should be more precise in our terms, methods and observations. We should specify whether we are dealing with quotations, partial quotations, interpretatively translated quotations, blended quotations (i.e. blending together more than one quotation from the same document), mixed quotations (i.e. quotations from two separate sources), paraphrases, or allusions. Each of the categories should be subdivided, according to whether the quotation or other category is accurate according to the extant Hebrew, Aramaic, or Greek of another document, whether it is attributed or unattributed to that source, whether the attribution is accurate or inaccurate, and whether the attribution is only a generic one (e.g. 'according to the scriptures'). The degree of certainty depends on observing these factors. Space will not permit a full development and illustration of this methodology; a few examples must suffice.

Before beginning, it is imperative to clarify a fact in comparing the Pseudepigrapha documents and New Testament writings. The documents in the New Testament contain *no quotations* from the Apocrypha, Dead Sea Scrolls, Philo's writings, Josephus' writings, the Jewish magical papyri, the Hermetica, and the Nag Hammadi Codices. The New Testament writers quote from only two collections of ancient Jewish documents: the Old Testament and Old Testament Pseudepigrapha.

(1) *Primus (the Old Testament as Canon)*

The highest possible evidence of a relationship between two documents is when one quotes from the other without translation, without any inaccuracies, and with a clear and accurate attribution. This situation occurs when a quotation in document A is accurate according to an extant document B, in the same language, and attributed correctly to B. In this category are found only quotations in a New Testament document that derive from a passage in a *Greek* Old Testament text. Hence, for example, Luke 20:42 contains a quotation from Psalm 110:1 (LXX 109:1); it is accurately quoted according to the LXX (the only difference — not an inaccuracy — is that the LXX contains the definite article before *Kurios*); and it is clearly and correctly attributed to David: it is *en biblō psalmōn*. It is, therefore, definite that Luke depended upon the Psalter when he wrote, and he used a Greek text similar to the one we possess.

There are obviously subdivisions to the primary category; these depend upon the level and amount of precision, inaccuracy, or incompleteness in all aspects of the quotation and attribution. Under this first category, as far as I know, are passages only from the Greek Old Testament. Since portions of the Greek New Testament may originally have been composed in Semitic tracts — especially testimony tracts — the extant Greek translation may represent a text that had obtained a quotation identical to a passage in an Old Testament document. Most important for a perception of the significance of the Pseudepigrapha for the New Testament, is the recognition that the *primus* quotations signify that when the New Testament writers composed their documents, almost all of the 'Old Testament' had become widely recognized as set, authoritative and inspired; and in that sense 'canonical'. This insight leads us directly to the next level of dependency between one document upon another.

(2) *Secundus (Jude and 1 Enoch)*

The second level of certainty is present when we discover a quotation in A not deriving precisely from the extant languages of document B, but correctly attributed to B. The difference between the first and second levels of certainty is due to an assessment of the degree of accuracy in the *quotation*. Sometimes the quotation may be different because our sources for document B are inferior to what was available to the author of A, or because the author of A was translating from one language to another, or because the author of A borrowed from an earlier translation. For example, the author of Matthew 2:17–18, attributes correctly to Jeremiah, a passage that 'he' (or his 'school') has translated; but he shifts the tenses of the verbs to strengthen his *Tendenz* for the fulfillment of prophecy. Note the comparisons between Jeremiah 31:15 and Matthew 2:17–18 (Jer 38:15 in LXX is different; the BH and LXX are often very different in Jer):[1]

BH	Gk NT
Jer 31:15	Mt 2:17–18
	Then was fulfilled the
Thus says the Lord:	saying by Jeremiah the prophet:
'A voice in Rama	'A voice in Ramah
is heard (nishmā')	*was heard (ēkousthē)*
wailing (and) bitter weeping.	weeping and much lamentation.
Rachel is weeping	Rachel is weeping
over her children;	(over) her children;
she refused (*mēʼªnāh*)	and she refused (*kai ouk ēthelen*)
to be comforted	to be consoled,
over her children,	
because they are not.'[2]	because they are not.'

Unless Matthew has resolved a tension in the Hebrew between 'is heard' (Ni. participle) and 'she refused' (a perfect), by pointing *nishmā'* as *nishma'*, against the MT, which is quite possible, he has aligned the tenses to clarify the fulfillment of the prophecy. The possible incomplete action of the participle, literally 'is being heard', becomes for Matthew 'was heard' (aor. passive), because of Herod's past action: He killed 'all the male children in Bethlehem' (Mt 2:16).

This same phenomenon may occur in another quotation in the New Testament. It is also in the *secundus* category. Jude 14–15 attributes to Enoch a prophecy (*eprophēteusen*) that we now know assuredly was in a book of Enoch that predated Jude. We know this for certain because at Qumran, probably from Cave 4, a fragment of precisely the passage quoted has been recovered, and the fragment is in an Aramaic hand of the first century B.C.E.[3] Comparisons between Jude's Greek, the extant Aramaic, the selfsame passages in Codex Panopolitanus and Pseudo-Cyprian, and the Ethiopic of 1 Enoch, raise the possibility that the author of Jude may have been a Palestinian Christian who did not depend upon a Greek version but translated himself from Aramaic.[4]

What is so important for us to observe now is that as in the example above from Matthew, so in the quotation of 1 Enoch in Jude, the text is altered to clarify that it refers to Jesus and that the prophecy is to be seen as fulfilled. Note the comparisons:

Ethiopic Enoch 1:9[5]	Aramaic Enoch (4QEn^c)[6]	Jude 14–15
		And Enoch prophesied (aor.) about these things seven generations after Adam, saying:
Behold, he *will* arrive (*maṣ'a*)[7]		'Behold (the) lord came (*ēlthen*, 2 aor.)
with the myriads[8] of the holy ones	[with the myri]ads of the[9] holy one[s,]	with his holy myriads,
in order to execute	[...]	to execute (*poiēsai*, aor. inf.)
judgment upon all.	[...]	judgment against all,
He will destroy the wicked ones	[...]	and to convict (*elegzai*; aor. inf.)
and censure all flesh on account of everything	[all f]lesh, regarding	all the ungodly ones of all their
that they have done,	the works [of ...]	ungodly deeds which
that which the sinners and the	[...]	they did godlessly (*ēsebēsan*; aor.),
	[... all] the boastful and hard [things ...]	and of all the hard things which
wicked ones		the ungodly sinners
committed	[...]	spoke (*elalēsan.* aor.)
against him.	[...]	against him.'

These comparisons are enlightening and impressive. First, the indefinite 'he' in the Ethiopic, which referred back to God and his future coming, is paralleled by *kurios* in the Greek. The alteration is clearly by the Christian Jews; as most interpolations and alterations by Christians of early Jewish writings, the alteration is caused by Christology.[10] He – that is Christ – is 'the Lord'. Second, both the Ethiopic and Aramaic have 'the holy ones',[11] while Jude clearly has the possessive, 'his' (it is also in Codex Panopolitanus and Ps-Cyprian). If Jude added the possessive, then the alteration seems again caused by Christology: Christ possesses the legions; they are 'his'. Third, what seems most impressive is that all the verbs in Greek are in the aorist tense, which signifies the event has been seen holistically as a past time. The aorists may be seen as cumulative aorists; hence, they denote the end of the process: 'he came'. The parousia is perceived as a fulfilled *future* event, and that is possible because of the Semitic verb tenses (*perfectum propheticum*), and the portrayal of the parousia in the light of the advent. For Jude, Christ came and accomplished his task, in the light of this he will return, as Enoch had prophesied about God. The Ethiopic verbs are taken by Ethiopic specialists to denote *incomplete action* ('he will arrive'). Hence, as was the norm for quoting 'the Old Testament',[12] so Jude freely alters − within acceptable bounds − a text to prove his interpretation.[13] As with Matthew 2, the prophecy is perceived as already fulfilled.[14]

Another issue must not be bypassed. Since Jude introduces the Enoch quotation with the verb to denote a prophesy (*eprophēteusen*) it is certain he considered the document inspired.[15] If Jude had a closed canon, and Enoch was outside it, then he acknowledged inspired writings outside the canon.[16] This twofold category of canon and of writings inspired by God should be commended to theologians today. If Jude had anything like a closed canon, it might have included 1 Enoch, as in the Falasha canon. But it is improbable that Jude had a *closed* canon; perhaps he had an open canon with inspired writings like Enoch, on the fringes. We need to recall that he wrote before Esther was finally admitted by the Rabbis at Usha. I take these observations to mean that we are challenged historically and theologically by the limits of 'our' closed canon. How can Christians discard as insignificant, or apocryphal, a document that is clearly pre-Christian, Jewish, and quoted as prophecy by an author who has been canonized?[17] The Pseudepigrapha raise more questions than we can at present answer.

We now must leave the *secundus* category of quotations. These quotations certainly show that text A is dependent on text B, and reveal the necessity and justified methodology in antiquity for altering a quotation in line with a presupposition. In most cases, as in Jude 14−15, the alteration of an earlier Jewish quotation is precisely because of the belief in the advent of the one-who-was-to-come. The commitment to Jesus as the Christ, the Messiah, shifted inherited parallel verbs and nouns according to the light shown upon the text, altering these traditions like light passing through a prism.

(3) *Tertius and Quartus*

Other categories for *quotations* are the following: *tertius*, a quotation in A which is an interpretive translation of a passage in a known document, B, but incorrectly attributed to another document C; *quartus*, a paraphrase in A which is obviously from document B and in some way attributed to it. The level of certainty wanes according to the imprecision or erroneous nature in the formulaic elements (quotation and its accuracy, attribution, if any, and its accuracy). We shall not be able to illustrate each of these categories now, turning instead to one that is very problematical for us.

(4) *Quintus (Jude and the Death of Moses)*

This fifth category applies to the following situation: a clear quotation in A, that may be accurate, according to a source (or sources) later than A, and ultimately derived from B, which is earlier than A and also unnamed. This category applies to the quotation in Jude 9:

> But when the archangel Michael, contending with the devil, disputed about the body of Moses, he did not presume to pronounce a reviling judgment upon him, but said, 'The Lord rebuke you.'
> (RSV)

The elements of the formula are: (a) a clear quotation, 'The Lord rebuke you' (*epitimēsai soi kurios* (set out in bold type face to signal a quotation in Aland, *et al.* (ed.), *The Greek New Testament*; and in the 'Index of Quotations' it is attributed to the 'Assumption of Moses'));[18] and (b) no attribution to a source, whether oral or written.

We can assume that Jude 9 is quoting from a *lost* Jewish writing or oral story because of two factors: first, a quotation is put into the mouth of Michael. Second, a narrative structure is obvious; Michael is struggling with the devil over the corpse of Moses. The devil has already said something, probably a charge against Moses, which warrants Michael's rebuke.

This category and this example are complex. Recently Bauckham presented a truly impressive defence for the position that Jude 9 quotes from the lost ending of the Testament of Moses. He even offers an attempt to reconstruct the lost ending.[19]

Jude 9 may very well be quoting from the ending of the Testament of Moses, which is extant in only one imperfect Latin manuscript.[20] But, we must never forget that the quotation is *not found* in the extant text of the Testament of Moses. We may hypothesize that the quotation was in the lost portion of the Testament of Moses, but at best, this position results from scholarly speculation and deduction from much later comments either on the life of Moses or on Jude itself.

The following observations lead me to hesitate in positing that Jude quoted from the lost ending of the Testament of Moses: (i) A review of the extant Jewish literature reveals a highly developed Moses cycle of traditions and documents, most of which seem concerned with reflections on Deuteronomy 35 (especially verse 6), and the place and manner of Moses' death and burial. Also, significant and related to this cycle is the Testament of 'Amram (4Q'Amram), Moses' father (Num 26:59).[21]

(ii) It is unwise to argue that because 'testaments usually end with an account of the subject's death and burial',[22] the Testament of Moses 'must have ended with a story of Moses' death and burial'.[23] This description does not fit the Testaments of the Twelve Patriarchs; none of them has a *story* about the patriarchs death and burial; what we are presented with is a simple formula, such as the following: 'Benjamin died last of all in his one hundred twenty-fifth year at a ripe old age, and they placed him in a coffin' (TBenj 12:2).[24] Other examples could be given, but suffice it to state that it is precarious to think comparatively and analogically between two documents; especially is this true when we realize how different in form and content are the extant testaments.

(iii) If the Testament of Moses 11:6−8 'seems to require an account of his burial in an unknown grave',[25] that demands neither that it contained an ending that can be reconstructed reliably, nor that Jude, then, quotes from such a reconstruction.

(iv) We must not be overly persuaded by the reasoning that the debate is resolved by recognizing that the Early Fathers claimed that Jude 9 is a quotation from the 'Assumption of Moses'. Some Fathers (viz. Clement of Alexandria, *Strom* 1.23.153, 1; 6.15.132, 2−3; Didymas the Blind, *EpJE* ii *a*;[26] Gelasius Cyzicenus, *Hist. Eccl.* 2.17.17, 2.21.7),[27] do tend to state or suggest that Jude is quoting from the 'Assumption of Moses'. But, other early scholars in the Church contradict this information, as we shall see; and we must ask which of these is trustworthy.

(v) Moreover, as is well known, the early lists of apocryphal books often name not only a *Diathēkē Mōuseōs* but also an *Analēpsis Mōuseōs* (e.g. List of Sixty Books, Pseudo-Athanasius, Nicephorous, the Slavic list).[28] I have not given up on the possibility that Charles was correct in assuming that the Testament of Moses and the Assumption of Moses may be 'two originally independent works';[29] if so we have, perhaps, the Testament of Moses, and Clement of Alexandria, and others, attributing Jude's quotation to a work now lost. I am not sure of this possibility, of course, but I am certain that to attribute Jude's quotation to an hypothetical reconstruction of the extant fragmentary Testament of Moses is to reconstruct — and perhaps to conflate (an egregious error) — from different and later sources. One needs to be reminded of the assumptions being made.

(vi) Jude does not designate the source of the quotation, it may conceivably be derived from a story circulating in oral traditions, or from a lost midrash on Deuteronomy 34, or one of the lost works similar to Jubilees,[30] *Liber Antiquitatum Biblicarum*, or another writing that was an 'Expansion of "Old Testament" Narratives', one of the lost Moses apocrypha similar to Qumran's Apocryphon of Moses (2QapMoses), the Book of the Mysterious Words of Moses,[31] or a passage in one of the lost histories of the Jews (viz. by Justin of Tiberius, or Jason of Cyrene).

(vii) The quotation found in Jude, 'The Lord rebuke you', is generic; and perhaps derives from Zechariah 3:2, 'And the Lord said to Satan (LXX: *ton diabolon*), "The Lord rebuke (*yigh'ar; epitimēsai*) you, O Satan" (LXX: *diabole*)!' (RSV). We need not search for Jude's quotations in writings related to this cycle of traditions; most, of course, are probably lost forever.

Perhaps I am far too conservative here, but the amount of traditions and documents written with Moses in mind, or attributed to Moses, leaves me unconvinced that Jude quoted from the lost ending of the Testament of Moses. I have learned never to discount the knowledge of Origen; and he attributed Jude's quotation to a document entitled 'the Ascension of Moses' (*in Adscensione Mosis*, in *Princ* 3.2.1).[32] I conclude, therefore, that Jude probably quoted, as Severus of Antioch (c. 465–538) stated, from a pseudepigraphical or apocryphal book (*tauta de en apokruphō bibliō legetai keisthai leptoteran echonti tēs geneseōs ētoi tēs ktiseōs aphēgēsin*).[33] While Jude may be insignificant in the study of the New Testament, it is clear that it is a major work, far more important than its size, for a perception of Early Christianity and the influence of the literature of Early Judaism upon it.

(5) *Allusions*

Next in the order of categories that help us to assess the influence of one document upon another is the whole range of *allusions*. Here we have many examples that need careful scrutiny. Limiting our attention to the eleventh chapter of Hebrews, we can observe two allusions to documents in the Pseudepigrapha. Hebrews 11:37 celebrates the faithful who have faced martyrdom, including those who were sawn in two (*epristhēsan*, a hapax legomenon in the NT). Undoubtedly, this verb alludes to the martyrdom of Isaiah, preserved for us in the Martyrdom of Isaiah: and Manasseh 'sawed Isaiah in half with a wood saw' (5:1).[34] Another possible allusion is in Hebrews 11:5, which refers to Enoch being taken up; this comment may refer only to Genesis 5, but in the light of the importance of 1 Enoch in Early Christianity it is possible the author alludes to the Enoch cycle, especially to 1 Enoch. Assessing these possibilities moves us into an appreciation of oral traditions; and these lead us on to an entirely different set of criteria.

Before leaving the issue of comparing one document with another, let us remember that secular texts are often quoted or alluded to by the early Christians. Four so-called pagan authors are quoted or alluded to in the New Testament: Aratus (*Phaenomena* 5; Acts 17:28), Cleanthes (Acts 17:28), Epimenides (*de Oraculis*; Tit 1:12) and Menander (*Thais* 218; 1 Cor 15:33).

Comparing One Document with Many Others

(1) *The Revealed Zeitgeist of Early Judaism*

The examples already cited are exceptions to the rule: the documents in the Pseudepigrapha are not primarily important because they are cited by the new Testament authors; they are significant because they reveal the *Zeitgeist* of Early Judaism and the matrix of earliest Christianity.

Experience has shown that frequently a full exploration of a reputed quotation in the New Testament of an earlier Jewish document shows, in the final analysis, a term, concept, or phrase shared among numerous documents. This discovery disappoints the researcher who was attempting to compare two documents, but it discloses the great significance of the writings in the Pseudepigrapha. They reveal the terms, concepts, ideas, expressions, and world view that were prevalent in Early Judaism.

It is unwise, therefore, to seek to see if Romans 7:7 is related directly to 4 Maccabees 2:5. These parallels in thought are caused by reflective exegesis on the same biblical passage, namely the law against coveting (cf. Ex 20:17, Deut 5:21). Similarly, it is unwise to pursue a detailed comparison of Matthew 22:32 with 4 Maccabees 7:19; both really contain a wide spread Jewish notion, namely that the Patriarchs are not really dead. Even more unfruitful is an attempt to link passages that are characterized by ancient wisdom motifs; for example, Luke 11:21−2 is not dependent on Psalms of Solomon 5:4. Both inherit the common Jewish knowledge that 'no one takes plunder away from a strong man' (PssSol 5:3).[35]

(2) *2 Timothy 3 and Jannes and Jambres*

A good example of the influence of many Jewish writings on a passage in the New Testament is found in 2 Timothy 3. Seeking for an historical analogy to the licentious men threatening the Christian community, the author of 2 Timothy refers back to Jannes and Jambres who opposed Moses. Even though their names are not given in Exodus 7:11, there is insufficient proof to conclude that the author of 2 Timothy knew the document now called Jannes and Jambres.[36] These two wicked magicians were well-known in Early Judaism. Indeed they became a paradigm of those who resist God, as we know from the Cairo Damascus Document.[37] The names of Jannes and Jambres were part of the popular lore of antiquity; for example, they were mentioned by Pliny (*Natural History* 30.2.11), Apuleius (*Apology* 90), and especially the author of the Acts of Pilate 5:1 (also called the Gospel of Nicodemus).[38]

(3) *Living Oral Traditions*

We must acknowledge and allow for what we know so well was a major formative influence on writers and thinkers in Early Judaism, even if we have, at best, only an indirect access to it.[39] I refer, of course, to the deep, ancient, yet vibrantly alive oral tradition.[40] Many of the passages in the Pseudepigrapha, notably the humorous stories in the Apocalypse of Abraham and 3 Maccabees, must assuredly once have had a different setting. Probably some were told with infectious animation around camp fires as dusk settled into night (see the 'Introduction', p. 1). Many such tales most assuredly originated in non academic settings (cf. Song);[41] examples that come to mind are passages in the Epistle of Jeremiah, Joseph and Aseneth, the Genesis Apocryphon (viz. the description of Sarah's beauty), and Susannah. Many lively tales never made their way from oral to written tradition, and we can well imagine why when we consider the embellishments all too readily at hand when recounting the attributes of Rahab (cf. esp. Heb 11:31*b*) and Abishag the Shunammite (1 Kgs 1). An example of such earthy folk wisdom may be behind the document whose fragments are sometimes called 'The Wiles of the Wicked Woman'.[42]

(4) *Jude 5–7 and a Popular Tradition*

Another example of one document being influenced by many writings, oral traditions, or well-known formulae is found in Jude 5–7, which refers to three examples of those who were faithless; the *unfaithful* ones who fell back and desired to return to Egypt (verse 5), the *angels* who fell from heaven (verse 6), and the inhabitants of *Sodom* and *Gomorrah* (verse 7). Bauckham argues correctly that the author of Jude 'has drawn on a traditional schema in which such examples were listed'.[43] The popular tradition – probably not a schema – is found especially prominently in Ben Sira, the Cairo Damascus Document, 3 Maccabees, the Mishnah (Sanh), Jubilees, and the Testament of Naphtali. The *unfaithful followers* of Moses are mentioned in Ben Sira, Cairo Damascus Document, and mSanhedrin. The reference to the *fallen angels*, called the Watchers, or their sons (the giants), occurs in Ben Sira, Cairo Damascus Document, 3 Maccabees, Jubilees, and the Testament of Naphtali. *Sodom* and *Gomorrah* appear in each of them, except the Cairo Damascus Document. Jude's order, however, is not paralleled in any of these documents; the author inherited it from *traditions* he learned in the synagogue, in the home, or elsewhere.

(5) *A Rich Inheritance for the New Testament Authors*

These are but a few of the innumerable examples that could be brought forward to illustrate the fact that any document, for example one in the New Testament, inherits from reservoirs of diverse traditions most of its themes, *termini technici*, semiotic language, and clustered linguistic perceptions and phrases. The New Testament writings are the products of a long historical and linguistic process.

The Pseudepigrapha and Dating the New Testament

Perception of the Erudition and Sophistication of Early Jewish Thought

The New Testament documents are usually dated by references to historical events, especially the burning of the Temple in Jerusalem in 70, or by comparisons with other documents in the New Testament. Most of us, for example, conclude that Mark was probably composed just before or just after the destruction of Jerusalem because of the probable references to it in chapter 13. Because they are deemed dependent on Mark, Matthew and Luke are dated somewhere between 80 and 90 C.E. This methodology is inexact; it can be circular, and it is usually blind to a fact mentioned earlier that warrants rephrasing: New Testament scholars have *no* New Testament; they have only documents to study, twenty-seven of them were later, much later than the first century, collected into a canon.

The preceding discussion leads on to another arena, one which is full of data for helping us perceive the probable dates of many early 'Christian' writings. The assumption that New Testament documents with highly developed terms and ideas must be late writings founders on the recognition that Early Judaism was characterized by amazing erudition and by brilliantly articulated and highly advanced concepts and perceptions.[44] The first generation of Jews converted to 'Christianity' was proficient in developed and sophisticated thoughts, and later Christians were capable of producing 'primitive' or mediocre writings.

The Development of Christology Through Transference and Specification

Both Moule and W. Marxsen[45] have argued very persuasively and perceptively that Christology did not evolve, with unexpected jumps and mutations, but it developed out of pregnant elements ready for maturation. Without undermining the obvious significant development of Christian thought and Christology from 30 to 150 C.E., I do wish to stress that in the 30s, and even during Jesus' public ministry, there were highly-developed ideas. What was needed was not so much more development, as *transference* and *specification*. The transference to Jesus of many of the ideas already highly-developed about the Lord God and his messengers;[46] the specification of Jesus as the one-who-was-to-come; for example, as the Messiah, as the Son of God, and as the Son of Man.

Against the perspective — often associated with one of the most influential and brilliant scholars of this century, namely Bultmann[47] — that Palestinian christological thought was later altered categorically when it moved out into the Greek and Roman world, two points need clarification. First, early Christian thought did not have to move outside Palestine to be significantly affected by Greek and Roman ideas. Even the terminology of the mystery religions was well known, and a Mithraeum has now been uncovered in Caesarea.

While this point is clear and now widely acknowledged, the influence of the mystery religions in Palestine should not be exaggerated. The Mithraeum in Caesarea is the only one found in Palestine, and it dates from the third century C.E.[48] The mystery religions were not successful in Palestine, because of their offensive idolatrous base,[49] and because the solution to humanity's predicaments and to the explanation of human existence, as M. Hengel argues, were already attractively elaborated in the 'apocalyptic doctrines of resurrection, immortality and judgment'.[50]

Second, Bultmann's position is now undermined by the recognition that the terms once thought foreign to Palestinian Judaism are now found well-entrenched in early Jewish thought. For example, *kurios*, 'Lord', is highly developed in pre-70 Palestinian Greek and Semitic thought; indeed it corresponds to the perpetual *qere* for the ineffable tetragrammaton. Likewise, 'son of God', if the examples Vermes cites can be reliably used to portray phenomena in pre-70 Galilee, was a title attributed to Ḥanina ben Dosa and Rabbi Meir.[51]

The *Birkath hām-Mînîm*

Finally, the dating of some New Testament documents may be affected by the realization that the *Birkath hām-Mînîm* did *not* necessarily include the Christian among the *Minim*, and that early Jewish Christians may not have felt they were included in the rejection of the *Minim* (see chapter 2, n. 56). There was no irreconcilable rift between Judaism and Christianity resulting from this, or any other edict emanating from Jamnia (Yavneh), which was felt everywhere in the Jewish communities. The relationship between Jews and Christians was complex; one should not generalize too readily and confuse the vast differences between communities widely separated geographically. As late as the beginning of the fifth century John Chrysostom (c. 347–407) was aghast that some Christians continued to frequent the synagogue services.[52] *Aposunagōgos* in the Gospel of John may have nothing to do with the *Birkath hām-Mînîm*.

If this line of reasoning is accurate and if Urbach, Kimelman, and Maier (see chapter 2, n. 56) are correct in arguing that the *Minim* did not include the Jewish Christians, then J. L. Martyn's claim that the Gospel of John's historical background must be seen in terms of synagogal polemic against the *Minim* (the Jewish Christians) needs to be altered significantly.[53] The issues of Jamnia's reforms, the intent of the *Birkath hām-Mînîm* in the first century in contrast to subsequent centuries, the use of *aposunagōgos* in John, and the possibility of persecution of the Johannine community by others (perhaps 'Jews') need to be clarified separately before they are related. Martyn's contributions to our understanding of the Gospel of John and its background have been significant; however, there is need for more precision in and some refinement of his argument in the light of recent work on Jewish liturgies.

The essence of what I am trying to say with regard to the importance of the Pseudepigrapha for our attempts to date the documents in the New Testament is that Early Judaism was extremely sophisticated and fully developed in its own sense by 70 C.E.; and, moreover, that the earliest followers of Jesus, who were Jews, brought with them into the new Jewish movement that would be called 'Christian' this sophistication. The greatest development of thought in Early Christianity would probably have occurred in Palestine and in the decades from 30 to 75 and not elsewhere from 75 to 150. Unless I am sadly mistaken this perception is a tendency evidencing itself now in the publications of the best New Testament scholars.[54] In addition to the two scholars already noted, namely Moule and Marxsen, Hengel should be singled out. In *Der Sohn Gottes: Die Entstehung der Christologie und die jüdische—hellenistische Religionsgeschichte* (Tübingen, 1975) Hengel claims, referring to the twenty years following the crucifixion, that 'more happened in this period of less than two decades than in the whole of the next seven centuries, up to the time when the doctrine of the early church was completed'.[55]

Our attempts to date three documents in the New Testament may be significantly influenced by the insights presented in the preceding discussion. These documents are Hebrews, James and Revelation.

Hebrews

For some time most introductions to the New Testament have assigned Hebrews to the latter part of the first century C.E. W. G. Kümmel, for example, dated Hebrews, 'between 80 and 90'.[56] The first reason he gives for this date is 'the persecutions which the community had experienced (10:32—34)'. These verses, however, do not give the impression of a time long ago, or forty years in the past. The words 'the former days' (*tas proteron hēmeras*, 10:32) could easily refer to any period prior to 70 C.E.

The second reason Kümmel gives for dating Hebrews is 'the spiritual proximity to Lk-Acts' which for him points 'in all probability to the post-Pauline period'.[57] This argument is singularly important for us. If one reads Hebrews only within the collection of writings now in the New Testament, the impression may very well be the one Kümmel obtains. But Hebrews should be read in the light of all documents anterior to and contemporaneous with it.[58] As we long ago freed Hebrews from the constrictions of being read and understood within the Pauline corpus, so we need to cut Hebrews loose from a myopia caused by seeing it only within a canon that postdates it considerably. Turning to Hebrews after reading Luke-Acts may give one impression, turning to it after reading 1 Enoch may give a different insight. Regarding the date of composition of Hebrews, it moves down into the early parts of the first century, and before 70.

Hebrews contains ideas found in — and possibly alludes to — the following works in the Apocrypha and Pseudepigrapha: 1 Enoch (1 En 70:1–4, Heb 11:5), Ben Sira (Sir 25:23, Heb 12:12; Sir 44:16, Heb 11:5; Sir 44:21, Heb 6:14), the Wisdom of Solomon (WisSol 4:10, Heb 11:5), and the Ascension of Isaiah (AscenIs 5:11–14, Heb 11:37). Its brilliance, its highly developed cosmology and eschatology, its comparisons of Christ to the angels and Moses, and especially the Christology that sees Jesus as the son of God, the forerunner of the wandering people of God, and the enthroned high priest, all reflect the world view and developed ideas of Early Judaism. There can be little doubt that the author of Hebrews is a Jew converted to Christianity.[59]

Constrictions of time and space permit only two arguments. (1) The author of Hebrews struggles to prove that Jesus is superior to the angels; and this angelology is developed in the literature of Early Judaism, especially in the Dead Sea Scrolls (viz. 1QM) and in the Pseudepigrapha (viz. 1 En, 3 En). He also expends considerable effort to prove Jesus' superiority to Moses, 'Yet Jesus has been counted worthy of as much more glory than Moses as the builder of a house has more honour than the house' (Heb 3:3, RSV). As is well known, the author then proceeds to argue that Jesus has been appointed by God as the enthroned high priest (cf. 5:5–10, 6:20, 7:23–8). He is now, states the author of Hebrews, 'seated at the right hand of the throne of the Majesty in heaven' (Heb 8:1, RSV).

This argument seems unpersuasive to those of us who think of Moses traditions as primarily concerned with *Halakoth*, and reflections upon the death and secret burial of Moses. There is another tradition about Moses; it is found in the Pseudepigrapha. This tradition emphasizes, even portrays, Moses' ascent to heaven, and his heavenly enthronement as 'God's viceregent who is *presently* ruling over the universe and validating as "divinely inspired" the Jewish nation.'[60] According to Ezekiel the Tragedian's *Exagôgê*, as preserved by Alexander Polyhistor through Eusebius' *Praeparatio Evangelica* (IX 28, 2–4; 29, 5–16), Moses receives a vision in which he sees 'on the summit of mount Sinai' a great throne upon which was 'seated a noble man'. This figure, God, as Moses reputedly relates, 'beckoned me, and I took my stand before the throne. He handed me the sceptre and he summoned me to sit upon the great throne. And he also gave me the royal diadem, and he himself descended from the throne.'[61] Certainly these clearly pre-Christian Jewish ideas and semiotic traditions can significantly help us to understand the background of the author of Hebrews and comprehend his intent and meaning.

(2) The reference to Melchisedek in Hebrews 6 and 7 is dependent, if not on Essene thought (11QMelch), certainly on the rich depository of Jewish speculation about Melchisedek, represented in many writings, including Philo's and Josephus' works.[62] The ending to 2 Enoch,[63] unfortunately omitted in Charles' edition of the Pseudepigrapha, describes Melchisedek's miraculous birth. His father had not caused his mother to be pregnant, and she dies before giving birth. Melchisedek is born fully articulate from a corpse. If this passage reflects Jewish ideas from the first part of the first century C.E.[64] – and this ending has a stronger claim to be Jewish than many other parts of 2 Enoch, as Andersen has argued[65] – then we have a most significant parallel to Hebrews 7:3, which states that Melchisedek was 'without father or mother or genealogy and has neither beginning of days nor end of life' (RSV). Since we are here dealing with a text preserved only in Slavonic we must admit that our reflections on this particular point are speculative; but they are, nevertheless, revealing.

With these impressions, I have turned again to *Hebrews* and have become convinced that it *probably antedates the burning of Jerusalem*. Hebrews 8:4 refers to priests who *now offer* up gifts according to the Torah (cf. Heb 9:9–10; 10:1–4). Hebrews 9:8 implies that the outer *tent* of the Temple is *still standing*. Hebrews 13:10 refers to priests who *now serve* the altar. With Moule, therefore, I wish to point to the long development of scriptural exegesis in Judaism – not in Early Christianity – that prepared the way for Hebrews' interpretation of Torah. With Robinson, G. W. Buchanan and Moule I would argue for a pre-70 date for Hebrews; Moule correctly claims that 'a very plausible setting may be found in the ardent Jewish nationalism which must have been kindled or enhanced by the opening of the Jewish war in A.D. 66'.[66]

James

The Epistle of James has also been customarily dated to the last decades of the first century C.E. Kümmel may serve again as an authority: 'The date of writing of James cannot be determined more exactly than toward the end of the first century.'[67] The main, and first argument, given is that the 'cultured language of James is not that of a simple Palestinian'.[68] Perhaps this comment is primarily directed against those who attribute the letter to James, the brother of Jesus. Nevertheless, one is surprised by the facile assumptions; are we to get the impression that Palestinian Jews who converted to Christianity had been both simple and uncultured? Kümmel is far too erudite and gifted to argue for that position. Since the works in the Pseudepigrapha reveal that Jews, including those in Palestine, could write in excellent Greek (including the difficult poetic meters), since the Shema was said in Caesarea in Greek, since some inscriptions in the Jewish cemeteries are in Greek, and since Bar-Kokhba wrote to his commanders in Greek, as well as in Hebrew and Aramaic, it is certainly unwise to state that a Palestinian Jew could not write in good and cultured Greek. The Pseudepigrapha, especially the Palestinian compositions like 1 Enoch, Jubilees, Pseudo-Philo, *Vita Adae et Evae*,[69] reveal the highly *cultured* status of Palestinian Jews.

Dating James before 70 C.E. is not a novel idea, although this tendency might become more popular due to Robinson's excitingly controversial arguments in *Redating the New Testament*.[70] It is difficult to prove that James is a Christian composition, and not a Jewish writing with Christian interpolations, or a Jewish *Grundschrift* revised and redacted by a Christian. The work is also impressively paraenetic, and the paraenesis to endure suffering points *not* to Jesus but to the Old Testament prophets (Jas 5:10). The newly-translated group of ethical tracts, philosophical works, and wisdom books in *The Old Testament Pseudepigrapha*, namely 3 Maccabees, 4 Maccabees, Pseudo-Phocylides, and Syriac Menander, illustrate impressively the highly-developed, universalistic, and surprisingly different moral ideas prevalent among Jews in the first century. There is absolutely no compelling reason to date James after 70; we may now have reasons to date it prior to the destruction of Jerusalem.

Revelation

Revelation, like Hebrews and James, is profoundly Jewish in thought and imagery. My attempts to discover two literary layers in Revelation and to date one of these to the Neronian persecutions have failed. Revelation is a unity. It should also be studied not as the last book in a later defined canon, but as an apocalypse in a continuum of apocalypses, stretching for centuries in each chronological direction.[71]

My attempts to find an original Jewish core to Revelation have proved fruitless;[72] also, comparisons of the earlier and roughly contemporaneous Jewish apocalypses, most of which are placed in the Pseudepigrapha, did not produce one clear quotation or literary dependency. Abundant parallels were found between Revelation and many documents in the Pseudepigrapha, especially 4 Ezra, 2 Baruch, the Apocalypse of Abraham and 2 Enoch. All of these apocalypses are dated before 100 C.E., although the latter two Slavonic Pseudepigrapha cannot yet be assuredly and reliably dated towards the end of the first century. Hence, comparisons between Revelation and the documents in the Pseudepigrapha do not indicate a pre-70 date; these confirm a date in the early nineties, or 90−5.[73] Revelation reflects the same *Zeitgeist* as 4 Ezra,[74] 2 Baruch, the Apocalypse of Abraham,[75] and 2 Enoch.[76]

Messianism and Christology: A Major Problematic Term

Function and Meaning

In the preceding discussion we have intermittently referred to the growing recognition of the Jewish background to some terms that took on a significant christological meaning in the early Christian communities. Repeatedly emphasized is the necessity of reading through the Jewish documents to ascertain the function, meaning and importance of the terms in a particular stratum or document. For example, while reading through the Greek of the misnamed Apocalypse of Moses one confronts frequent dialogues between Eve and Adam. The former often refers to her husband as *Kurie mou*, ('my lord') *Kurie mou Adam*, ('my lord, Adam'). Without undermining the recognition that *ho Kurios* had obtained deep theological meanings in Early Judaism long before the advent of Christianity, and without digressing to explore the subtle meanings of this term in Eve's dialogues, we can readily perceive that *ho Kurios* was used outside theological confessions and that it had secular meanings which were also honorific.

How different it is to turn from reading the Apocalypse of Moses and the thoughts, feelings and perceptions this experience provides — and we should also recognize that many of these are subconscious and alter inarticulate preconceptions — and then to turn to the Centurion's words addressed to Jesus: *Kurie* (Mt 8:6, 7). We have probably a *secular* recognition of honour and authority (Mt 8:7—9) that is often missed by the use of this pericope in Matthew and the emphasis on faith (*pistis*), which is a Matthean *Tendenz*, as is well-known.[77] The subtle and significant insights obtained by reading through the Pseudepigrapha are lost if you come to this pericope from the function and meaning of *Kurios* in, for example, Romans 1:4.

Son of Man

The most intractable problem in the study of christological terms is the title 'Son of Man'. Research has produced two firm conclusions: first, in Aramaic and Syriac *bar nash(a)* is almost always a surrogate for man, or infrequently a circumlocution for the first person pronoun singular. Second, in the Early Church Jesus was accorded the title the 'Son of Man'. Matthew even changes Mark's 'I' (viz. Mk 8:27) to the 'Son of Man', (Mt 16:13). In the attempt to understand how, when and why the title took on a significant christological connotation, two Jewish documents have loomed large, Daniel and 1 Enoch.

For at least a decade it has been fashionable for New Testament specialists to avoid using the latter document, 1 Enoch 37—71.[78] This reticence has been due to a recognition that 1 Enoch is a document with so many complexities that it can entrap or mislead, even embarrass, the New Testament scholar. During this century two scholarly positions have undermined our use of 1 Enoch 37—71.

(1) *Charles and the Relegation of Enoch's Elevation*

Charles *emended* the ending of this section, or Book of the Similitudes (or Parables) of Enoch, so that Enoch is told, 'This is the Son of Man who is born unto righteousness' (1 En 71:14).[79] There is no textual basis for this emendation; and as Charles himself noted, the text reads, 'Thou art the Son of Man'. The emendation was caused by Charles' misunderstanding; he thought that the transformation of Enoch was awkward and in tension with the rest of 37—71.[80] Charles' prominence in the field of the Pseudepigrapha and his emendation misled New

Testament scholars to ponder over the identity of the Son of Man in 1 Enoch. The texts are clear; *the Son of Man is Enoch*. Now, we New Testament scholars need to assess the significance of that fact for our own work.

(2) *Milik and an Unfulfilled Promise*

Since the 50s J. T. Milik promised us he could prove that 1 Enoch 37−71 is not Jewish, but indeed a Christian composition that considerably postdates the New Testament period (50−150). His genius and pioneering leadership in the study of the Dead Sea Scrolls caused a moratorium on the use of 1 Enoch 37−71 for a study of the term 'Son of Man' in earliest Christianity (especially before 70).

(3) *An Irony: A Consensus Communis*

With the publication of his defence of this position, *SNTS* seminars were focused upon his arguments and position (see Appendix p. 102−10). It became obvious that Milik had not proved his position, as Fitzmyer pointed out as soon as *The Books of Enoch* had been published.[81] Repeatedly the specialists on 1 Enoch have come out in favour of the *Jewish* nature of this section of 1 Enoch, and its first-century C.E. origin, and probable pre-70 date. The list of specialists on 1 Enoch arguing for this position has become overwhelmingly impressive: Isaac, Nickelsburg, Stone, Knibb, Andersen, Black, VanderKam, Greenfield and Suter.[82] The *consensus communis* is unparalleled in almost any other area of research; no specialist now argues that 1 Enoch 37−71 is Christian and postdates the first century.

This conclusion means that *1 Enoch 37−71 is Jewish, Palestinian and probably predates the burning of Jerusalem in 70*. Now, there is much to do. We need to start afresh and ask what is the function and meaning of *walda sab'e, walda be'esi*, and *walda 'eguala 'emmaheiaw* (the three terms for 'son of man') in 1 Enoch 37−71. Should any or all of these terms be capitalized? Does the phrase in 1 Enoch 37−71 denote not a celestial being, but the elevation of a human figure, as M. Casey has contended?[83] What segment of Jewish society would concur with the ideas absorbed by 1 Enoch? How widespread were these ideas? What relationship existed between these terms and the other terms in 1 Enoch 37−71 (e.g. the 'Messiah', the 'Anointed One', or 'anointed')? What is the meaning of the demonstrative 'that' before the 'Son of Man' in 1 Enoch 37−71, and is it significant for understanding the prevalence of the definite article before this term in the Synoptic Gospels? This problem is recognized by Moule as one of the 'neglected' areas in our research.[84] New Testament scholars will not be content to discern only the relation between 1 Enoch 37–71 and the New Testament documents; they will demand research upon the possibilities that the Book of the Parables of Enoch may have influenced Jesus and not only his earliest followers.

CONCLUSION

New Testament scholars are already convinced of the importance of the Old Testament Pseudepigrapha for their own work. In the preceding pages I have sometimes spoken polemically against tendencies obviously atypical of many scholars, but unfortunately found in the work of some scholars who have not had the privilege to study intensively the literature of Early Judaism. Perhaps my comments have focused too much on methodologies, presuppositions, and perceptions; but I have thought this procedure appropriate, suggesting ways for detailed research on the few examples given.

Among the significant explorations left for future work are the importance of the Pseudepigrapha for (*inter alia*)

(1) lexicography;[1]
(2) a perception of the daily religious life in Palestine;[2]
(3) the study of paraenesis and ethics;[3]
(4) a recognition of the prevalence of the use of parables;[4]
(5) the conception of the Kingdom or the Rule of God;[5]
(6) an understanding of the Jewish (4 Ezra, 2 Bar, ApAb) and Christian (Rom) expressed need to argue for the righteousness of God;[6]
(7) an exploration of the parallels between Jewish and Christian theodicies,[7] especially regarding the delay of the eschaton or the parousia;
(8) and an improved articulation of the development of Jewish exegesis, especially the relation between 'expansions' to the Old Testament and other methods, notably Pesherim, Talmudim, Targumim, Midrashim and legend.[8]

Only brief comments have been uttered regarding the complicated relationships between Jewish messianism and early Christology. For example,[9] W. Wrede's *Das Messiasgeheimnis in den Evangelien* is at once brilliant and simplistic.[10] It is far too simplistic regarding the complex relationship between the *Urgemeinde* and Mark's redaction of tradition; and most significantly for us, it presents a view of Jewish messianism that fails to allow for the complex, often contradictory views of the Messiah, messianic figures, quasi-messianic figures, and amorphously conceptualized salvific figures in Early Judaism.[11] There is sufficient evidence to contend that some early Jews held firmly to the belief that the Messiah's presence will be revealed only by God himself;[12] a self-proclamation, as well as any demonic or human confession, reveals a messianic pretender. As the author of the Psalms of Solomon stated, God alone knows the identity of the Messiah (17:42), and *in God's own time* the 'king, the son of David' shall be raised up by God (17:23).

Four concluding, and personal, thoughts: first, I must stress how strange it is to pick up books on Early Judaism written before 1947 and to read, for example, about Palestinian Judaism and Egyptian Judaism as 'les deux formes du Judaïsme'.[13] How odd it is to be told that Early Christianity is so different from Early Judaism because the Christian doctrine cannot be extracted from it, and that the difference is 'le point capital des origines chrétiennes par rapport au Judaïsme'.[14] It is wise not to describe such methods or conclusions – they were penned by a truly gifted, industrious and revered scholar – it is better to perceive how different and improved is the work being published today. The main catalyst is certainly the discovery and recognition of such early Jewish documents as the Dead Sea Scrolls and the Pseudepigrapha.

Second, Christianity's inheritance from Early Judaism is rich and complex.[15] We are entering a new phase in research on Early Judaism and Christian Origins. The preceding discussion is merely prolegomenous.

Third, the historian does not have the guidance of Nature, who can serve the scientist by proving or disproving an hypothesis. Einstein's theory of relativity was strengthened and perhaps proved by the precession of Mercury's perihelion, the sun's bending of light, and radiation's red shift. The historian works in more darkness, aided by flickers of light bouncing off (perhaps from) a new discovery, especially off a once-lost document. Often these discoveries shatter constructed paradigms and models of portions of history. New discoveries may produce the nightmare that our 'respective hobby-horses have irretrievably run off in different directions'.[16] Yet the author of these words, Albert Einstein, urged us to recognize the goodness and righteousness in the search for truth: 'Subtle is the Lord, but malicious he is not.'[17]

Fourth, surveying reflectively the literature being produced on the New Testament writings and their backgrounds, the following thought seems appropriate in concluding. Perhaps Jesus of Nazareth did teach his disciples to call God *Abba*, because 'there are needs which result in speech but are not needs *for* speech. Language is a vehicle, almost never destination.'[18] And so, perhaps the words of the 'pseudepigraphers' are *invitations* to obtain meaning or at least to live meaningfully in a palpably meaningless world, and to an encounter with the One who seeks to approach from beyond.

APPENDIX: THE *SNTS* PSEUDEPIGRAPHA SEMINARS FROM 1976 to 1983

1976 (Durham, N.C., Duke University): The Testaments of the Twelve Patriarchs

In August 1976 at Duke University the *SNTS* inaugurated a new seminar that focuses upon the importance of the Old Testament Pseudepigrapha for New Testament research. The two documents most pertinent for this focus of discussion are the Testaments of the Twelve Patriarchs, because of the lengthy and fruitful debate over its Jewish or Christian character, and 1 (Ethiopic) Enoch, because of the importance for Christology of the Son of Man passages in chapters 37–71, and because one book in the New Testament, Jude, considered it authoritative and inspired.

The first seminar was directed to the T12P primarily because of the importance of J. Becker's recent books,[1] the appearance of two important collections of studies, one edited by W. Eltester[2] and the other by M. de Jonge,[3] and the anticipation of the *editio maior* of the Greek text by M. de Jonge.[4] The latter scholar was invited to present a paper, since he is an esteemed authority and acknowledged expert on the T12P; and since he is the leading proponent of the claim that the document is Christian and dates from the second century C.E. H.C. Kee was invited to present the second paper, because he has contributed the introduction to and translation of the T12P for *The Old Testament Pseudepigrapha*, and because he concludes that the document is Jewish and dates from the second century B.C.E. Both specialists accepted the invitation; the following account intends to abbreviate the highpoints in the discussions between these two scholars and among the members of the seminar.[5]

I. Recent Research on the T12P

M. de Jonge demonstrated why recent research on the T12P has turned again to textual criticism. Seven additional Greek witnesses have been discovered since the edition by R.H. Charles,[6] and one of these (MS Sinai Gr. 2170, ff 8r–88r), given the *signum j*, has been found since the publication of H. J. de Jonge's *Stemma*.[7] Manuscripts *h, i* and *j* are narrowly related, particularly *h* and *j*.

Even more impressive than the increase in Greek witnesses is the multiplication of known Armenian manuscripts, from twelve known by R. H. Charles[8] to fifty-one now accessible to M. E. Stone, who is preparing an edition of this version.[9]

The two most debated problems, in terms of the relation between the Greek and Armenian versions, are the date of the Armenian translation (A) and its place in the *stemma*. Chr. Burchard[10] and M. E. Stone[11] conclude that A is very early, dating perhaps from the fifth, sixth or seventh century, because of the archaic character of the language. M. de Jonge, however, notes that A joins a number of Greek witnesses in giving a short text in TZeb 5–9. In the tenth chapter of *Studies* he tried to prove that A is later than the short Greek text.[12] The fact that the oldest Greek manuscript preserving the short text dates from the eleventh century links up with the fact that the oldest external evidence for A dates from the same century. Along entirely different lines H. J. de Jonge tried to prove that A cannot have originated before the ninth century.[13]

The debate cannot be resolved conclusively until other questions can be answered. Can Burchard or Stone discover evidence of the Armenian translation or of the short Greek text prior to the ninth or eighth century? Can either show that the language of the Armenian is not simply a tenth-century copying of the archaic style? Is de Jonge's demonstration of the priority of the longer text in TZeb convincing? Until these and similar questions are adequately researched and discussed, scholars will find little objective evidence to persuade them to follow Stone, and place the origin of A in the fifth century, or to follow de Jonge, and relegate A to the tenth century. Where A is to be placed in the *stemma* obviously results from this debate. H. J. de Jonge places it with family II,[14] before manuscript *e*, the earliest Greek witness for the short version, and after the group of manuscripts designated *g, l, m*, etc., which are witnesses for the longer version with which it has many readings in common.

M. de Jonge, on the basis of common research with M. E. Stone, claims that the Armenian version helps solve the question of the extent and content of the original text. The Armenian translation consistently omits paraenetic material, and is an extraction from the Greek.[15] This conclusion is demanded by the consistency of the method of extracting and the evidence that the Armenian derives from one Greek text.

A significant result of the textual studies by the scholars at Leiden is that one should no longer speak about a paradigm consisting of manuscript α and β, as did R.H. Charles;[16] the important division is between two families, both of which derive ultimately from uncial Greek texts. If these conclusions are sound, then Becker's text-critical operations and suggestions need considerable revision,[17] since they are based upon the misleading α−β dichotomy.

The *editio maior* will give a critical text. Where a decision between family I (Greek only) and family II (all other witnesses) is difficult or impossible, the text of family I is printed. An appendix will give a full list of all major divergencies between the two families and indicate when the editors choose the family I text, out of convenience or conviction.

In order to demonstrate the validity of his own thesis on the T12P, M. de Jonge turned to the TIss, which has seven chapters. He rejected Becker's contention that behind chapters 1 and 2 there lies an original story in which there is mention of only one mandrake (cf. 1:14, ἕνα μανδραγόραν),[18] and that two insertions were added that emphasized the number two (viz. 1:7a, 2:1−3). The number two is used inconsistently throughout; if a later scribe had added the theme of two he would most likely have been less inconsistent.[19] Two apples are demanded later in the text (cf. 2:2, τὰ δύο μῆλα); the comparison is between the apples and the *two* sons of Rachel. M. de Jonge argued that the extant text is not so poor as western minds might initially think; the author has followed the account in Genesis 30:14−18, including the exact order of the sons.

Chapters 3 to 5 of TIss present the patriarch as the perfect pious man whose conduct is characterized by ἁπλότης. He marries late (3:5), and has sexual intercourse only for the procreation of children.[20] With acknowledgement of what he regards as the excellent research published by J. Amstutz, who deals with the T12P in detail,[21] M. de Jonge argued that ἁπλότης is not a secondary element in this testament but is a major thread in the original fabric. It is the main theme of 3:1−2 and the reason Issachar was blessed by his father Jacob (ὅτι ἐν ἁπλότητι πορεύομαι). There is no need to opt for the possibility of a *Grundtext* with redactions; the present text is a reasonably meaningful whole.[22]

M. de Jonge concluded his presentation by turning to the problem with which his name has been linked for the last thirty years: the question concerning the Jewish or Christian (including Jewish-Christian) character of the document. He admitted frankly that he did not know at the moment what should be said about the character of TIss. The lone clearly Christian passage is 7:7*b*; it is vaguely possible that a Christian interpolated here, but it is probable that a Christian redacted throughout the T12P. M. de Jonge correctly emphasized that simply removing a few passages because they are 'clearly Christian' is improper; often such phrases are linked with other units linguistically but not necessarily ideologically similar. He was able to demonstrate that in some places removing a phrase that seemed Christian — to the perspective of us so far removed chrono-logically and conceptually from the original scribe, regardless of a second-century B.C.E. or second-century C.E. date — effected ramifications elsewhere in the document.[23] M. de Jonge convincingly showed that an hypothesis of minor Christian interpolations, self-contained and easily removed, would not suffice. The data are more complex.[24] Wide agreement followed de Jonge's confession that he simply refused to force Christian monks working between the tenth and fourteenth centuries into a particular mould.

G. Nickelsburg inserted into the discussion a question that has concerned many of us who participated in the 1975 SBL Seminar on the T12P which focused on the TJos.[25] If the Qumran fragment of a Testament of Naphtali represents the TNaph that is part of the T12P, then is it not reasonable to assume that the T12P are Jewish in character and pre-Christian in date? Why would an author attribute a testament to Naphtali, who is relatively insignificant? If he had composed testaments of the other eleven, a testament for Naphtali would be by design, not choice.[26]

M. de Jonge's reply showed that he had reflected in depth on this question. His answer had four emphases. The Qumran fragment has not yet been published, although its presence was announced by J. T. Milik in 1957;[27] hence, de Jonge has not been able to read it. Second, de Jonge is not certain the fragment comes from a Testament of Naphtali. Third, even if it is a Testament of Naphtali, it may not be identified with, or even similar to, the TNaph that is now part of the T12P. Finally, it is conceivable that an author would be attracted to Naphtali and dedicate a testament to him. He is the messenger *par excellence* (cf. TNaph 2:1, 'Since I was light on my feet like a deer, my father, Jacob, appointed me for all missions and messages', εἰς πᾶσαν ἀποστολὴν καὶ ἀγγελίαν·). Genesis 49 speaks disapprovingly of Simeon and Levi especially in verse 7 ('Cursed be their anger ... I will divide them in Jacob and scatter them in Israel', RSV); but it blesses Naphtali in verse 21 ('Naphtali is a hind let loose, that bears comely fawns' (or 'who gives beautiful words')).[28]

II. The Ethical Dimensions of the T12P as a Clue to Provenance

H.C. Kee began his presentation in agreement with M. de Jonge on three points. The T12P have a long complicated literary history: the starting point is the midrashic expansion of Genesis 49; the end product is the extant T12P with Christian redaction, which itself survives in a range of different textual traditions, as the manuscripts and versions show; the attempts to prove a direct relationship between the T12P and the Qumran messianic passages have been unconvincing. At least two major differences separated Kee from de Jonge: for Kee the T12P are essentially Jewish, and they originated around 100 B.C. E. Kee is convinced that the provenance of the T12P is neither Qumranic nor Jewish-Christian; his attempt at a different solution to the probable provenance of the T12P is through analysis of key concepts; for example, 'law', 'custom' and 'command', as represented by ὁ νόμος and ἡ ἐντολή.

Two of the nine uses of ἐντολή in the T12P coincide with non-Jewish concepts of law; and law is not used to refer to the dietary restrictions found in the Torah.[29] For example, the cloven hoof is a symbol of double-mindedness (cf. διπρόσωπος, TAsh 2:8), practically the most unethical conduct imaginable, except for incest, which is reprehensible because it violates natural law. *Nomos* is employed with reference to revelation not regulation (cf. TLevi 12:2 'as they ceaselessly read the Law of God', ἀναγινώσκοντες ἀδιαλείπτως τὸν νόμον τοῦ θεοῦ·).

Nomos is not used absolutely, as one would expect if it meant Torah, but it is almost always defined as God's law, which is the law of nature, the order of the universe (cf. TLevi 14:4). Law is not perceived as related to a particular *Heilsgeschichte*; covenant and Moses are of minor importance. Rather, law is presented along the lines of Jewish wisdom literature. When law as timeless principle is linked with eschatological expectation, there is perhaps a partial confirmation of G. von Rad's claim that apocalyptic is linked with wisdom.[30] Brotherly love is grounded not in Berith but in common humanity; the apodictic demands of YHWH are noticeably absent. In contrast to the Jewish pragmatic and casuistic exhortations stand such abstract terms in the T12P as σύνεσις (embodiment of will), σωφροσύνη (the potency of inward power for righteousness), εὐσέβεια (piety), ἀσέβεια (impiety), ἁπλότης (single-mindedness). These concepts cumulatively link the T12P with middle Stoicism.[31]

The concept of the two spirits in the T12P (cf. TJud 20:1, ὅτι δύο πνεύματα σχολάζουσι τῷ ἀνθρώπῳ, τὸ τῆς ἀληθείας καὶ τὸ τῆς πλάνης·), has been usually related in some way to Qumran dualism (cf. 1QS 3.13ff).[32] Stoic influence on the T12P would provide yet another evidence of the hellenistic impact on Judaism in the Graeco-Roman period, since a good case may perhaps be made for Stoic influence upon the concept of the spirits at Qumran.[33]

The use of διαθήκη in the T12P tends to corroborate the above suggestions regarding provenance. *Diathēkē* in the T12P means 'testament' not 'covenant'. The ethical exhortations presuppose a common humanity not a covenant people.

Kee concluded that although de Jonge has made a good case for Christian midrashic expansion, a Christian origin can be ruled out. With the exception of a few interpolations, Kee finds nothing that could not have originated in second-century Judaism. The T12P were written in Greek, because of the Greek place names, proper names, such terms as ἱππόδρομος (TJos 30:3), and the use of assonance and alliteration in the present Greek text. The document was composed apparently some time after 100 B.C.E. within a thoroughly hellenized Judaism, which was a genuine synthesis of Hellenism and a form of Judaism that regarded itself as faithful to the 'true' intent of the Law, not a forced hellenization of Judaism such as the Seleucids wished to accomplish. The learning underlying the document and the evidence of scholastic endeavours suggest that the T12P was written within a 'school'. The most likely place is Alexandria, although a Syrian (Antiochene) or Palestinian site is possible.

III. Methodology and Theology

As chairman of the seminar I asked both de Jonge and Kee to begin our final discussion by focusing upon a few passages which would help explain the difference between an interpolation and a redaction. Similarly each member of the seminar was requested to be prepared to discuss the theological peculiarities of Christianity (and Jewish Christianity) so that we could evaluate openly the relative strengths of de Jonge's and Kee's positions.

Kee began the final session by discussing his criteria for isolating an interpolation. TLevi 10:1−2 contains an interpolation by a Christian. The setting and content is clear; Levi passes on to his sons that which has been transmitted to him from his ancestors. The emphasis in this chapter is upon Israel as the people of God. Verse

2*b* is an interpolation because it disrupts the flow of thought, contains an idea in tension with the context – the thought is anti-Jewish – and can be removed easily. TLevi 10:2 is as follows:

> And behold I am clear from your ungodliness and trans-gression, which ye shall commit in the end of the ages [against the Saviour of the world, Christ, acting godlessly], deceiving Israel, and stirring up against it great evils from the Lord.
>
> (Charles' trans.)

Turning next to TLevi 14:2 Kee circumscribed another interpolation: 'For our father Israel is pure from the transgressions of the chief priests [who shall lay their hands upon the Saviour of the world].' This passage has been interpolated; it interrupts the thought, describes an anti-Jewish act, and is grammatically independent of the contiguous passages.

M. de Jonge disagreed with Kee. With regard to chapter 10 he pointed to a parallel in TBenj 9:4. As far as he can tell all further parallels are found in Christian sources.[34] Moreover, chapters 10, 14–15 and 16 in TLevi give three times an acknowledged form critical frame of the T12P; each is a Sin–Exile–Return passage. Kee agrees with this claim by de Jonge, but argues that the pattern is present even when the allegedly Christian interpolations are removed. The passage Kee wishes to remove from chapter 14 is not preserved in the Aramaic fragment mentioned by Milik.[35] Checking this fragment, which has been published only in part, proves little since 14:2 is not preserved; only 14:3–4 is extant.

A heated debate centred upon the features of interpolations and redactions; this discussion produced considerable light which is summarized as follows.[36] *Interpolations* are insertions into the text that disrupt the flow of thought or add specific details, especially in defining Israel's rejection of God or his agent. They can be removed because of their linguistic structure, which is usually genitival, parenthetical, or otherwise self-contained. They might contain terms, symbols, or ideas foreign – or even antithetical – to the context, or they might make specific the Christian way of understanding a text. For example, Kee points to TLevi in which the 'sin' is specified in the interpolations as the rejection of the Messiah, who is Jesus of Nazareth. Without this specification, the wickedness of the nation remains a strong element in TLevi.

Redactions are passages embedded into the fabric of the document and cannot be excised. Early sources are so reworked from a new perspective that they cannot be distinguished from the more recent sections.

These definitions are pragmatically effective in many situations; yet it is often impossible to distinguish between an interpolation and a redaction. Frequently it is difficult to find the precise borders of an interpolation, and an apparent interpolation might be a passage in which the redactor has failed to achieve the usual integration, transition or flow of thought. The discovery of an interpolation does not disclose that a document is to be characterized as an interpolated text; interpolations are often made to documents which are redactional in character. De Jonge, for example, allows for the possibility that there may be later Christian interpolations — after all our oldest Greek witness is of the tenth century — but these interpolations would be Christian additions to a Christian document. Kee contends that there are interpolations by a Christian to a Jewish document. Both scholars agree that we must be careful to proceed with the assumption that the interpolation—redaction paradigm is often a false distinction, that we should attempt to perceive the entire document and not a series of random samples, and that we must constantly allow for the laconic nature of the few documents that have been preserved from the period 100 B.C.E. to 200 C.E.

The discussion did not belabour the obvious impossibility of discovering whether a pseudepigraphical passage is Jewish or Christian (and Jewish-Christian). Specialists on the Pseudepigrapha are well aware that their data are too ambiguous on this issue. Intermittently, however, the members of the seminar acknowledged appreciation of R. A. Kraft's paper read the preceding day in the *SNTS* plenary session on the Pseudepigrapha.[37] One emphasis by Kraft was particularly significant for our discussions and should be repeated here. Kraft pointed to the fact that many pseudepigrapha contain Christian passages, whether interpolations or redactions, and are preserved and transmitted to us only through Christian circles; the proper methodological presupposition for them, he claimed, should be that the document is Christian until proved otherwise. M. de Jonge enjoined this principle for the T12P. Kee thought that the principle was here used illegitimately; preservation of material related to the T12P at Qumran proved that this document (or earlier versions of it) was cherished by two communities, one clearly Christian and the other undeniably Jewish. Perhaps it would be wise to credit Kraft with signalling a moratorium on the presupposition that the burden of proof is with de Jonge and others regarding the Christian origin of a pseudepigraphon. There should be no charge that the burden of proof lies with either interlocutor; the proof is always within the data itself.

IV. Conclusions

Seminar discussions do not evolve toward set conclusions; yet I sensed some points of consensus: (1) the T12P was not written by the Qumran sectarians; (2) it was composed in Greek; (3) as extant it is clearly Christian but there is a Jewish foundation; (4) post-Nicene Christians interpolated the document; and (5) it is a major witness either to Jewish paraenesis just prior to Christianity, or to the profoundly determinative impact of Jewish ethics upon 'Christian' paraenesis in the second century C.E.[38]

The 1977 *SNTS* Pseudepigrapha Seminar will meet in Tübingen and will concentrate upon 1 (Ethiopic) Enoch. The focus of the presentations will be J. T. Milik's recent book on the Aramaic material.[39]

1977 (Tübingen; Eberhard-Karls Universität): The Books of Enoch

The *SNTS* Pseudepigrapha Seminar, which is organized to explore the importance of the Pseudepigrapha for a better understanding of Christian origins and the New Testament writings, met for the second time in 1977.[1] The focus of the seminar was upon the Books of Enoch; only the highlights of the session are summarized briefly below.

I. Unexamined Manuscripts of 1 (Ethiopic) Enoch

Four sessions were assigned to the seminar in the 1977 *SNTS* Conference. Tuesday morning, 23 August, Professor Ephraim Isaac spoke about the significance of twenty-one virtually unexamined manuscripts of Ethiopic Enoch,[2] and about the ramifications of his research on this document for J. T. Milik's position, published in *The Books of Enoch: Aramaic Fragments of Qumrân Cave 4* (Oxford, 1976).

Isaac drew attention to 'two of the oldest existing manuscripts' of 1 (Ethiopic) Enoch: the oldest and most important manuscript is Tānāsee 9–Kebrān 9 which dates from the fourteenth or fifteenth century;[3] the other is EMML 2080, which dates from the fifteenth century.[4] Isaac claimed that the former manuscript contains many previously unknown and extremely important variants. These were summarized for the scholars in attendance,[5] and will be published in a forthcoming article.

On the basis of his critical study of these and other Ethiopic manuscripts of Ethiopic Enoch, Isaac expressed his opinion that Milik had been too dependent upon the editions by J. Flemming and R. H. Charles. He claimed that few Ethiopic specialists will accept Milik's dating of Ethiopic Enoch to the sixth century. Isaac preferred a date between 350 and 550 C.E. for the translation into Ge'ez. One of the reasons Milik argued for the sixth century is the reference to 'winged angels' in 1 (Ethiopic) Enoch 61:1; Isaac stated that Kebran 9 does not contain this reading. Numerous other examples were presented. Isaac argued that 1 (Ethiopic) Enoch, or portions of it, had been translated directly from an Aramaic document. He rejected Milik's claim that the Parables of Enoch are dependent upon the New Testament.

II. Nickelsburg's Insights

Nickelsburg, the official respondent to Isaac's paper, began the second seminar session with several reactions and suggestions. He stated that Isaac's position centres on one point: conclusions now are premature since manuscripts of Ethiopic Enoch have been recovered that prove to be, in some cases, superior to those used by Charles and earlier editors. He questioned the novelty of some of Isaac's examples, pointing out that some are represented in the Greek recension. He argued that in chapters 97–107 there are numerous passages that convince him that the Ethiopic version is based on a Greek rather than directly on the Aramaic version. The remarkable correspondence between the Son of Man in 1 (Ethiopic) Enoch 37–71 and the Gospels is primarily that in both he is *judge*. The link is significant; Nickelsburg then agreed with Isaac that Milik has failed to demonstrate that the Parables of Enoch are influenced by the New Testament.[6]

III. Challenging Developments in the Study of 2 (Slavonic) Enoch

While Isaac prepared the contribution of 1 (Ethiopic) Enoch for the new English edition of the Pseudepigrapha published by Doubleday & Company, Inc. of New York, F. Andersen was commissioned to contribute the materials on 2 (Slavonic) Enoch. At the third session of the seminar on 24 August, he turned our attention to two un-published manuscripts of 2 (Slavonic) Enoch, MS BAN 45.13.4 (A) and MS BAN 13.3.25 (J).[7] The former has been hitherto unknown to western scholars; the latter hardly noted by A. Vaillant,[8] since even Sokolov never had direct use of it. Andersen argued that there are strong reasons to doubt the consensus that has evolved from Vaillant, especially regarding the priority of the short recension and the late date of the longer passages.

Among Milik's numerous statements on 2 (Slavonic) Enoch that should not remain unchallenged are the following: (1) Milik accepts Vaillant's claim that the 'short' text was later expanded into the 'long' one. The complicated relationships between all extant manuscripts preclude such facile conclusions; moreover, the terms 'long' and 'short' fail to serve scholarship because specialists disagree which manuscripts are really 'long' and 'short', and the terms cannot refer to the length of a manuscript, many of which preserve only a portion of 2 (Slavonic) Enoch. (2) Milik contends that the 'short form ... represents the original text of the version' (p. 107). This position is not helpful since Vaillant, whom Milik follows, stated that MS U is the best of the 'short' recension, but some scholars have claimed that this manuscript, because it is more ample than N (the base for 'B' in Charles' *APOT*), represents an 'intermediate' recension. Moreover, 'short' manuscripts differ considerably among themselves. It is unwise to reject as corrupt a unique reading. Fuller material R, J, P, P[2], the 'long' recension, may be either medieval expansions or original words lost from the 'short' manuscripts. Far too many scholars have seen only the first of these possibilities. Andersen is convinced that he has found examples of the second possibility.[9] (3) Milik claimed that the 'original text of the version' was made 'from Greek into the old western Slavonic of Macedonia, if not Pannonia' (p. 108). Although Milik refers to Schmidt at this point, he is obviously dependent upon Vaillant, whom he has misunderstood: 'Ce vieux slave est nettement du vieux slave occidental, de Macédoine, sinon de Pannonie' (p. xiv). Milik apparently did not know that Macedonian is an eastern dialect in the South Slavonic group. He is also apparently ignorant of the pioneering work in Russia by Meshchersky, who argues against Vaillant's conclusion regarding the provenance of 2 (Slavonic) Enoch. The original location of the translation of 2 (Slavonic) Enoch from Greek to Slavonic remains unknown. (4) Milik claims that the Greek text of 2 (Slavonic) Enoch was extant in the thirteenth century because 'it is quoted in the Greek treatise entitled the *Debate of the Panagiote and the Azymite*' (p. 108). He inherited this claim from Vaillant (p. xvii) but without acknowledgement. The literary connections between 2 (Slavonic) Enoch and the *Debate* are unclear; similar material is also found in 3 Baruch. (5) Milik's discussion of the transmission history of the text (p. 108) is confused and uninformed. (6) Milik's discussion of the 'long' recension is misleading; he lists only six manuscripts of 2 (Slavonic) Enoch with any exactitude. Twenty-three manuscripts are now known; and a collation of J reveals that some of Milik's statements are incorrect. (7) Milik claims that 'no trace' of 2 (Slavonic) Enoch 'has been found in early Christian literature' (p. 109). Origen, as other scholars have argued, may have known 2 (Greek?) Enoch. A fuller discussion and an open mind are needed. (8) Milik claims that the short recension 'preserves the original Greek text fairly faithfully' (p. 109). Andersen wonders why Milik can be so confident when not one word of the supposed Greek original has survived. As the supposed work of a Constantinople monk, 2 (Slavonic) Enoch is baffling, especially because of the total absence of any palpable Christian idea in it. Hence, Andersen disagrees with Vaillant (and Rubinstein) that it is a Christian work; he concurs with Pines and Scholem that it is a Jewish composition. Milik, however, ignores this important debate. (9) Milik's dating of the Greek source of 2 (Slavonic) Enoch to the ninth or tenth century rests ultimately on an emendation which is purely conjectural. (10) Milik sees in the Melkisedek legend the clearest traces of late Christian ideas. Andersen is surprised by the lack of Christian ideas in the Melkisedek legend, points to the fact that there are strong contradictions of the legend as preserved in Hebrews (in 2 (Slavonic) Enoch he has a mother!), and stresses the wide interest in Melkisedek among early Jews as now proved by the recovery of 11Q Melkisedek. Andersen points to the Russian I.D. Amusin's arguments that the Melkisedek tradition in 2 (Slavonic) Enoch is certainly pre-Christian.[10] In summary, Andersen rejects Milik's position on 2 (Slavonic) Enoch and laments that his statements may further inhibit the study and inclusion among the early Jewish writings of a truly remarkable work.

IV. Discussion and Conclusion

The fourth session on 25 August was an open and free-wheeling discussion that is difficult to summarize. Scholars were eager to study both papers and urged their publication. No scholar seemed persuaded by Milik's position on 2 (Slavonic) Enoch or by his dating of the Parables of Enoch. It was agreed to focus the Paris sessions upon the dating of these chapters and the general importance of 1 (Ethiopic) Enoch for understanding the New Testament. It was hoped that M. Knibb and G. W. E. Nickelsburg could be persuaded to present papers that would be circulated prior to the sessions.

1978 (Paris; Châtenay-Malabry): 1 (Ethiopic) Enoch and Luke and the Dating of the Parables of Enoch

The *SNTS* Pseudepigrapha Seminar met three times during the 1978 *SNTS* Conference, which was held on the fringes of Paris at Châtenay-Malabry. Knibb and Nickelsburg, recognized authorities on 1 (Ethiopic) Enoch, presented papers on the subjects requested by the Tübingen group. The chairman circulated copies of each paper to the participants,[1] among whom were two other specialists who are currently working on 1 (Ethiopic) Enoch,[2] namely E. Isaac and M. Black. Isaac has completed the contribution on 1 (Ethiopic) Enoch for the new English edition of the Pseudepigrapha published by Doubleday, and plans to publish a facsimile edition of Tānāsee 9−Kebrān 9 (see preceding discussion); Black collaborated with Milik on *The Books of Enoch*, republished the Greek version,[3] and is preparing a commentary on 1 (Ethiopic) Enoch.

I. 1 (Ethiopic) Enoch 92−105 and Luke

On 25 July 1978 the first session of the seminar was devoted to Nickelsburg's paper 'Riches, the Rich, and God's Judgment in 1 Enoch 92−105 and the Gospel According to Luke'. Because it is printed,[4] it is necessary to summarize only the major points. The starting point of Nickelsburg's paper was the remarkable parallels between Luke's special material and the last chapters of 1 (Ethiopic) Enoch that were the focus for an article by S. Aalen in *NTS*.[5] Aalen did not conclude his article with an explanation of these parallels, but left the question open for future research (p. 12). In an additional note, however, he reveals his own personal judgment that Luke borrowed from 1 (Ethiopic) Enoch and asked, 'Was the relationship in question more than a literary one? Was Luke personally acquainted with the man who translated 1 (Ethiopic) Enoch? Or was he perhaps himself this man?' (p. 13).

Nickelsburg refined Aalen's list of parallels and divided them into minor and major. The latter indicate that there is some contact between 1 (Ethiopic) Enoch and the traditions in Luke. The last chapters of 1 (Ethiopic) Enoch are 'a piece of in-group literature' (cf. 92:1), reflecting oppression by and rejection of the rich. Luke, in contrast, addresses the rich, exhorting them to share their wealth. He also stresses more a concern for the poor. The abundance of similar material about riches and the rich in not only L but Q and Mark raises the possibility that some of these traditions derive ultimately from Jesus of Nazareth. Finally, the similarities between 1 (Ethiopic) Enoch 92ff and Luke indicate that there is some contact between this section of 1 (Ethiopic) Enoch and the traditions in Luke.

The chairman asked for reactions to Nickelsburg's statement that 'in their emphases and contents, and to some extent, their forms, the sections of Luke in question find their closest parallels in extant literature in 1 (Ethiopic) Enoch 92 – 105'. He expressed the opinion that this statement seemed accurate; the theological treatment of riches and the rich shared by 1 (Ethiopic) Enoch and Luke is not found in the major pseudepigrapha and certainly is not in the Treatise of Shem, the History of the Rechabites, and the Odes of Solomon. M. de Jonge agreed that these concerns are not typical of the Testaments of the Twelve Patriarchs.

M. Knibb argued that one real difference between 1 (Ethiopic) Enoch and Luke is that only in the former is the concern about the rich of really fundamental importance. Knibb admitted the parallels cited are impressive but preferred to think that these are probably due to common and abundant prophetic tradition. Isaac agreed with Knibb and drew attention to the many Old Testament verses that feature the oppression of the poor by the rich.

Considerable discussion centred around the claim that 1 (Ethiopic) Enoch 92 – 105 represents an 'in-group' oppressed by the rich. Hartman stressed that in Luke the traditions receive a new function; the rich are included in the exhortations. Leaney stated that in the Epistle of James the rich oppress the poor, but in Luke – Acts the rich are not the enemies of Christianity. Perhaps Luke is softening the attitude of an 'in-group' so that Christianity can appeal also to the upper strata of society.

Isaac asked if 1 (Ethiopic) Enoch 92 – 105 mirrored a sociological group. Nickelsburg replied that he saw the 'in-group' as an oppressed group, not a sect, that saw themselves as outcasts. Knibb agreed that the ideas in 92 – 105 are not sectarian, and voiced the opinion that this section dates from the beginning of the second century B.C.E., before the persecution under Antiochus Epiphanes.

II. Dating the Parables of Enoch

On 26 July the second session of the seminar was devoted to Knibb's paper 'The Date of the Parables of Enoch: A Critical Review'.[6] The genesis of his study occurred when a few years ago he found it impossible to respond adequately to the question, 'Is there any hard evidence for dating the Parables?' The focus of his paper was upon Milik, who removes the Parables from the period of Early Judaism and places them near the end of the third century C.E.[7] Systematically Knibb analysed and rejected Milik's arguments. Knibb argued persuasively to almost all in attendance that the Parables are both Jewish and Semitic. The reference to the Parthians in 56:5−8 should not be seen as depicting the incidents either in the third century C.E. or first century B.C.E. Any attempt to date the Parables because of this passage is 'unsatisfactory and unconvincing'. Moreover, 56:5−57:3 may be an independent piece either inherited by the author of the Parables or interpolated later. Milik's argument that this section of the Parables (56:5−7) was 'obviously inspired' (p. 95) by the Sibylline Oracles (5:104−10) is forced and unpersuasive.

Knibb offered his own opinion that the Parables depend upon the earlier Enochic literature, and were composed near the end of the first century C.E. The absence of fragments of the Parables from the Qumran caves seems 'to point fairly strongly to the view that this section of Enoch was composed after the Qumran site was abandoned in A.D. 68'. Secondly, the Son of Man passages fit most naturally into the end of the first century since the most significant parallels are with 2 Baruch and 4 Ezra 3−14 (and perhaps Jn 5:27).[8]

Nickelsburg responded to Knibb's paper. He agreed that the Sibylline Oracles are not a good parallel to 1 (Ethiopic) Enoch 37−71, and reiterated that the function of the Son of Man as judge in these verses is significant.

M. Black then expressed his opinion regarding the date of the Parables. In an article in *The Expository Times* he had argued that the 'negative arguments, in particular the silence of Qumran and of versional and patristic tradition, seem absolutely decisive for the mediaeval origins' of the Parables.[9] Most participants, especially in light of C. L. Mearns' published reaction to the above quotation from Black,[10] expected him to support Milik's position. Black's comments were significantly different and a pleasant surprise for many. He stated that he now saw the Parables as Jewish and post-Christian, perhaps a Jewish reaction to Christianity from around 100 C.E.[11] He commented further that Milik's position rests on slender foundations, that the Parables seem to have Semitic roots but it is unlikely that they ever existed either in Hebrew or Aramaic, that 1 (Ethiopic) Enoch 56:7 ('But the city of my righteous shall be a hindrance to their [the Parthians'] horses.')[12] best refers to the Parthian capture of Jerusalem in 40 B.C.E.

Knibb replied that it was good to have a clarification of Black's position, that it was difficult to agree with Black about the non-existence of a Semitic base to the Parables, and that 56:7 is too imprecise to support Black's conclusion and may not be original to the document.

III. Discussion

On 27 July the final session of the seminar was devoted to general discussion and future plans. M. de Jonge began the third session with two questions: are Nickelsburg and Knibb far apart from each other; and is it possible that the Parables derive from a Greek *Vorlage* that used Semitic material but may not have been written in a Semitic language? Nickelsburg replied that he believes that *something like* the 'Son of Man' materials in the Parables was extant by the first century C.E. The Parables, as Knibb stated, depend upon the Book of the Watchers (1 En 1–36); moreover, in the Parables the Elect One assumes some functions of God found in the Book of the Watchers.

Knibb replied to de Jonge's second question. He admitted that such a supposition is possible, but the evidence that points to a Semitic original runs throughout the Parables. Knibb advocated a Semitic original for the whole of 37–71. He agreed that essentially he and Nickelsburg were not far apart; certainly, I must add, not as far apart as Charles, with his early first-century B.C.E. date,[13] and Milik, with his third-century C.E. date.

A general discussion of messianic figures in early Jewish literature drew attention to the multiplicity of titles and functions. It was lamented that textbooks still talk about the existence of only two figures, the Son of Man and the Messiah, in pre-Christian Jewish texts. It is obvious that such distinctions as a heavenly or terrestrial messiah are less than representative, and that such titles as Son of Man and Messiah were malleable concepts frequently related and sometimes used interchangeably.

The participants agreed that the sessions were rich and important. Next year's seminar will be organized by the chairman in consultation with others. It was suggested that attention to the central issue of messianism in the Pseudepigrapha would be an appropriate topic for the 1979 sessions.

IV. Conclusion to the Seminars on the Books of Enoch

The main conclusions that represented the consensus of the scholars participating in the Tübingen seminar were the recognition of the complexity of the manuscript traditions of both 1 (Ethiopic) Enoch and 2 (Slavonic) Enoch and the frequent untrustworthiness of available editions and translations. It was agreed that Milik should have worked more directly with the Ethiopic and Slavonic evidence, and that it would have been better for him to have published only the Aramaic fragments with a succinct introduction two decades earlier. There was general excitement over the discovery or use of important manuscripts of 1 (Ethiopic) Enoch and 2 (Slavonic) Enoch and over the textual labours by Isaac and Andersen. *No* scholar concurred with Milik's date for the Parables.

The shared conclusions of the sessions in Paris were more precise. (1) 1 (Ethiopic) Enoch 92–105 comes from an 'in-group' that was being oppressed by the rich. (2) The closest parallel to Luke's special interest in the poor and the neglect of them by the rich is in 1 (Ethiopic) Enoch 92–105. (3) These verses of 1 (Ethiopic) Enoch should not be considered sectarian. (4) Examining the parallels between 1 (Ethiopic) Enoch and Luke is a significant means towards a better understanding of the latter, its theology and its sources. (5) The links between the Parables and the Sibylline Oracles are generic and insignificant for dating the former. (6) The Parables are Jewish. (7) Most importantly, no one agreed with Milik's late date for the Parables; these date from the early or later part of the first century C.E. This conclusion is significant; yet the real issue remains open. Are these Jewish Parables pre-Christian and a source for understanding either Jesus' *ipsissima verba* or the theologies of the Evangelists? Or, are they post-Christian and a significant development independent of the canonical gospels, or a Jewish reaction to Christianity?

1979 (Durham, England; University of Durham): Methodological Issues — The Messiah, 'Christos', and the 'Anointed One'

The *SNTS* Pseudepigrapha Seminar met for the fourth consecutive year in August 1979 at the University of Durham in Durham, England. The title of the 1979 seminar was 'The Pseudepigrapha and the New Testament: Methodological Issues — The Messiah, "Christos", and the "Anointed One"'. The seminar was focused on an assessment of the importance of the various messianic titles and ideas in the Old Testament Pseudepigrapha and their significance for a better understanding of the origins of Christology, especially the christological ideas and titles in the New Testament. Three seminar sessions were organized so that more time than in the previous years would be devoted to open discussion.

I. The Earliest Christian Use of χριστός

On 21 August M. de Jonge introduced a discussion of 'The Earliest Christian Use of Christos'.[1] Among his general and introductory considerations especially significant were the following: (1) we must avoid the confusion and misrepresentation caused by using the technical term 'Messiah' to denote any (more or less) human eschatological mediator; (2) we should use the actual terms found in our source (or sources), recognizing that these terms also occur in non-eschatological contexts, and that different terms may be employed to describe the same figure; (3) the widespread Jewish expectation of God's final act is not always conceived in terms of a mediating figure, whether 'human', 'angelic', or 'divine'; (4) in early Jewish eschatology the concept of the Messiah was not central; in contrast, in early Christian theology christology dominates; (5) almost all of the Old Testament Pseudepigrapha have come down to us through the mediation of Christian scribes and we must always keep this fact in our perspective and methodology.

M. de Jonge argued that it is almost unbelievable that the earliest Christians chose 'Christos' as the most popular title for Jesus. He agreed with N. A. Dahl that 'the name Christ received its content not through a previously-fixed conception of messiahship but rather from the person and work of Jesus Christ'.[2]

For de Jonge the main question is 'Why was "Christos" specifically connected with the death of Jesus?' Except for 1:1 all occurrences of 'Christos' in Mark are between 8:29 and 14:61. It is never a self-designation for Jesus. In 8:29 Peter's confession is corrected with another term, the 'Son of Man', who must suffer and then is exalted (Mk 8:34–8). The so-called messianic secret is not specifically a Christos secret.[3] Mark inherited the title 'Christos',[4] but he tried to qualify it in terms of the 'Son of God' and the 'Son of Man', and to connect it with Jesus' death and resurrection. The need for this re-definition is emphasized by the disciples' need for instruction and the complete misunderstanding among the Jewish leaders (cf. Mk 15:32).

A passage that needs more detailed discussion is Mark 12:35–7, which is the question about David's son. The πῶς (verse 35) and πόθεν (verse 37) indicate that the scribes' designation of ὁ χριστός as υἱὸς Δαυίδ is being criticized. The answer to πῶς is by means of a quotation from Psalm 110:1. The passage is a critique of the title 'Christos'. It is not denied that Jesus is υἱὸς Δαυίδ; what seems central is the discussion of kingship. For Mark Jesus is certainly the Messiah; yet in 12:35–7 Jesus uses the term only implicitly for himself. Mark is trying to show that χριστός is in need of further explanation, and other terms are necessary. For Mark the premier title for Jesus is 'Son of God', not 'Christos' or 'Son of David'.

The Marcan redaction reflects two phenomena in Early Christianity: the need for instruction regarding 'Christos' in the Christian community, and the necessity for polemic against the scribe's conception of the Messiah.

The search for the pre-Marcan stage of the development of the concept of 'Messiah' or 'Christos' leads us both into a maze of unanswered questions and back into the messianism of the early Jews in Palestine.[5] Some of the questions are the following: do the open-ended and implicit references to Jesus as Messiah and the simple use of Psalm 110:1 in Mark indicate a pre-Marcan stage? How should one explain Jesus' avoidance of the title 'Christos' according to Mark? Was Jesus crucified as 'King of the Jews', and does that brute fact explain the pre-Pauline use of 'Christos'?[6] Can Mark's portrayal of disciples who do not understand, and the polemics against the 'scribes', which reflects Mark's own situation, be used in reconstructing Jesus' time, in particular his relations with the disciples and the Jewish authorities?

M. de Jonge's methodological approach, whereby both Jewish sources and Christian literature were scrutinized simultaneously and similarly, was accepted as essential in our historical research. The responses to the introductory remarks and questions elicited a lively discussion, of which the high points may now be summarized. L. Hartman emphasized that in Jewish literature the Messiah has virtually no functions; he asked how one can explain the contrast in the New Testament documents? E.P. Sanders agreed that in Judaism the Messiah does virtually nothing; he asked why Paul picked up this term 'Christos' from his predecessors? M. de Jonge accepted Dahl's explanation (see n. 6) and argued that Paul defines Christos. Sanders asked what term would be appropriate for Theudas. He pointed out that Josephus called him a pseudo-prophet (γόης τις ἀνὴρ θευδᾶς ὀνόματι ... προφήτας γὰρ ἔλεγεν εἶναι *Ant* 20.97).[7] M. de Jonge warned against the bias of Josephus, who referred to Jesus as χριστὸς λεγόμενος (see the variant in *Ant* 18.63; I assume this reading is original and was later altered by Christians to ὁ χριστὸς οὗτος ἦν).[8]

M. Hooker asked us to consider the possibility that 'Messiah' is not a title, and that there were no ready-made titles. She asked, 'Now how do you express your faith in Jesus? Is not 'Messiah' a convenient adjective? (cf. Isa). D.R. Catchpole pointed out that it is singularly inappropriate for 'Christos' to die; hence we must include in our reflections the possibility that an emphasis upon 'resurrection is behind the unique Christian development of the term. Sanders responded by asking why σωτήρ would have not been more appropriate. Hooker added, 'Why did not the earliest Christians have a means for saying that God has been working through this person?' There was a consensus that we are confronted with a major problem of getting from the Christian *content* back into the Jewish non-descriptive 'titles' or terms (or should we proceed chronologically from Judaism to Christianity?).

R. Pesch claimed that the most important text for our search into the background of 'Christos' is Mark 12:35 − 7. It is clear that Mark has interpreted the title or term, and that Christos remains open. Mark wants us to see the Messiah in terms of the Son of Man. The concept of the Messiah has been developed in terms of the expectation of the Son of Man.

II. The 'Anointed One' in the Pseudepigrapha and Qumran Scrolls

On 22 August de Jonge introduced our second session. The subject was the 'Anointed One' in the Pseudepigrapha and Qumran Scrolls. In the Pseudepigrapha the following documents were discussed: the

Psalms of Solomon, *Liber Antiquitatum Biblicarum*, 1 (Ethiopic) Enoch, 4 Ezra and 2 Baruch.

In the Psalms of Solomon 17 the Christos is seen in terms of God's kingship and as the ideal king, the son of David; and emphasis is upon the king as a wise man. He is called *christos kurios* (17:32). Only in Psalm 18 is Christos developed in the direction of a 'technical' term.

In *LAB* there is no mention of a future 'Anointed One'. Samuel is anointed priest and prophet (51:6−7); but he serves David (*quousque dent cornu christo suo, et aderit potentia thronis regis eius*, 51:6).[9] Samuel later anoints David (59:3), and *dixit Samuel: Ecce nunc sanctus christus Domini*?[10] David then chants a psalm about God's protection; it contains the important line: *et quando nominatus est christus Domini obliti sunt mei.*[11] David is seen as a type of messianic figure; perhaps such ideas lie behind Mark 12:35−7.

In the Parables of Enoch (see the proceedings of the 1977 and 1978 seminars) we are introduced to a complex celestial figure (or figures); among the names (or titles) used are the Chosen One, the Son of Man (with different Ethiopic terms), the Righteous One, and the Anointed One. The major passages are the following: 1 (Ethiopic) Enoch 48:10, which is influenced by Psalm 2:2, 'For they have denied the Lord of the Spirits and his Messiah';[12] 1 (Ethiopic) Enoch 52:4, 'And he said to me, "All these things which you have seen happen by the authority of his Messiah so that he may give orders and be praised upon the earth".'[13] Both times the reference is to 'his Messiah' not to 'a' or 'the' Messiah.

In 4 Ezra there are three main passages: 4 Ezra 7:26−30 contains the idea of 'my son the Messiah (*bry mshyḥ*')'[14] who will be revealed (along with the hidden city and land, cf. verse 26) together 'with those who are with him' (7:28; cf. 6:26, 13:52, 14:9). For four hundred years he will bring joy to those who have been 'delivered from the evils'. This period is followed by a universal death, which includes the death of the Messiah, and a primeval silence of seven days (7:30).

4 Ezra 12:31−4 interprets the action of the lion in the Vision of the Eagle and the Lion in 11:1−12:3. The Lion pronounces judgment. In 12:32 we see the significant explanation, *hic est unctus, quem reservavit Altissimus in finem.*[15] In this passage we have an absolute use of 'Anointed One', with an emphasis on judgment, temporary rule, and heavenly origin.

The same traditional elements, with the significant exception of the designation the 'Anointed One' and his temporary rule, is found in chapter 13. This complicated chapter concerns the vision of the

'Man from the Sea'. M. de Jonge concluded that he was again struck by the great variety within the work itself. There is no consistent picture of the 'Anointed One'. A detailed delineation of this concept cannot be discerned (*page* U.B. Müller, *Messias und Menschensohn*).

In 2 Baruch three passages are significant. In 29:3–30:1 the 'Anointed One' is paralleled with Behemoth and Leviathan. The role of the Messiah is passive. M. de Jonge suggested that the 'return' of the Messiah in 30:1 may correspond to 4 Ezra 7:29, and that there may be Christian influences on the terminology here.

The interpretation of the vision of the forest, the vine, the fountain and the cedar in 2 Baruch 35:1–37:1 entails the following clarification: 'at that time the dominion of my Anointed One, which is like the fountain and the vine, will be revealed' (39:7).[16] In 2 Baruch 40 a final conflict is depicted between 'my Messiah' and the 'last ruler'. The dominion of the Anointed One will 'last forever until the world of corruption has ended' (40:3).

According to 2 Baruch 70:9 everyone who escapes the last wars and disasters 'will be delivered into the hands of my Servant, the Anointed One'. In 2 Baruch 72:2–3 'my Anointed One' summons the nations and destroys those who had ruled over Israel. The Anointed One will finally sit 'down in eternal peace on the throne of the kingdom' (73:1). M. de Jonge asked, 'Do 4 Ezra and 2 Baruch witness to the existence of a fluid set of connotations, derived from and influenced by sets of passages from scripture that are connected with a royal eschatological figure, who may be referred to as the "Anointed One" or the "Messiah"?' Several scholars, in particular M.A. Knibb, tended to affirm this possibility.

M. de Jonge reminded the members of the seminar that the Qumran community awaited the coming of a true priest and a true king, and that some scrolls also mention a prophet. He argued that the Qumran texts

> ... expect a number of figures sent by God, to none of whom the designation 'anointed one' belongs exclusively. It is not the persons as such that are important, but their calling and function, because it is through them that God shows his continuing care and his power to overcome all opposition. The central point is that God will bring about a change in the history of his people and that thenceforward, Israel will have a true prince and or a true high priest or prophet.[17]

He emphasized the great varieties of thought at Qumran and that it is hazardous to explain Qumran messianism in terms of historical development (*pace* J. Starcky).

T. F. Glasson disagreed with de Jonge regarding 4 Ezra. He argued that there is no inconsistency in the document. The 'Messiah' is to have an earthly reign; and it will not come to an end. M. de Jonge replied by referring again to 4 Ezra 13 and the description of the messianic age, which is influenced by Daniel.

Several scholars urged de Jonge to speak about the concept of the 'Messiah' in the Testaments of the Twelve Patriarchs. He stated that there was a dual expectation that was expressed in terms of the Levi and Judah motif. In the future there would be an ideal priesthood and an ideal kingship, and Levi is far more prominant than Judah, but there is never a clear statement that the Messiah is to come from Levi. He urged us to consider the possibility of Christian alterations of Jewish traditions here (see the 1976 proceedings above).

Charlesworth argued that when you include for consideration the early rabbinic literature it becomes abundantly clear that there was no ruling concept of the 'Anointed One'. He asked, 'Is it not possible that many of our documents, such as 4 Ezra, 1 (Ethiopic) Enoch, *LAB* and 2 Baruch, are the editorial and literary products – but diverse – of one particular social group, the scribe?'

N. Walter stressed that in Early Judaism 'the things to come' are the important concept, not the one who is to bring them about. In the New Testament the emphasis changes to he-who-is-to-bring-them-in. He suggested that our problems begin with the desire to connect Jewish messianism neatly with Christology. M. de Jonge replied that he agreed fully.

Knibb turned the discussion back to 4 Ezra. He argued that 4 Ezra is a unity, but the author has drawn on diverse ideas. He did not think he was referring to two different figures, who were to act at the end of time, the end of the age. B. Schaller agreed that 4 Ezra is the work of one author who inherited various traditions. He argued that we must differentiate between theology and piety; the latter is not systematic. We have traditions; the question is where they come from.

R. Leivestad replied that Qumran is important precisely because we know the group from which the writings have come. The Qumran community really expected a Messiah, and a messianic king. M. de Jonge answered, 'No'. The Messiah at Qumran is not clearly Davidic. The data is more complex; there is a great variety at Qumran. Leivestad answered de Jonge by pointing out that in several documents at

Qumran there is expectation of a Davidic Messiah, note especially 1QSa and CD.

Knibb added that the priestly Messiah is more important than the Davidic Messiah, and Leivestad agreed. Charlesworth claimed that we must now take note that the priest has veto power over the king in the Temple Scroll.

B. M. Metzger confessed that the more he studied 4 Ezra the more difficult it became to place the author into a particular setting or circle. Knibb offered his opinion that the author was from a learned group on the fringes of early rabbinic thought in the late first century C.E.

L. Hartman asked a penetrating question, 'How did these books function?' Certainly the authors did not 'publish' them. Were they copied by friends? Were they ever used in synagogues?

Charlesworth stressed that the pseudepigrapha are more important in some ways than the Dead Sea Scrolls because some of them come from non-Palestinian settings. The same situation applies to the New Testament writings.

M. de Jonge stated that the Qumran community could not get around the Davidic concept of the Messiah. The exorcistic and related traditions were Davidic; and that is significant also for our attempts to understand Jesus and the exorcisms attributed to him. Note especially the claim that he was the Son of David.

III. Messianism in Early Judaism and Christology in Early Christianity

Charlesworth introduced the third and final session of the seminar. He began by presenting a consensus − to which he gave full support − that appeared to be shared by most members of the seminar. He articulated it as follows:

(1) There is no unified concept of 'the (or a) Messiah' either in the Pseudepigrapha or in the other early Jewish writings.[18]

(2) New Testament scholars focusing upon the Christologies in the New Testament need to be more aware of the diversity of reflections on 'the (or a) Messiah' and related figures within Judaism. They should be more cognizant of the absence of a normative definition of 'the (or a) Messiah' in Early Judaism.

(3) The apparently contradictory statements about 'the (or a) Messiah' in such documents as 4 Ezra are neither the result of redactional activity nor the product of two or more sources inelegantly combined. These tensions seem to result from the author's dual focus:

on the one hand he looked at the 'Old Testament' descriptions of 'Messiah' and on the other he focused upon 'the end of the times', which was conceived as rapidly approaching.

(4) Since there were no set concepts of the Messiah, the Son of Man, or the Elect One, it is misleading to state that the authors of the apocalypses (1 Enoch, 4 Ezra, 2 Baruch) combined these concepts. It is more representative to state that the authors combined fluid elements related to these terms or titles.

(5) The Apocrypha and Pseudepigrapha represent some important aspects of Early Judaism that must not be overlooked in the study of Early Judaism and Early Christianity. These books are important for research on the earliest Christians, because they are roughly contemporaneous with them, define or develop many of the ideas, symbols and terms inherited by them, often have a universal extension and breadth like them, and contain much of the diasporic perspective that defined the early Christian mission.

(6) The authors of the documents in the Pseudepigrapha seem to be attending more to the dawning of *God's* final act in history than to the figure or mediator God would choose to inaugurate this act. They were hence more eschatologically oriented than messianically focused. The early Christians had a different emphasis: concern about the Messiah was usually the central focus, concern for the eschaton was usually of secondary importance. Most authors of pseudepigrapha were not interested in messianism; most authors of New Testament writings were preoccupied with Christology. The distinguishing emphasis should be recognized by New Testament specialists. The difference is caused by the kerygma in which Jesus is proclaimed as the Messiah, the Christos.

(7) Reflection on the content of the end time (but not the concept of the Messiah) is typical of the authors of the pseudepigrapha: 'Just as no one can explore or know what is in the depths of the sea, so no one on earth can see my Son or those who are with him, except in the time of his day' (4 Ezra 13:52). This concept (Charlesworth was convinced) may inform us regarding such passages as Mark 13:32.

After this opening statement there followed a general discussion. J. C. O'Neill stated that we are clearly confronted with a revolution of language in early Christian circles. There is more of a discontinuity than a continuity. M. de Jonge replied that a discontinuity implied continuity. No one started off speaking Chinese in Palestinian circles. There was an interweaving of ideas and terms in the texture of thought. There were all sorts of lines and threads in the various traditions. No scribe started from scratch. As long as we consider these individual lines as fluid concepts and not set concepts we are all right. The 'Anointed One' in 90% of the texts is associated with Davidic traditions. The 'royal' Messiah needs definition. It was defined in terms of theocracy; he is essentially a mediator of God. The same situation occurs in early Christianity.

The royal 'Anointed One' in the Psalms of Solomon is the wise man who explains the Torah. The figure is led by the spirit, according to *LAB*. Does that picture provide some continuity in terms of the discontinuity? The early Christians said Jesus is he; he is the one imagined.

Leivestad argued that there is a messianic secret in Mark. Catchpole replied that the messianic secret concerns when Jesus was disclosed to be the Messiah.

Sanders claimed that we will not reach a consensus on a particular messianic motif. The real issue concerns how we should use the documents in the Pseudepigrapha so that they pay off positively. Do these documents contain the theme of the dispersion? Where did the early Christians find this idea? Sanders suggested that we need to formulate areas for exploration.

Pesch thanked the group for the sessions, and admitted he found the discussions insightful and fruitful. He had obtained some answers to questions forced upon him while he was writing his commentary on Mark. The concept of the Messiah entails a special relationship with the Father. According to Mark, John the Baptist baptizes Jesus and then the spirit descends upon him. The Messiah is explained in the baptism pericope as *the one with the spirit*. Jesus is called a prophet in Mark, and he is an exorcist. All of these motifs are important, as we have seen, in terms of early Jewish messianism. Most prominently in Mark Jesus' Messiahship is seen in terms of the concept of the Son of God.

M. de Jonge thanked Pesch and admitted he was encouraged by these positive results.

1980 (Toronto; Trinity College): Hymns, Odes and Prayers

The fifth consecutive annual meeting of the *SNTS* Pseudepigrapha Seminar was held in Trinity College, Toronto, Canada on 26, 27 and 28 August 1980. Two main papers were presented; since each has been published it will be possible to abbreviate the report.

I. Hymns and Prayers

On 26 August Charlesworth read a paper on 'Hymns and Prayers: In Search of the Importance of the Pseudepigrapha for Understanding the New Testament'. There were three sections to his paper. First, he reviewed research on the early Jewish and Christian hymns and prayers since 1900. He attempted to assess the advances made by scholars, giving particular attention to the discovery of additional sources, the development of a more sophisticated methodology, and the recognition of the proper perspectives.

Second, he assessed the importance of the hymns and prayers in the Pseudepigrapha for a better understanding of the New Testament. He discussed the parallels between the Odes of Solomon and Philippians 2:6–11, the continuum of praise and expression of need from the Hodayoth to the Hellenistic Synagogal Prayers, and the theological sensitivity of Jewish hymns and prayers.

Third, he raised two main questions: Is a Jewish hymn clearly quoted by a New Testament author? Is there a significant theological result from the observation that Jewish apocalypses often contain hymns (2 Bar 10:6–19, 11:1–7, 14:8–10, 35:2–5, 75:1–8) and especially prayers (1 En 84:1–6; 4 Ezra 8:20–36; 2 Bar 38:1–4, 48:2–24, 54:1–22; 4 Bar 6:6–10, 6:12–14, 9:3–6; ApZeph 9:1–10, 12:5–10)?

Charlesworth's paper, in a revised and expanded form, is now published: 'A Prolegomenon to a New Study of the Jewish Background of the Hymns and Prayers in the New Testament', in *Essays in Honour of Yigael Yadin*, ed. G. Vermes and J. Neusner (*JSJ* 33:1–2; Oxford, 1982), pp. 265–85.

II. Apocalyptic Thought and Early Christian Prophecy

On 27 August D.E. Aune read a paper on 'Connections Between Realized Eschatology, Prophecy and Apocalyptic in the Odes of Solomon, the Fourth Gospel and the Apocalypses'. He began with a number of stated assumptions: (1) the Odes of Solomon were originally written in Syriac (a change in his position) and are the earliest extant literature in Syriac; (2) the Odes were written sometime during the half-century extending from the last quarter of the first century to the first quarter of the second century C.E.; (3) the Odes are thoroughly Christian, though they exhibit strong conceptual and ideological ties to Early Judaism, particularly the type represented by the Dead Sea Scrolls; (4) the Odes are linked conceptually, not only with the Dead Sea Scrolls, but also with the Fourth Gospel, the letters of Ignatius and the systems of thought represented by Marcion and Valentinus; (5) there is no literary relationship between the Odes and the Fourth Gospel or the Apocalypse of John, though all three share traditional and conceptual affinities; (6) the Odes are essentially liturgical compositions intended for recitation within the framework of community worship.

Aune attempted to demonstrate the following proposals: (1) the Fourth Gospel is dominated by realized eschatology but also contains a modicum of apocalyptic eschatology, while the reverse is true of the Apocalypse; yet the fact that these two types of eschatology are complementary is revealed in the Odes of Solomon; (2) the hymns of the Apocalypse, the primary location of realized eschatology in the Apocalypse, are not traditional liturgical compositions, but rather the free compositions of the author (though he uses traditional themes and phrases). The Odes of Solomon appear to be the type of liturgical compositions upon which the Apocalyptist modelled his own hymns; (3) realized eschatology is a phenomenon whose primary *Sitz im Leben* is the cult, and therefore one can expect to find such an eschatological orientation expressed primarily in liturgical compositions (such as the Odes of Solomon, the Hymns of the Apocalypse, in spite of their 'pseudo-hymnic' status, and the Hodayoth); and there more readily, frequently, and consistently than in other types of religious literature.

Aune's paper, in a shortened version, is now published: 'The Odes of Solomon and Early Christian Prophecy?' *NTS* 28 (1982), 435–60.

III. Discussion

On 28 August there was a general discussion of the two main papers. Unlike the discussion-oriented sessions of the previous year in Durham, the discussion in Toronto was less structured and thoughts were exchanged rapidly and freely. It is possible, nevertheless, to summarize a few detailed exchanges and two general points of consensus.

Aune argued that the Odist only used one term for 'prophet' and that is *ḥzy'*, which means 'seer'. The passage is found in Ode 7:18–19.

> The Seers (*ḥzy'*) shall go before Him,
> And they shall be seen (*wnthzwn*) before Him.
> And they shall praise the Lord in His love,
> Because He is near and does see (*wḥzy'*).

Gruenwald replied that *ḥzy'* can refer to pilgrims who visit the Temple. Aune appreciated and considered this suggestion. He tended, however, to see *ḥzy'* in Ode 7 as a deliberate choice by the Odist to develop an idea through paronomasia, which is clearly evident in three of the lines above. He also suggested that the Odist may have chosen *ḥzy'*, which does have prophetic and cultic meanings, to develop the idea that the seer is seen by God (cf. now *NTS* 28 (1982), 439).

After some discussion the members of the seminar tended to agree that the Odes are from the time period suggested by Aune and are clearly Christian. In order to focus discussion in the most fruitful way, it was decided not to discuss whether the Odes are 'gnostic', or 'not-gnostic'.

Charlesworth asked the group if any one knew a significant parallel in Jewish or Christian literature to the concept in Ode 19 that God has breasts (*tᵉrein tᵉdhawhi dᵉ'abbâ*, 19:4*b*). The members cited several distant parallels, but agreed that a negative answer was demanded. The Odist contains a unique idea here.

Two Points of Consensus

There was firm agreement with F. C. Grant's following claim: 'For the proper understanding of the New Testament, e.g., the study of the ancient Jewish liturgy is of paramount importance. Ancient Judaism was by no means a decadent, moribund, sterile, formalistic religion − though there have not been lacking Christians, alas, who would have it so!'[1]

Second, there was a consensus that many scholars frequently and erroneously equate earliest Christianity with the New Testament. The error is twofold. First, there is the obvious confusion between the wide variety in earliest Christianity and the later edited and selected writings. Second, there is the problem of what we really mean by the New Testament text; textual criticism shows us that we must not confuse our present so-called critical text (and there is now more than one available) with the earliest writings themselves, the autographs. In the Diatessaron seminar, which I had the privilege of co-chairing for a few years, it became clear to most of us that we should be very careful when talking about the New Testament text. N. Birdsall has emphasized that we must be open to the long process of editing the New Testament text through the second century and the unknown decades at the end of the first century. The first point is especially significant for our work on the early Jewish writings. It is now very difficult to be clear as to what are the criteria that help us distinguish between a Christian and a Jew in the first century of the present era.

1981 (Rome; Domus Pacis): The Pseudepigrapha and the Apocalypse

The sixth consecutive annual session of the *SNTS* Pseudepigrapha Seminar was held on 25, 26 and 27 August 1981, in Domus Pacis, Rome. Three papers were read and discussed.[1]

I. The Judgment Scene

On 25 August T. F. Glasson presented a paper entitled, 'The Judgment in Revelation 20 and in Related Writings'. He pointed out that the judgment scene of Revelation 20:11–15, with its great white throne and general resurrection, became definitive in Christian teaching, and is made famous, for example, in the paintings on the ceiling of the Sistine Chapel. It is generally thought that such a judgment day was a commonplace in the thought of Early Judaism. Lists of references are given from the Old Testament and from apocalyptic writings purporting to support this opinion. However, none of the Old Testament passages describes a general forensic judgment following a resurrection; and there is no supporting evidence from early Jewish sources. Joel 3 and Daniel 7 use legal imagery but it is imagery. The Old Testament Day of the Lord originally involved the punishment of God's enemies. This implication is found in the Qumran Scrolls, in which the servants of God are the instruments of judgment.

There is ambiguity in the term judgment (*mishpāt*) which can, among its many meanings, indicate a catastrophe, a battle, or a judicial sentencing of demons, kings, oppressors and gentile nations. The term may or may not include a resurrection of individuals from the dead. Such wide variety is confusing and stricter definitions are needed.

A forensic judgment of all humanity, living and dead, is what judgment day conveys today and attention should be directed to this assumption. Even in the New Testament writings this comprehensive judgment is not involved in the references to the judgment theme. This kind of judgment, however, is depicted in documents roughly contemporaneous with Revelation. The clearest is in 4 Ezra 7:30–140 (see also SibOr 4.41–2 and 184ff and 2 Bar 83). The Similitudes of Enoch may also belong to this period and this section, chapters 37–71, needs examination.

Glasson argued that the judgment of all individuals is found among gentiles centuries earlier than among the Jews. In Egypt and Greece we find the belief that a judgment took place at the end of each earthly life. The idea of a judging of all men is described in the most general terms in the glossator's addition to Ecclesiastes 12:14, at a period when Greek ideas could have exerted an influence on Jewish thought. Different divisions in Hades or Sheol involve a postmortem discrimination of some kind. 1 (Ethiopic) Enoch 22, with its four compartments, nevertheless, points to a future 'day', though this is punishment rather than judicial inquiry and is applied explicitly to one class only.

It is easy to see that once the thought of a universal judgment of individuals came into Jewish thinking, this would inevitably gravitate to the final 'Day of the Lord', which by that time was securely established as the climactic event. And so a judgment which had become associated with the punishment of fallen angels, nations, and apostate Jews, would gather to itself a more comprehensive crowd of defendants and would ultimately become a universal assize, even though the trial of a country's entire population would be unthinkable as far as earthly analogies are concerned. By the time of Paul we have a day of wrath indicated in Romans 2:6–16 when the secrets of all will be divulged, though Paul does not spell this out in any pictorial fashion, such as characterizes some of the later apocalyptic writings we have mentioned.

Glasson argued that the coming of God in the Old Testament and more especially in the apocalyptic writings is depicted in very realistic terms. In Jewish literature God is portrayed on a mountain or on a throne. In Christian thought this conception is altered by the fact that Jesus was recognized as the Lord of many early Jewish passages; the promised theophany became the doctrine of the parousia.

Glasson was asked if he thought a resurrection was depicted in Daniel. He replied that Daniel 12 portrayed a partial resurrection, as does 1 (Ethiopic) Enoch 22.

MacRae offered the insight that in early Jewish writings the judgment is only of the wicked. The concept of judgment was understood as condemnation. Subsequently the concept of judgment grew to include also rewards. Glasson agreed, indicating that he saw a development in the meaning of *krisis* from condemnation to judgment.

Denis pointed out that the Testament of Abraham has a general judgment. Glasson agreed, but argued that this document does not belong among the early apocalypses; it postdates 100 C.E. He also claimed that there is no parousia in the Jewish apocalypses, and warned that the late idea of a great assize must not be read back into early Jewish passages. Glasson's paper was published in *NTS* 28 (1982), 528–39.

II. The Twelve Tribes

On 26 August A. S. Geyser presented a paper on 'The Twelve Tribes in Revelation'. His points may be summarized as follows:

(1) The number twelve occurs more often in Revelation than in any other work inside or outside the New Testament. The word φυλή in the meaning of 'tribe' appears more than twice as often in Revelation as in all the rest of the New Testament. From these two observations alone it is evident that the book is primarily concerned with the *twelve tribes* of Israel, and notably with their restoration as a kingdom under the rule of God and the Davidic Messiah. To this end 12,000 from each of the twelve tribes will be sealed against the cosmic annihilation which will precede the eschaton.

(2) The 'twelve apostles' are also involved in the restoration. Their names and those of the twelve tribes mark the foundation stones of the new Jerusalem; and they possibly participate in the heavenly court of the twenty-four elders. This court of twice twelve is in constant evidence during the entire central scene of the book, and from their introit in 4:1 to their exit after 19:9 twelve references are made to them.

(3) The new Jerusalem is presented in measures and entities of twelve, and the tree of life in its centre bears twelve varieties of fruit twelve times per annum.

(4) The restoration is expected to take place soon and here on earth. The number twelve has a symbolic value of fulfilment and completion. It signifies that the time is fulfilled. The same urgency as that of John the Baptist and Jesus' proclamation of the Kingdom marks the message of the restoration of the twelve tribes in Revelation.

(5) The emphasis in Revelation on the twelve tribes relates the book to the Letter of James, 1 Peter, Q, M and Mark's Judean source; but by the same token this emphasis differentiates it markedly from Paul's letters, Luke's two books, and the Fourth Gospel. Paul does not mention the twelve tribes, and only once refers to the Twelve of Jesus;

moreover this is in a passage which sounds like a quotation from a (Jerusalem?) catechism. The Fourth Gospel does not feature the restoration of the twelve tribes, it refers to the Twelve by preference as 'the disciples'.

In his Gospel and Acts Luke calls the Twelve mostly 'the apostles', and his reference to the twelve tribes is only in his report of Paul's speech before Agrippa, and in the Throne Logion which is Q material. Perhaps the representative of the gospel to the gentiles purposely avoided reference to twelve precisely on account of its association in the Judean and Judeo-Christian mind with the restoration of the twelve tribes. Conversely, Revelation, James, 1 Peter, Q, M and Mark's Judean source must be products of the Jewish 'Church' and its extensions beyond the borders of Judea proper. Their confession of Jesus as Messiah and his parousia apart, this 'Church' was more closely related to Jewish apocalyptic circles like that of Qumran than to the mainstream Christian Church of the later first century.

(6) A Jewish apocalyptic ambience was, nevertheless, the cradle of all the Church. It was born from and into the expectation of the restoration of the twelve-tribe-kingdom of David. What are the origins of this conviction?

The greatest common denominator of the pious Jewish mind was the triad: twelve tribes, Jerusalem, and the Davidic king. It was born with the investiture of David as king of the southern and then of the northern tribes, his transfer of the ark to Jerusalem, and the covenantal promise in 2 Samuel 7:16 that his kingdom shall have no end. During all the misfortunes of Israel and Judah the faith in this covenant never flagged. The prophets before, during, and after the Exile developed it; it evolved into Jewish apocalyptic thought. Ezekiel's vision of the resurrection of the dead bones (chapter 37) is also the vision of the restoration of the twelve tribes.

(7) More than any other apocalyptic work, Daniel influenced Revelation, even though it does not envisage the restoration of the kingdom in terms of twelves; its favourite symbol was seven. There must have been some stimulus for the revival of the expectation explicitly of the twelve tribes after Daniel. Perhaps the stimulus came from the successes of the first Maccabees, for from then on it proliferates in most apocalyptic works, including those from Qumran in particular.

(8) The number twelve appears in Revelation for the first time as a multiple: the twenty-four elders in the heavenly court. Daniel has a

comparable court scene, but does not count its members. Heavenly courts in other apocalypses, however, do show a leaning toward twelve and its multiples. Daniel's court was composed of two bodies, one of angels, the other of the representatives of the people of these angels. Both of them are under Israel's patron, the archangel Michael.

(9) Why are the members of this college called 'elders' in Revelation? A deliberative and consultative body watching over the affairs of a community in the hellenistic world is certainly a *gerousia* or *senatus*. It seems to follow, therefore, that Israelite tradition has influenced the name 'elder' in Revelation. The first elected body to represent the children of Israel before God were the elders, seventy-two (12x6) in number (cf. Ex 24). The elders who in Isaiah 24:23 witness to the glory of God on Mount Zion are, as can be read from the context, representatives of the people. In Israelite tradition elders became representatives of the people before God. Jesus' appointed Twelve were intended for the heavenly *gerousia*. With the patron angels of the tribes they formed the heavenly court of Revelation.

(10) Quite a few Qumran Scrolls witness to courts of twelve and their multiples; but none so remarkably as 4QpIs. Apart from listing some of the precious stones that went into the new Jerusalem, it also parallels Revelation's court of twenty-four. There is a difference; the court of Revelation does not judge. It witnesses to the judgments of God, and lauds every act by which he clears the cosmic scene for the re-establishment of the twelve-tribe kingdom. Their function in Revelation resembles that of the courts of Isaiah 24 and Daniel 7. As representatives of their people they do what these should have done all along; they worship God steadfastly and constantly.

(11) Like the heavenly court and like Qumran's and Ezekiel's temple, Revelation's new Jerusalem is duodecimal in order to accommodate the twelve tribes and an unspecified number of faithful gentiles under the rule of God and his Messiah from David. With the new Jerusalem the book completes the triad of the covenantal promise of 2 Samuel 7:16.

(12) The Servant of Deutero-Isaiah was also to be 'a light unto the nations'. This idea generated a steady interest for the God-fearing gentile in Jewish circles. Provision for the righteous gentile is made not only in the psalms of Maccabean times, but also, among others, in 1 (Ethiopic) Enoch, Jubilees and 4 Ezra. Qumran makes no provision for them, but Revelation does, even in the new Jerusalem.

These gentile witnesses for the faith are not countable in numbers. Paul knew their number only as the 'full number' which has to come in before the arrival of the Kingdom for Israel. The exact number of the 'thirteenth tribe' remains God's secret.

Geyser's paper has been published: 'The Twelve Tribes in Revelation: Judean and Judeo-Christian Apocalypticism', *NTS* 28 (1982), 388–99. Also see Geyser's 'Jesus, the Twelve and the Twelve Tribes in Matthew', *Neotestamentica* 12 (1978), 1–19.

III. The Voice and Early Christology

On 27 August Charlesworth drew attention to nineteen 'Classical Jewish Apocalypses' and thirteen 'Jewish Apocalypses Significantly Expanded by Christians'.[2] He argued that all too often we have not approached Revelation properly. We should not come to it from the New Testament corpus; we should proceed to it from the large corpus of Jewish apocalypses. When one sees Revelation in the light of the continuum of Jewish apocalyptic thought new insights and understandings are obtained. Attention was drawn to only one example.

According to Revelation, Ἰωάννης reports that καὶ ἤκουσα ὀπίσω μου φωνὴν μεγάλην ὡς σάλπιγγος λεγούσης (Rev 1:10–11). Exegetes have ignored the literal meaning of verse 10*b* and have been more interested in commentating on verses 10*a* and 11*b*. Yet verse 12 again returns to the imagery of a voice: Καὶ ἐπέστρεψα βλέπειν τὴν φωνὴν ἥτις ἐλάλει μετ᾽ ἐμοῦ· καὶ ἐπιστρέψας εἶδον. The verse is usually paraphrased or translated freely; for example, the translators of the NEB miss the imagery: 'I turned to see whose (*sic*) voice it was that spoke to me; and when I turned I saw'. The verse should be taken literally: 'And I turned around in order to see the Voice who spoke with me; and when I turned around I saw'.

The main reason commentators have missed the imagery is because they assume no one turns around to see τὴν φωνήν. Yet, precisely the literal meaning may well be intended by the apocalyptist John. He had turned around to see 'the Voice'. A search for the precise meaning of this imagery has led to the discovery that by the time of Revelation (c. 95 C.E.). the concept of an hypostatic voice had developed in hellenistic Judaism, probably within and without Palestine. In lines analogous to those along which ὁ λόγος, *DBR, BT QWL* and ἡ σοφία had developed, ἡ φωνή moved from the simple concept of 'a voice' through personification to hypostatization. He (probably not she) became conceived of as a being in God's heavenly courts.

One of the most impressive examples of the concept of the hypostatic voice is found in the Apocalypse of Sedrach 2:5 (2:2−4 in Wahl's Greek text).[3]

> And Sedrach said: 'What (is it) my Lord (Κύριέ μου)?' And the Voice (ἡ φωνή) said to him: 'I was sent to you so that I may carry you up this way into the heaven'. But he (Sedrach) said: 'I wish to speak with God face to face, (but) I am not able, Lord (Κύριε), to ascend into the heavens.' And the angel (ὁ ἄγγελος), having stretched out his wings (ταῖς πτέρυξιν αὐτοῦ), took him and ascended into the heavens, and raised him up as far as the third heaven, and the flame of the divinity stood in it.

Here the Voice is clearly an angel, with wings, who is even called *Kurios* by Sedrach. The Voice is conceived here as hypostatic. The problem is not with the interpretation but with the date. Although the Apocalypse of Sedrach is a depository of early Jewish traditions, it is certainly Christian and late. This pseudepigraphon shows that ἡ φωνή was eventually portrayed as a being; but it is too late to be used as *prima facie* evidence for a first-century concept of a hypostatic voice.

Evidence of probably Jewish and perhaps first-century perception of a Voice is found in the Apocalypse of Abraham 9:1−4.

> Then a Voice came speaking to me twice, 'Abraham, Abraham!' And I said, 'Here I am.' And he said, 'Behold, it is I. Fear not, for I am Before-the-World and Mighty, the God who created previously, before the light of the age. I am the protector for you and I am your helper.'[4]

Here in a strain of thought reminiscent of other concepts − notably ὁ λόγος, *dbr* and σοφία − the Voice is portrayed as a being and one who created the world. Significantly, somewhat analogously to the Revelation of John, the idea of a Voice comes at the beginning of the 'Apocalypse' to Abraham. As with the Apocalypse of Sedrach the problem is not with the interpretation, but with the date of the tradition. The Apocalypse of Abraham is extant only in Slavonic, and it is not easy to trace the Slavic pseudepigrapha back into Early Judaism (see chapter 2 and the section on 'Slavic Pseudepigrapha', pp. 32−6). Scholars have generally agreed that the Apocalypse of Abraham, or at least the portion of it in which the apocalypse occurs, is to be dated to the latter decades of the first century C.E. There are good reasons to conclude, therefore, that the passage quoted above is Jewish and predates or is contemporaneous with Revelation.

The conjecture regarding the early date for the concept of the hypostatic Voice is strengthened by the discovery of a passage in 2 Baruch 13:1.

> And it happened after these things that I, Baruch, was standing on Mount Zion and, behold, the Voice (*ql'*) came from the heights (i.e. the heavens); and he said to me: 'Stand upon your feet Baruch, and hear the word of the mighty God.'[5]

The Voice is not the word of God, but the Voice from God. He (probably not she) is subsequently called 'Lord' (*mry'*, 15:1, 16:1, 17:1). The dialogue is between the Voice and Abraham.

With 2 Baruch we do not confront the problem of date. Almost all specialists have concluded that this work predates or is contemporaneous with Revelation. It is clearly Jewish.

Other texts were mentioned by Charlesworth; one that is from the first century B.C.E. (Torrey, Pfeiffer, Delcor) or first century C.E. (Philonenko, Kee, Collins) or either (Spittler) is the Testament of Job. This Jewish work probably also reflects the concept of the Voice.

> And in the night as I was in bed a loud voice (μεγάλη φωνὴ, cf. Rev 1:10) came to me in a very bright light saying, 'Jobab, Jobab!' And I said, 'Behold (here) I am.' And he said, 'Arise, and I will show you'. (3:1−2).[6]

Charlesworth argued that the concept of 'the Voice' as a divine being was probably inherited by the author of Revelation. If so, what is significant is that the concept is now shifted from Judaism to Christianity, thereby adding clear proof of the Christian character of Revelation for those critics who still suggest it is a Jewish work edited by a Christian. John turned around βλέπειν τὴν φωνὴν ἥτις ἐλάλει; but ἐπιστρέψας he saw ἑπτὰ λυχνίας χρυσᾶς, and most significantly ἐν μέσῳ τῶν λυχνιῶν ὅμοιον υἱὸν ἀνθρώπου.

Charlesworth stated that he had become convinced − from the above observations and reasons he plans to publish − that the apocalyptist John identifies ἡ φωνή as υἱὸν ἀνθρώπου, who for him is certainly ἀρνίον ἑστηκὸς ὡς ἐσφαγμένον (5:6). The importance of this discovery for an understanding of the earliest christologies and the Jewish origins of Christology could be great.

MacRae asked Charlesworth if he considered the terms personification and hypostatization as somewhat synonymous. He replied that they are distinctly different, even though both can refer to a conception or term that has developed into a 'being'. MacRae then agreed and suggested that one major distinguishing peculiarity of hypostatization is that a term or concept is moved beyond the strictures inherent in its basic meaning. Charlesworth agreed; to state that the Voice speaks is to move no further perhaps than personification; but when the Voice is said to walk, is sent out by God, is described as having wings, and is called an 'angel' or 'Lord' then we have moved beyond personification to hypostatization.

R. Hamerton-Kelly added to what he considered a fruitful and insightful exchange by pointing out that the contours among basic meaning, personification, and hypostatization are vague and somewhat amorphous. Charlesworth agreed, stating that it has been very difficult to decide when references to a voice being heard are no more than hearing the voice of someone, when phrases like 'a voice came to me' are more than merely an idiomatic expression for hearing someone's (probably an angel's) voice, and when 'the voice came' is not a paraphrase for 'the voice of God came' (cf. Apocalypse of Paul 14). He re-emphasized, however, that hypostatization of the Voice is evident in more than one early Jewish document, and that fact leaves us with the problems of discerning when it is behind ambiguous words in other texts and what is the precise intention or background of Revelation, chapter one.

Charlesworth also emphasized that the decision concerning whether a word or phrase is to be taken literally, metaphorically, or to be considered personified or hypostatized demands nothing less than a thorough and repeated reading and studying of the full document or documents in which the term or phrase appears, and that this research must be pursued with the text not a translation. For example, a phrase such as ἄρτος ζωῆς (JosAsen 8:5, 9; 15:5, etc.) or ὁ ἄρτος τῆς ζωῆς (Jn 6:35, 48) may have a metaphorical (or even soteriological and christological) meaning, as it does in the Gospel of John; or ζωῆς may be a genitive attribute that designates the effect caused by eating bread, i.e. it gives life, as it does in Joseph and Aseneth. Focus upon the texts themselves readily reveals that these real distinctions are not so logically or clearly made as in our abstracted theoretical reflections.

IV. Conclusion

At the conclusion of the seminar sessions the chairman asked for the election of assistants and advisors to help prepare the annual sessions. He requested that two scholars be chosen, one who would be German-speaking and the other French-speaking. The seminar members unanimously elected M. de Jonge and A.-M. Denis. The topic for the 1982 seminar will be Joseph and Aseneth.

1982 (Leuven, Paus Adriaan VI College): Joseph and Aseneth

The seventh consecutive session of the *SNTS* Pseudepigrapha Seminar was held at Leuven in August 1982. Two papers were read, one by Chr. Burchard and the other by H. C. Kee.[1]

I. Joseph and Aseneth and the New Testament

On 24 August Burchard read a paper on 'The Importance of Joseph and Aseneth for the Study of the New Testament'. It has now been revised and will appear in *New Testament Studies*. There were three main sections to his presentation.

(1) F. Düsterdieck correctly noted in his commentary on Revelation in 1859 that the παρθένοι in Revelation 14:4 are males, and that παρθένος is an appropriate term for males in Early Judaism as we learn from Joseph and Aseneth (cf. 4:7). New Testament scholars were not interested in this pseudepigraphon until G. D. Kilpatrick in 1952, followed by J. Jeremias in 1954, discussed it.

After this brief *Forschungsbericht* Burchard asked why it had taken New Testament scholars so long to recognize the importance of Joseph and Aseneth for their special area of research. Several reasons may be given: (i) Joseph and Aseneth was never mentioned in ancient Jewish or Christian literature; (ii) the Greek and Latin texts were not edited until 1889–90; (iii) The editor, P. Batiffol incorrectly thought the pseudepigraphon had been composed in the fifth century. Although he corrected his error later Joseph and Aseneth was unfortunately considered a Byzantine text.

(2) Burchard argued that scholars today correctly recognized that Joseph and Aseneth is Jewish and was composed in the Diaspora, probably in Egypt, before 117. He argued that the pseudepigraphon does not reflect a sectarian viewpoint, and is important for understanding the

Jewish milieu in the Diaspora from which many early Christians were recruited. He pointed to the significant lexicological links between Joseph and Aseneth and the New Testament writings, to the phenomenological significance of the sacred meal in the document and in the New Testament writings, and especially to the study of the conversion of Aseneth, which is seen as a 'new creation', for conversion to Christianity.

(3) Burchard reviewed the many recent suggestions by New Testament scholars, such as those by P. Stuhlmacher, O. Hofius, E. Brandenburger and G. Fischer, that Joseph and Aseneth is important for interpreting the New Testament writings. He offered the following fresh suggestions:

The passage in Joseph and Aseneth that mentions blessed bread, cup and ointment does not reflect a special religious meal in Jewish antiquity, whether known or unknown. They refer to the special Jewish way of using food, drink and ointment. The Jewish benedictions associated with each of these basic elements in human subsistence are operative for this and the coming world because the person who utters the blessing is endowed with life, wisdom and truth.

Burchard, agreeing with J. Jeremias against Kilpatrick, argued that Joseph and Aseneth does not help us understand the background or model of Jesus' Last Supper. He also disagreed with Kuhn's marginal use of Joseph and Aseneth in reconstructing the setting described in Mark 14:22–4 (and par.). According to Burchard Joseph and Aseneth is irrelevant to the origin of the Last Supper precisely because it does not refer to a cultic meal. Joseph and Aseneth does help us understand why the 'central rite of that new religious movement, Christianity, was a solemn form of consuming ἄρτος and ποτήριον', and why gestures concerning the two were remembered.

Burchard spoke on the relationship between Joseph and Aseneth (esp. chapter 16 and 15:13–17:4) and John 6. He rejected his earlier position (1965) in which he expressed the opinion that John inherits a view similar to the one found in Joseph and Aseneth – eating manna for daily food provides immortality – and then shifts it to emphasize that Jesus is the true manna. John 6, which is John's version of the institution of the eucharist, is similar in function to Joseph and Aseneth 16. Both are 'aetiologies of sacramental foodstuffs believed to bring about eternal life after death as opposed to food which does not'. Differences are evident, of course, between the two documents; for example, Joseph and Aseneth applies 'bread of life' to a substance, John to the person of Jesus. The different purposes and sociological settings cause some of the differences between Joseph and Aseneth 16 and John 6. John could have confronted the Jewish critics − Jesus is not the Messiah because he did not produce manna as had Moses − by narrating how Jesus, the Word and God's only son, was sent down from heaven as bread. John then would have adopted a Jewish tradition, which told how celestial food − not the biblical manna − had once been provided by God's highest angel. John would then have evoked Jewish tradition, which we know from Joseph and Aseneth, to confront Jewish objection.

Burchard argued that Joseph and Aseneth is significant for understanding 1 Corinthians 10−11, Paul's reflections upon and account of the Last Supper. Impressively reminiscent of Joseph and Aseneth 16:14 is Paul's argument in 1 Corinthians 10:31 that the manna and water have a supernatural origin and salvific effect. It is easy to imagine that a Jew who had attributed 'his eternal fate to some *sacramentalia* such as the blessed bread, cup, and ointment' would have reinterpreted these after he had come to believe in Christ as Lord with the bread and cup at the Lord's Supper. Accordingly Paul's general theme in 1 Corinthians 10 is not sacrament (*pace* H. von Soden), but conversion and perseverance; and now we know why 1 Corinthians 10 easily follows from 9.

The discussion that followed Burchard's presentation was brief because of time. Numerous points for clarification were raised and it became abundantly clear that Burchard had indeed mastered the study of Joseph and Aseneth. The seminar members thanked Burchard for his brilliant presentation and concurred that Joseph and Aseneth is extremely important for the study of Christian Origins and in particular for the understanding of the New Testament writings.

II. The Historical Setting of Joseph and Aseneth

On 25 August Kee presented a paper on 'The Socio-Cultural Setting of Joseph and Aseneth'. Kee agreed with Burchard that Joseph and Aseneth is to be considered an example of the hellenistic romance, that it is not a missionary tract, that it should not be labelled Pharisaic, Sadducean, Essene, Therapeutic, Zelotic, Philonic, or apocalyptic, and that it addresses the Jews, both born and naturalized, reminding them of their privilege and advantages.

Employing the research published by B. E. Perry in his *The Ancient Romances: A Literary-Historical Account of Their Origins* (Berkeley, 1967), Kee attempted to clarify the position that Joseph and Aseneth is an example of an ancient romance. Kee agreed with Perry that the 'purpose of an author, not his means nor the specific content and mechanical features of his book, is the only feasible criterion by which to classify it among genres' (*Ancient Romances*, p. 30). Emphasizing with Perry that a genre is not a concretized form into which the creatively new story is poured, but a configuration of typical features which enable the interpreter to discern that which is characteristic and distinctive about an author's adaptation of the genre, Kee listed the typical features of an ancient romance (200 B.C.E. to 200 C.E.). These are as follows:

> The work serves as propaganda for a cult.
> It depicts a conversion experience.
> Conversion leads to a sacred marriage.
> The literary style shifts between narrative and poetical or liturgical forms.
> The plot is moved along by inner and external conflicts of the hero or heroine, with deliverance accomplished by divine action.
> The climax of the story involves the death and re-birth of the hero or heroine, a theophany, and the self-dedication of the hero or heroine to the god.

Joseph and Aseneth is one of the few ancient romances that has *each* of these features.

Kee disagreed with Burchard's conclusion that according to Joseph and Aseneth the 'Divine Life is not mediated through the Law, through special revelation or mystical experience; it is obtained through the right use of the food and ointment and by the avoidance of the pagan way of partaking of them.'[2] Kee voiced agreement with Philonenko's argument that Joseph and Aseneth must be seen in terms of the wide-ranging parallels with ancient mythological and mystical material.

Kee argued that the main purpose of Joseph and Aseneth cannot be to urge gentiles to convert; because circumcision, which was 'the major factor in the conversion process', is conspicuously absent in the document. Many features in Joseph and Aseneth are left un-explained by the argument that it was written to confirm Jews and make proselytes.

Kee's unique contribution – in contrast to Burchard, Philonenko and other scholars – evolves out of his sensitivity to the *transformation* of Aseneth. In answer to Joseph's prayer on her behalf she will be transformed by God in the following ways:

she will be renewed by God's spirit;
she will be formed anew by God's hidden hand;
she will be made alive again by the divine life;
she will eat and drink of the heavenly substances;
she will be numbered among God's people;
she will enter the rest prepared by God.

Aseneth's personal transformation is paralleled only in the Isis and Asklepios cults of the second century C.E., and it is conveyed in the romances analogous to Joseph and Aseneth. Kee is convinced that it is the perception of reality known to be characteristic of the Isis cult, as F. Dunand described them, 'which seems to have deeply influenced the author of this pseudepigraphon in his telling of the heavenly encounter of Aseneth and its consequence for her destiny'.

Aseneth's appearance is fundamentally changed after the vision of the visit from heaven. Her companion now 'prostrates in awe before her, as she had done before the man from heaven (18:11)'. She is prepared to marry Joseph, God's first-born son. Her new beauty is hers forever (21:4), and her parents are astounded by the change (20:5).

Kee did not argue for a 'direct cause-and-effect relationship' between the Isis cult and Joseph and Aseneth, yet he claimed that 'it is the changing image of Isis which seems to have developed in ways that shed light on the portrait of Aseneth and her conversion in our document'. Isis had changed from an agent of creation and fertility to a goddess identified with Ma'at, the goddess of Wisdom. By the second century C.E. Isis had become 'both symbol of philosophical wisdom (in the treatise of Plutarch) and mediator of the transformed life (in Apuleius)'.

Kee emphasized that the central feature of Joseph and Aseneth is 'the epiphanic experience of the God of light, whose presence illumines the faithful seeker and transforms that individual, so that he (Joseph) or she (Aseneth), whether of Jewish or pagan origins, shares in the divine life'.

Kee agreed that Joseph and Aseneth is important for an understanding of Christian Origins. The closest literary analogy in the New Testament to Joseph and Aseneth is Acts, whose author 'has adopted for his purposes the hellenistic romance'. Kee's paper has been published in *NTS* 29 (1983), 393–413.

III. Debate and Conclusion

On 26 August there was a lively debate between Burchard and Kee. Each voiced major points of agreement, but differed considerably regarding the purpose of Joseph and Aseneth. Burchard admitted that Kee had raised some new questions that he would have to address in the future. He remained unconvinced, however, by Kee's argument regarding the relationship between Joseph and Aseneth and the Isis cult.

The members of the seminar agreed that Joseph and Aseneth comes from a type of Egyptian Judaism that predates 117 C.E. The probing questions proved how little we know about the religious background of Joseph and Aseneth and how complex and latitudinous Egyptian Judaism had become by 117. Certainly it is unrepresentative to argue now, as Charles had done,[3] that Philo is representative of Egyptian Judaism.

The seminar members decided to focus the 1983 discussions on the question of canon with particular attention to Jude. Barnabas Lindars nominated Richard Bauckham, who has completed a book on Jude; and M. de Jonge nominated B. Dehandschutter, who has been studying the relationships between 1 Enoch and Jude and has also completed a commentary on Jude. The chairman accepted the nominations, and agreed to try to elicit the assistance of these young scholars.

1983 (Canterbury; University of Kent): 1 Enoch, Jude and the Canon

For the eighth consecutive year the *SNTS* Pseudepigrapha Seminar met; the sessions were held on 23–5 August 1983, at the University of Kent in Canterbury, England. The three sessions were well attended,[1] and were led by Dehandschutter, Bauckham and Charlesworth.

I. Jude and 1 Enoch 1:9

On 23 August Dehandschutter argued that Jude 14–15 quotes from 1 Enoch 1:9 (certainly not Ethiopic Enoch), but much uncertainty surrounds the search for the original form of the quotation. He claimed that πᾶσαν ψυχήν (Aland) in verse 15 should be corrected to πάντας τοὺς ἀσεβεῖς (with Nestle). This 'correction' is in line with the reading in 1 (Ethiopic) Enoch, 'He will destroy the wicked ones';[2]

and this reading is probably original for Jude. Dehandschutter disagreed with Milik that the text of Jude had been accommodated to 1 Enoch. Pseudo-Cyprian supports this reading, with *et perdere omnes impias*. The reference to Pseudo-Cyprian raises other problems, including the possible evidence of a Latin version of 1 Enoch (as Zahn suggested) from which Pseudo-Cyprian was quoting.

Dehandschutter also argued that κύριος in verse 14 is original in Jude and may represent the reading of 1 Enoch, even though it is not found in the Ethiopic, Greek version (1 Greek Enoch), and Pseudo-Cyprian (the Aramaic here is lost). Dehandschutter was convinced that there is no reason to assume that the author of Jude added κύριος to his quotation from 1 Enoch.

Morton Smith disagreed with Dehandschutter's last point. He suggested that perhaps κύριος was added by the author of Jude to explain the subject of the verb that was relatively clear in 1 Enoch (perhaps in Aramaic). There is not sufficient reason to conclude that 'Lord' was in the text of 1 Enoch.

Dehandschutter replied that he was convinced that Jude was working from a Greek version of 1 Enoch. Bauckham entered the discussion at this point, emphasizing that there are reasons to support the conclusion that Jude was working from an Aramaic text of 1 Enoch. One must remember, moreover, that the author of Jude used a Hebrew version of the Old Testament and not the Septuagint.

Glasson pointed to a well-recognized phenomenon. Many authors of the New Testament writings inherited a theophany and shifted it to a christophany. This alteration is certainly evident in Jude's quotation from 1 Enoch. A.-M. Denis raised the question that κύριος in Jude may not mean Jesus.

Morton Smith turned again to the text of Jude. He stressed that the appearance of ἦλθεν before κύριος must certainly be explained since it is wrong.

Charlesworth clarified that only Jude has ἦλθεν. Pseudo-Cyprian has *venit*, 1 (Greek) Enoch has ἔρχεται, 1 (Ethiopic) Enoch has 'he will arrive' (so Isaac). Milik's restoration [*y'th*], could just as well be either ['*t'*], *'athā*, 'he came (arrived)', or ['*TY*], *'āthēi*, 'he is coming (arriving)', or 'he shall come (arrive)'. Smith was correct to draw attention to the problem of ἦλθεν in Jude.

Dehandschutter suggested, and all agreed, that the problems are with the Greek, which is influenced by the Semitic language. The verbs are imprecise. Casey emphasized correctly that ἦλθεν can be understood as a prophetic perfect; that is, a future act is seen as completed.

II. Jude and the Testament of Moses

On 24 August Bauckham read a paper in which he attempted to show that the author of Jude in verse 9 quoted from the lost ending of the Testament of Moses.[3] He was convinced that the ending of the Testament of Moses, which is not preserved in the only extant manuscript of this document, could be restored.

He argued that the patristic and later evidence for the story of the contest between Michael and the Devil for the body of Moses derives from two different versions of the story, which were found in the Testament of Moses and the Assumption of Moses. Once the two versions are distinguished, the story Jude knew can be reconstructed fairly accurately, and can be seen to belong to a genre of similar stories of contests between Satan and an angel of God.

Bauckham went on to argue that when the story is properly reconstructed, the point of Jude's reference to it becomes much clearer.

Bauckham suggested that since the author of Jude uses the Testament of Moses, and since the Testament of Moses was not widely known in the early Church, his use of it is an indication that Jude comes to us from a Palestinian Jewish-Christian context.

There was considerable discussion regarding the lost ending of the Testament of Moses, which is preserved in only one incomplete manuscript. Charlesworth admitted that he was impressed with Bauckham's argument, but was also unconvinced. The ending of the Testament of Moses is lost, and any attempt to reconstruct it is speculative, especially when one perceives the abundance of early Jewish documents written precisely with Moses in mind – or concerning Moses – and the vast amount of oral traditions regarding Moses and his death.[4]

III. Jude, Inspiration and the Canon

On 25 August, after Charlesworth's plenary address on 'The Old Testament Pseudepigrapha and the New Testament', the seminar was focused on some of his comments on the canon, which was the remaining topic for discussion. Hence the seminar members were asked to ponder the following question: What are the ramifications to the observation that Jude, a book in 'the canon', quotes as prophecy a book not in 'the canon'?

Smith stated that there was *no canon* and *no normative Judaism*.

Until the time of the destruction of the Temple there was, however, an officially recognized religion, and that fact enables us to talk about groups that are sects. By law, he stressed, there was one official cult.

As far as canon is concerned the Law was closed, the Prophets were recognized as such but as far as the Temple is concerned there was no closed canon of the prophets. The 'Christian' group accepted Enoch among the latter 'collection'.

Glasson argued that Jude and his group found 1 Enoch authoritative. These were literally the words of Enoch. It is a matter of inspiration, not one of canon.

Denis replied that the canon was fixed at Jamnia. It seems that the Christians, represented by the New Testament documents, had already tended to accept the Old Testament books now considered canon as canonical. The New Testament authors, with the exception of Jude, do not quote from the non-Hebraica.

Smith continued by claiming that the Temple did not accept the authority of the Prophets. The Pharisees were a very small sect. Josephus simply did not know what the majority of Jews knew or thought about the belief in the after life, and other major ideas. He added that the cult of Yahweh centred in the Temple was accepted by the Romans as the religious cult of the Jews; in that sense it was 'normative'.

Casey replied that the Roman viewpoint is not the only or major viewpoint. We are not primarily interested in what the Romans thought about the Jews, but what the Jews thought about their traditions and books.

Cahill argued that the adjective 'normative' is not an historical term or concept. It is a theological term. We must ask does it serve us well? For example, is clarity served by talking about a 'normative' Islam? The term 'normative' must be rejected as useless in our historical research.

R. Murray agreed with Cahill. Not only is 'normative' a useless adjective, but 'sect' is also misrepresentative. We should talk about groups; there were no heresies, no sects.

Bauckham turned attention to the verb the author of Jude used to introduce the quotation from 1 Enoch: προεφήτευσεν. Jude thought Enoch was an inspired prophet. Jude goes on to endorse Enoch's inspiration. He then raised the question of the 'pagan' quotations in the New Testament (e.g. in Acts 17:28, Tit 1:12, and 1 Cor 15:33) and asked about the relevance of these quotations to Jude's use of 1 Enoch.

Cahill reminded the group of the fact that Early Judaism was alive with *oral* traditions, such as those attributed to so-called pagan cultures. He suggested that our preoccupation with form criticism and the search for layers may have misled us here. We must be more sensitive to oral traditions.

Bauckham stated that the New Testament authors shared the same world view as the authors of the Old Testament Pseudepigrapha, yet they — except for Jude — did not quote from them. Why?

Charlesworth replied that in order to be sensitive to these issues and perplexing questions we must continue working not only on the writings in the New Testament but also on *all* the writings and traditions related to Early Judaism and Early Christianity. To what extent can we comfortably refer to the New Testament writings as non-Jewish documents? To what extent should they be considered a part of Judaism and within the history of Judaism?

Cahill claimed, without being offensive, that the Christian claim on the Old Testament is 'one of the greatest acts of stealing in history'. We all know that in the first century a split in Judaism occurred, and that this split was caused by one's relationship to Jesus. The division was caused by the attitudes taken to Jesus.

IV. Conclusion

As the time for the seminar to end rapidly was upon us, the chairman said that next year, the first time in eleven years, he could not attend the *SNTS* sessions.[5] M. de Jonge will chair the 1984 session, and the topic for discussion will be 4 Ezra. The chairman also said that he would ask the *SNTS* Secretary to recognize de Jonge and Denis as co-chairmen with him.

NOTES

Introduction

1 R. Price, *A Palpable God* (New York, 1978), p. 3.

2 The significance of the eye in the phenomenological application of language is broached in J. H. Charlesworth, 'Kierkegaard and Optical Linguistics', *Kierkegaardiana* 7 (1968), 131–4.

3 The translation is by E. Isaac in *The Old Testament Pseudepigrapha*, ed. Charlesworth (Garden City, New York, 1983), vol. 1, p. 48.

4 The earliest form of Egyptian writing clearly evolves out of pictorial art and is pre-alphabetical. The Slate Palette of Narmer, for example, dates from around 3,000 B.C.E., and through drawings and small hieroglyphs symbolically represents a story. All that can be conjectured from this palette is that the 'falcon-god Horus (i.e. the king) leads captive the inhabitants of the papyrus-land' (p. 7). For facsimile and discussion see A. Gardiner, *Egyptian Grammar: Being an Introduction to the Study of Hieroglyphs* (Oxford, 1927, 1957[3], repr. 1979), pp. 6–8.

5 See the excellent studies on 'The Sociology of Apocalypticism and the "Sitz im Leben" of Apocalypses', by G. W. E. Nickelsburg and M. Hengel in *Apocalypticism in the Mediterranean World and the Near East: Proceedings of the International Colloquium on Apocalypticism; Uppsala, August 12–17, 1979*, ed. D. Hellholm (Tübingen, 1983).

6 Against Sartre's arguments that we choose words to articulate what we have thought, I have argued that word and thought are inseparable. As we tend toward a particular meaning our thought appears, not before but with words. Of course, 'word' must be defined in a full phenomenological sense to include, for example, music and silence. See Charlesworth, 'Merleau-Ponty's Phenomenological Description of "Word"', *Philosophy and Phenomenological Research* 30 (1970), 609–13. I take this position to be exceedingly important for our present search, for if word and thought were distinguished paradigmatically, then we would only be seeing the ancients' words and not the thought.

7 Compare, for example, the size of the lexicons by Kittel (Hebrew) with Lane (Arabic), and Jastrow (Aramaic) with R. Payne Smith (Syriac).

1. The Pseudepigrapha: New opportunities and challenges for the Biblical scholar

1 Charlesworth (ed.), *The Old Testament Pseudepigrapha* (2 vols., Garden City, New York, 1983–5).

2 G. K. Wiencke (ed.), *Luther's Works* (Philadelphia, 1968), vol. 43, pp. 272–3.

3 B. M. Metzger, 'An Early Protestant Bible Containing the Third Book of Maccabees: With a List of Editions and Translations of Third Maccabees', *Text-Wort-Glaube: Studien zur Überlieferung, Interpretation and Autorisierung biblischer Text (K. Aland Festschrift)*, ed. M. Brecht (Arbeiten zur Kirchengeschichte 50; Berlin, New York, 1980), pp. 123–33.

4 See C. F. D'Arcy, 'A Brief Memoir', in R. H. Charles, *Courage, Truth, Purity* (Oxford, 1931), pp. xiii–xxxv.

5 Translation by A. F. J. Klijn in *The Old Testament Pseudepigrapha*, vol. 1, p. 639.

6 In 1933 Erich Ludendorff telegraphed to the Reichspräsident von Hindenburg the following message: 'Sie haben durch die Ernennung Hitlers zum Reichskanzler unser heiliges deutsches Vaterland einem der größten Demagogen aller Zeiten ausgeliefert. Ich prophezeie Ihnen feierlich, daß dieser unselige Mann unser Reich in den Abgrund stürzen und unsere Nation in unfaßbares Elend bringen wird. Kommende Geschlechter werden Sie wegen dieser Handlung in Ihrem Grabe verfluchen.' C. Zentner, *Der Zweite Weltkrieg* (Stuttgart, 1981), p. 6.

7 G. Vermes, 'The Impact of the Dead Sea Scrolls on Jewish Studies During the Last Twenty-Five Years', *JJS* 26 (1975), 1–14; repr. in W. S. Green (ed.), *Approaches to Ancient Judaism: Theory and Practice* (BJS 1; Missoula, Mont, 1978), pp. 201–14 and in G. Vermes, *Jesus and the World of Judaism* (London, 1983), pp. 100–114.

8 M. Kähler, *Der sogenannte historische Jesus und der geschichtliche, biblische Christus* (Leipzig, 1896, repr. 1956; ET by C. E. Braaten, Philadelphia, 1964).

9 Only to a certain extent is P. Riessler's *Altjüdisches Schrifttum ausserhalb der Bibel* (Heidelberg, 1928; repr. 1966) an exception to the rule that the Pseudepigrapha was no longer an important and major field of research. Furthermore, Riessler's collection, unlike those of Kautzsch and Charles, is not a distinguished study of documents. It is essentially a collection of translations. Also, the handy series entitled Translation of Early Documents (1916–) is a popular spin-off from the distinguished research of the preceding period.

10 Vermes (*Approaches to Ancient Judaism*, pp. 201–14), for example, argues that the true revival of interest in the Pseudepigrapha is 'essentially due to the impetus of Qumran' (p. 208). He states further that 'before Qumran' the Pseudepigrapha 'were rarely conceived of as properly belonging to the realm of Jewish studies' (p. 206).

It is significant that Vermes also argues that the lack of recognition for the Pseudepigrapha was because of the paucity of these documents in Hebrew and Aramaic, and the dogmatic proclamations of the Tannaim.

11 P. Benoit, in 1946, reflecting on the *Formgeschichtliche Methode*, argued against the prevailing tendency to denigrate any historical elements in the gospels: 'Le souci d'histoire n'est peut-être pas *le* motif dominant qui a présidé à la formation de la tradition évangélique; il est du moins *un* des motifs, et qui mérite de figurer à côté des autres, apologétique, polémique, et le reste.' P. Benoit, 'Réflexions sur la "Formgeschichtliche Methode"', *RB* 53 (1946), 481–512 (repr. in *Exégèse et Théologie* (3 vols., Paris, 1961–8), vol. 1, pp. 25–61; the quotation is on p. 48). For ET see *Jesus and the Gospel*, trans. B. Weatherhead (2 vols., New York, 1973–4), vol. 1, pp. 32–3. N. A. Dahl, also in 1946 in his inaugural lecture at the University of Oslo, broke with the emphases of his teacher Ragnar Asting, and while acknowledging that the gospels 'do not pretend to be retrospective historical accounts' of Jesus and 'are incapable of producing a biographical account of his life' yet 'it must have been in the assembly of the faithful that one recounted how Jesus traversed the countryside healing the sick and casting out demons, how he had been opposed and unrecognized, and how he had come to the aid of his disciples. These events were not recounted because of a detached historical interest; nevertheless, the stories betray a concern to remember past events.' N. A. Dahl, 'Anamnesis: Memory and Commemoration in Early Christianity', first publication in French in *ST* 1 (1948), 69–95 and reprinted in Dahl's *Jesus in the Memory of the Early Church* (Minneapolis, Minnesota, 1976), pp. 11–29, quotations are on pp. 27–9. E. Käsemann, in 1953, in a famous essay pointed out the complexities and interrelationships of history, tradition, interpretation and comprehension. He showed that reliable Jesus tradition was embedded in the kerygma, and that the 'question of the historical Jesus is, in its legitimate form, the question of the continuity of the Gospel within the discontinuity of the times and within the variation of the kerygma' (p. 46). Käsemann's article appeared in *ZTK* 51 (1954), 125–53; cf. the ET 'The Problem of the Historical Jesus', in Käsemann's *Essays on New Testament Themes*, trans. W. J. Montague (SBT 41; London, 1964), pp. 15–47.

12 E. Käsemann, 'Die Anfänge christlicher Theologie', *TTK* 57 (1960), 162–85; cf. ET 'The Beginnings of Christian Theology', in *Apocalypticism*, ed. R. W. Funk (JThC 6; New York, 1969), pp. 17–46, cf. p. 40 for the claim that Jewish apocalyptic thought 'was the mother of all Christian theology'.

13 This thought is developed in my 'A History of Pseudepigrapha Research: The Re-emerging Importance of the Pseudepigrapha', *ANRW* 2.19.1 (1979), pp. 54–88.

14 The contents of these collections are discussed in three of my publications: 'Translating the Apocrypha and Pseudepigrapha: A Report

of International Projects', *BIOSCS* 10 (1977), 11–21; 'New Developments in the Study of the *Ecrits Intertestamentaires*', *BIOSCS* 11 (1978), 14–18; and *The Pseudepigrapha and Modern Research with a Supplement* (SCS 7S; Chico, California, 1981).

15 Isaac in *The Old Testament Pseudepigrapha*, vol. 1, p. 50.

16 M. A. Knibb, *The Ethiopic Book of Enoch: A New Edition in the Light of the Aramaic Dead Sea Fragments* (2 vols., Oxford, 1978), vol. 2, p. 166.

17 See my 'The *SNTS* Pseudepigrapha Seminars at Tübingen and Paris on the Books of Enoch', *NTS* 25 (1979), 315–23. See Appendix, pp. 102–10.

18 J. T. Milik (ed. with M. Black), *The Books of Enoch: Aramaic Fragments of Qumrân Cave 4* (Oxford, 1976) esp. see p. 96.

19 See the valuable discussions by M. Hengel, *Die Zeloten* (Leiden, 1976²) and D. M. Rhoads, *Israel in Revolution 6–74 C.E.: A Political History Based on the Writings of Josephus* (Philadelphia, 1976).

20 Acts 24:14 – *hoti kata tēn hodon hēn legousin hairesin*. Epiphanius *AdvHaer* 29:1 – *houtoi gar heautois onoma epethento ouchi Christou oute auto to onoma tou Iēsou, alla Nazōraiōn ... ekalounto de Iessaioi dia ton Iessai*. For the Greek text of *AdvHaer* see K. Holl (ed.), *Epiphanius (Ancoratus und Panarion)* (GCS 25; Leipzig, 1915), vol. 1, pp. 321–6. I prefer to call the early followers of Jesus 'the Palestinian Jesus Movement'. Students have found this name helpful; it is abbreviated PJM.

21 I think that beneath what is at present a Christian document entitled 'The History of the Rechabites' (formerly the Testament or Apocalypse of Zosimus), especially in chapters 7 to 9, are traditions, perhaps even a remnant of a Jewish document, that may predate 70. See my comments in *The Pseudepigrapha and Modern Research with a Supplement*, pp. 223–8, 299–300. These ideas are developed further in my 'The History of the Rechabites', *The Old Testament Pseudepigrapha*, vol. 2, in press. For the Greek text and an English translation see *The History of the Rechabites*, volume 1: 'The Greek Recension' (Texts and Translations 17, Pseudepigrapha Series 10; Chico, California, 1982).

In *The Territorial Dimension of Judaism* (Berkeley, London, 1982), W. D. Davies suggests that 'the Rechabites stood in some connection with the Nazirites' (p. 57). The relationship, if any, between the Rechabites and the Nazirites, as well as the Essenes, deserves our research.

22 P. Hanson in *The Dawn of Apocalyptic* (Philadelphia, 1975, 1979²) significantly increased our knowledge of the sociological dimensions of the conflict among the priestly groups.

23 'Aber die Zadokiden bildeten doch den Kern und Hauptbestandteil der Priesterschaft in der nachexilischen Zeit' (vol. 2, p. 479). E. Schürer, *Geschichte des jüdischen Volkes im Zeitalter Jesu Christi* (3 vols., Leipzig, 1901–9³/⁴; repr. 1964). In the old English translation of Schürer's masterpiece the quotation can be found in II.II,

p. 33 for bibliography, see chapter 2, n.3. The translation above is my own.

24   A. Büchler, *Der galiläische 'Am-ha'areṣ des zweiten Jahrhunderts: Beiträge zur inneren Geschichte des palästinischen Judentums in den ersten zwei Jahrhunderten* (Vienna, 1906, repr. 1968). The tension between the *'am ha-aretz* and the *ḥaber*, therefore, dates from 'der nachhadrianischen Zeit' and can be associated with the 'Lehrern des Bêth-din in Ušâ' (p. 5).

25   S. Zeitlin, 'The Am Haaretz: A Study in the Social and Economic Life of the Jews Before and After the Destruction of the Second Temple', *JQR* N.S. 23 (1932), 45–61. The *'am ha-aretz*, the vast majority of the Jewish population (p. 47), according to the early Tannaitic literature 'refers to the people of the land, the farmers who tilled the soil' (p. 46). These farmers were not ignorant of the Torah; but because of the extreme demands made upon them by the soil and climate, they had little time 'to cultivate themselves and become educated in Jewish lore' (p. 59). Zeitlin's article was reprinted in *Solomon Zeitlin's Studies in the Early History of Judaism: History of Early Talmudic Law* (New York, 1978), vol. 4, pp. 210–24; the corresponding pages for the above idea and quotation are 212*a* and 222.

26   The heat and demand of hard labour take their toll; intellectual curiosity and scholarly industriousness presuppose a relaxed and healthy body. The mind and spirit are part of the body. Werner Heisenberg, the brilliant physicist and one-time president of the Alexander von Humboldt Foundation, wrote of his experiences during the spring of 1918, when as a sixteen-year-old he laboured on a farm at Miesbach: 'I remember that I had Kant's "Critique of Pure Reason" with me ... I discovered very soon that when you work on a farm the whole day you can do nothing but sleep in the evening' (p. 10). A. Hermann, *Werner Heisenberg 1901–1976*, trans. T. Nevill (Bonn-Bad Godesberg, 1976).

27   A. Oppenheimer, *The 'Am Ha-aretz: A Study in the Social History of the Jewish People in the Hellenistic-Roman Period*, trans. I. H. Levine (ALGHJ 8; Leiden, 1977).

28   A significant passage is in Tosephta, Seder Zeraim, Demai, II, 18 (incorrectly cited as I, 18 by Zeitlin, p. 46, n. 4); see pp. 218–20 for the context in S. Liebermann, *Tosefta Ki-Fshuṭah: A Comprehensive Commentary on the Tosefta* (New York, 1955), Part I: 'Oder Zera'im'. The key phrase is *bn ḥbr shlmd 'ṣl 'm h'rṣ*, 'the son of a *ḥaber* who studies with an *'am ha-aretz*'. Zeitlin (p. 46) claims this phrase 'disproves the notion that the term Am haarez refers to ignorant people'. Oppenheimer (p. 3, n. 10) rejects this interpretation: 'There is no proof that the reference here is to an 'am ha-aretz who taught Torah to a ḥaver's son. It more probably refers to the teaching of a handicraft.' The problem cannot be resolved so facilely and in a footnote. The passage quoted above in fact continues: *bn 'm h'rṣ hlmd 'ṣl ḥbr*, 'the son of an *'am ha-aretz*, he who studies with a *ḥaber*'. This passage deserves a full discussion.

R. S. Sarason translates the pertinent passages as follows: 'The son of a *ḥaber* who was apprenticed to [so Lieberman, *Tosefta*, Part I, p. 219, 1.52] an *'am ha'areṣ*, the servant of a *ḥaber* who was apprenticed to an *'am ha'areṣ* — behold, these remain in their presumed status until they are suspected. The son of an *'am ha'areṣ* who was apprenticed to a *ḥaber* [and] the servant of an *'am ha-areṣ* must take upon themselves [the obligations of *ḥaberut*]' (pp. 91–2). See Sarason's valuable study, *A History of the Mishnaic Law of Agriculture*, section 3: *A Study of Tractate Demai* (SJLA 27; Leiden, 1979). Sarason supports Oppenheimer's interpretation; he claims that Demai II, 18–19 concerns 'the son or servant of a *ḥaber* who (temporarily) studies a trade with an *'am ha'areṣ* in the latter's domain' (p. 93).

29 E. E. Urbach points out that the men of Qumran called their opponents numerous derogatory names but never *'am ha-aretz*, and attempts to show that Hillel may have referred to the Qumran covenanters with the pejorative term. See Urbach's classic, *The Sages: Their Concepts and Beliefs*, trans. I. Abrahams, (2 vols., Jerusalem, 1975), pp. 584–5.

30 S. S. Spiro discusses the enigma of the *ḥaber* in his 'Who was the *Ḥaber*? A New Approach to an Ancient Institution', *JSJ* 11 (1980), 186–216.

31 J. Neusner, 'The 'Am Ha'Areṣ in the System of Uncleanness', *A History of the Mishnaic Law of Purities*, Part XXII: *The Mishnaic System of Uncleanness* (SJLA 22; Leiden, 1977), pp. 151–2, also see pp. 216–17.

32 Of the *didrachmon*, which was the name given to the Jewish tax (*fiscus Judaicus*, compare *fiscus Asiaticus* and the *fiscus Alexandrinus*) that directed the Temple tax to the temple of Capitoline Jupiter, E. M. Smallwood insightfully writes: 'Strangely enough, there is no evidence for the impact of this change on the Jews of Palestine — neither for their reaction to it nor for any details of the collection of the tax itself' (p. 371). We need to examine the possible effects of this tax — as well as the earlier one, the Temple tax — on the Palestinian Jew. Certainly one result was the strengthening of the high priesthood economically and politically. See Smallwood's careful study, *The Jews Under Roman Rule from Pompey to Diocletian: A Study in Political Relations* (SJLA 20; Leiden, 1981 (repr. with corrections of the 1976 edition)).

33 While some scholars hesitate to label the Dead Sea Scrolls as Essene writings, the best specialists have now accepted this attribution. We should acknowledge the similarities between these Scrolls and the reports about the Essenes by the ancient authors, the slanted nature of some later reports about the Essenes, the differences between actual records and secondary reports, and the probability that the Qumran community represented a peculiar type of the Essenes. We dare not make the mistake of assuming all Essenes thought identically, or that the Dead Sea Scrolls are monolithic. They reflect over 200 years of development! See Charlesworth, 'The Origin and Subsequent

History of the Authors of the Dead Sea Scrolls: Four Transitional
Phases Among the Qumran Essenes', *RQ* 38 (1980), 213−33. H.
Lichtenberger has been demonstrating the importance of the develop-
ment of theology, or alteration of ideas, in the Qumran community.
See his *Studien zum Menschenbild in Texten der Qumrangemeinde*
(SUNT 15; Göttingen, 1980); 'Atonement and Sacrifice in the Qumran
Community', in W. S. Green (ed), *Approaches to Ancient Judaism*,
vol. 2 (BJS 9; Chico, California, 1980), pp. 159−71; and with B.
Janowski, 'Enderwartung und Reinheitsidee: Zur eschatologischen
Deutung von Reinheit und Sühne in der Qumrangemeinde', *JJS* 34
(1983), 31−62.

34 The production of pseudepigrapha was not a peculiarity of Early
Judaism; it was a well-known phenomenon in the hellenistic period.
See H. J. Rose, 'Pseudepigraphic Literature', in *The Oxford
Classical Dictionary*, ed. N. G. L. Hammond and H. H. Scullard
(Oxford, 1972²), p. 894. Also see my comments in 'Introduction
for the General Reader', *The Old Testament Pseudepigrapha*, vol.
1, pp. xxi−xxxiv. Also see the selection of studies collected by
N. Brox (ed.), *Pseudepigraphie in der heidnischen und Jüdisch-
Christlichen Antike* (WF 484; Darmstadt, 1977).

35 W. A. Meeks, *The First Urban Christians: The Social World of the
Apostle Paul* (New Haven, London, 1983), p. 7. Meeks, of course,
was thinking about the texts of 'the early Christian movement'. I
have applied his thought to the documents of Early Judaism.

36 Andersen in *The Old Testament Pseudepigrapha*, vol. 1, pp. 205−9.

37 1 Enoch 106:11; the Latin is from Charles, *APOT*, vol. 1, p. 279.

38 B. S. Childs, *Introduction to the Old Testament as Scripture*
(Philadelphia, 1979), pp. 75−6. Also, see the featured reviews and
critiques of Child's method in the *Journal for the Study of the Old
Testament* 16 (1980).

39 See especially the discussions on the literary dimension of hellenistic
culture by H. I. Marrou, *A History of Education in Antiquity*, trans.
G. Lamb (New York, 1956); by W. Jaeger, *Paideia: The Ideals of
Greek Culture I−III*, trans. G. Highet (New York, 1939−45,
1954²); and by B. Mack, 'Under the Shadow of Moses: Authorship
and Authority in Hellenistic Judaism', *Society of Biblical Literature
1982 Seminar Papers*, ed. K. H. Richards (Chico, California, 1982),
pp. 299−318, esp. see pp. 300−1.

2. The Pseudepigrapha, Early Judaism and Christian Origins

1 Y. M. Grintz, 'Apocrypha and Pseudepigrapha', *EncyJud*
(Jerusalem, 1971), vol. 3, col. 182. Picking up Vermes' 'Jewish
Studies and New Testament Interpretation' I have had second
thoughts on the way I have written this monograph. Perhaps my
points should have been more cutting, and my approach to New
Testament scholars polemical. Perhaps I should boldly have written
that most 'of you' were trained incorrectly. Perhaps I should have
stated that 'you' were taught to think that the New Testament is a

sacred canon of books (and not, as 'you' should have seen it, as a portion of the literature of Early Judaism or Christianity), that the New Testament belongs to the Church (and not, as it must be understood as 'a fraction of the literary legacy of first-century Judaism') (Vermes, p. 13), and that the essential writings of importance for New Testament specialists are canonized in the Old and New Testaments (and not, as is certain, found both there and in the *sadly separated collections* called, for example, the Dead Sea Scrolls, the Apocrypha, the Pseudepigrapha, the Philonic Corpus, Josephus' works, the Tannaitic writings, and others). I have not employed the I-you paradigm of discourse, because I am convinced, as Vermes states that 'we have now a more open, positive and constructive approach by New Testament scholars towards post-biblical Judaism' (pp. 10–11). Vermes, 'Jewish Studies and New Testament Interpretation', *JJS* 31 (1980), 1–17; now reprinted in *Jesus and the World of Judaism* (London, 1983), pp. 58–73.

2 This and the following quotation are from R. H. Charles and W. O. E. Oesterley's 'Apocalyptic Literature', *Encyclopaedia Britannica* (Chicago, London, Toronto, 1956), vol. 2, pp. 103–4.

3 Schürer, *A History of the Jewish People in the Time of Jesus Christ*, trans. S. Taylor and P. Christie (Edinburgh, 1898), Div. II, vol. 2, p. 115.

4 Schürer, *The History of the Jewish People in the Age of Jesus Christ: A New English Version*, rev. and ed. G. Vermes, F. Millar, M. Black, with P. Vermes (Edinburgh, 1979), vol. 2, p. 481.

5 G. F. Moore, 'Christian Writers on Judaism', *HTR* 14 (1921), 197–254. This exposé of the presuppositions employed by Christian scholars begins as follows: 'Christian interest in Jewish literature has always been apologetic or polemic rather than historical' (p. 197). I note *now* a trend among some Christian scholars to appreciate and comprehend the literature of Early Judaism.

6 E. P. Sanders, *Paul and Palestinian Judaism: A Comparison of Patterns of Religion* (Philadelphia, 1977), esp. see pp. 24–59. Sanders argues that, 'Besides Bousset, the two individual authors who have had the most to do in implanting Weber's theory of Jewish soteriology deeply in New Testament scholarship have been Paul Billerbeck and Rudolf Bultmann' (p. 42).

7 F. Weber, *Jüdische Theologie auf Grund des Talmud und verwandter Schriften* (Leipzig, 1897²). (This book was edited after the author's death by F. Delitzsch and G. Schnedermann.)

8 H. L. Strack and P. Billerbeck, *Kommentar zum Neuen Testament aus Talmud und Midrasch*, (4 vols., Munich, 1922–8). See Vermes' devasting critique of these volumes and of G. Kittel's *Theologisches Wörterbuch zum Neuen Testament*, (9 vols., Stuttgart, 1933–76) in *JJS* 31 (1980), 5–9; now reprinted in *Jesus and the World of Judaism* (London, 1983), pp. 62–6. Also see L. Siegele-Wenschkewitz, *Neutestamentliche Wissenschaft vor der Judenfrage: Gerhard Kittels theologische Arbeit im Wandel deutscher Geschichte* (TEH 208; Munich, 1980).

9 W. Bousset, *Die Religion des Judentums im neutestamentlichen Zeitalter* (Berlin, 1903; revised continuously, see 1924[4], repr. 1966).

10 R. Bultmann, *Das Urchristentum im Rahmen der antiken Religionen* (Zürich, 1949; ET: *Primitive Christianity in its Contemporary Setting*, trans. R. H. Fuller (London, New York, 1956)).

11 The Old Testament Pseudepigrapha and the New Testament Apocrypha and Pseudepigrapha are modern collections of ancient writings. See my discussions in Charlesworth, with J. R. Mueller, *The New Testament Apocrypha and Pseudepigrapha: A Guide to Publications with Excurses on Apocalypses* (Metuchen, N.J., London, in press).

12 R. E. Brown posits 'five stages in the composition of the Gospel', *The Gospel According to John* (2 vols., Garden City, N.Y., 1966.; London, 1971), vol. 1, p. xxxiv.

13 Some of these late documents obviously contain traditions that date from the first centuries C.E., and these traditions are important for a perception of Early Judaism and Early Christianity. Among this group just listed, the ones most likely to contain not only early traditions but also early sources, albeit redacted somewhat, are 3 Enoch, Testament of Solomon and Testament of Adam. On the one hand, traditions are categorically different from written sources, or redacted works; on the other hand, the century in which a tradition moves from the oral to written stage in no way dates the tradition to that century. Early traditions are found preserved in many late Christian and Jewish works (see n. 14). The Mekilta, and not only early (disparaged 'sectarian') Jewish documents, contains the Jewish belief in determinism: 'We find that the names (*šmytn*) of the righteous (*ṣdykym*) and their deeds (*wm 'šyhm*) are revealed before God even before they are born (*'d šl' nwṣrw*), as it is said: "Before I formed thee in the belly I knew thee", etc. (Jer. 1.5)' (Tractate Pisḥa). See J. Z. Lauterbach (ed.), *Mekilta de-Rabbi Ishmael* (Schiff Library of Jewish Classics; Philadelphia, 1933), pp. 134–5.

14 The Slavs were characterized by a rich imagination that evidenced itself in many apocryphal writings, related loosely to the Old and New Testaments. See Charlesworth, *The New Testament Apocrypha and Pseudepigrapha*. A. de Santos Otero, *Die handschriftliche Überlieferung der altslavischen Apokryphen* (2 vols., PTS 20, 23; Berlin, New York, 1978, 1981). See the major survey of medieval dualism by S. Runciman, *The Medieval Manichee: A Study of the Christian Dualist Heresy* (Cambridge, 1947; repr. 1955, and reissued in 1982 with an updated bibliography and valuable 'Preface to 1982 Reissue' on pp. vii–viii). On the Bogomils see especially I. Ivanov, *Bogomil Books and Legends* (Sofia, 1925 (in Bulgarian)); D. Angelov, *Bogomilism in Bulgaria* (Sofia, 1980[3] (in Bulgarian)); and D. Obolensky, *The Bogomils* (Cambridge, 1948). Also see the numerous publications by N. A. Meshchersky and É. Turdeanu cited in Charlesworth, *The Pseudepigrapha and Modern Research with a Supplement*; the informed and careful contribution by F. I.

Andersen on 2 Enoch in *The Old Testament Pseudepigrapha*, vol. 1, pp. 91–221; and Turdeanu's collection of essays entitled *Apocryphes Slaves et Roumains de l'Ancien Testament* (SVTP 5; Leiden, 1981).

What is sorely needed is a specialist who knows the biblical literature and languages and can also master Slavonics. Someone analogous to M. E. Stone, who from his mastery of Early Judaism and Armenian studies has been able to pore over the Armenian literature in search of early Jewish documents and traditions. See Stone's numerous publications cited in Charlesworth, *The Pseudepigrapha and Modern Research with a Supplement, passim*, and his most recent 'Jewish Apocryphal Literature in the Armenian Church', *Muséon* 95 (1982), 285–309. It must be emphasized that many writings of Early Judaism have been lost forever, others have been found through chance discoveries (for example, of manuscripts from the caves near Qumran, from the fringes of what was the Roman Empire, or in the great European libraries), other documents remain as yet undetected in libraries, not-yet-discovered places, and in Slavonic, Armenian and Syriac literature. A careful search of each of these should prove fruitful.

15 Translations of the Russian Primary Chronicle are according to S. H. Cross and O. P. Sherbowitz-Wetzor and published in *The Russian Primary Chronicle: Laurentian Text* (The Mediaeval Academy of America 60; Cambridge, Mass., 1953), esp. see sections 174–9 on pp. 150–3. For the text see *The Complete Collection of Russian Manuscripts Published by the Permanent Historical-Archeological Committee of the Academy of Sciences of the USSR*. Tome 1: *Laurentian Chronicle*; volume 1: 'Tale of Bygone Years' (Leningrad, 1926²); the relevant sections of 174–9 are on columns 174–80. I am most grateful to Professor Andersen of the University of Queensland and Dr S. Pugh of Duke University for assistance with the Russian Primary Chronicle; I do not wish to suggest, however, that they are responsible for any errors I may have inadvertently committed.

16 'Metaphysical dualism', as I wrote in 1968, 'signifies the opposition between God and Satan; cosmic dualism denotes the conception of two opposing celestial spirits or two distinct and present divisions of the universe.' See my 'A Critical Comparison of the Dualism in 1QS 3:13–4:26 and the "Dualism" Contained in the Gospel of John', *NTS* 15 (1968–9), 389–418; republished in *John and Qumran*, ed. Charlesworth (London, 1972), pp. 76–106.

17 At Qumran, according to 1QS 8.1 the Council of the Community (*ᵃṣath hayyaḥadh*) shall consist of twelve men (*shᵉnîm ʿāsār*) and three priests. At best, the ideological parallel to Yan and the twelve is remote; 'twelve' had become an important number in numerous traditions, e.g. the twelve sons of Jacob (made popular in the Testaments of the Twelve Patriarchs), the twelve tribes, the twelve apostles.

18 The Russian Primary Chronicle was copied by a certain Monk

Laurence (Laventis) in 1377 from an earlier text, a chronicle which dated from earlier in the fourteenth century. The original chronicle must postdate the ninth century, because it explains the origin of Rus, which began as a state in the ninth century. For the date for this and other Russian literature see V. I. Borkovsky and P. S. Kuznecov, *Historical Grammar of the Russian Language* (Moscow, 1963), p. 18 (in Russian). As Jewish apocalypticism was pressed out of Judaism by oppression from Persians, Greeks and Romans, so Bogomilism originated from peasants 'whose physical misery made them conscious of the wickedness of things', Runciman, *The Medieval Manichee*, p. 93.

19   Meshchersky, 'Concerning the Problem of the Sources of the Book of Slavonic Enoch', *Short Reports of the Institute of the Peoples of Asia* 86 (1965), 72—8 (in Russian). The short recension of 2 Enoch refers to the solar calendar, the long recension alone has the names of the Babylonian lunar months, namely Nisan and Tammuz. These and other observations lead Meshchersky to conclude, quite convincingly, that the 'short redaction ... is perfectly free from these additions and, therefore, without a doubt (*bez somneniya*) represents an earlier phase in the development of the text of the Book of Enoch' (p. 97). Meshchersky, 'Concerning the History of the Text of the Book of Slavonic Enoch', *Bizantijskij Bremennik* 24 (1964), 91—108 (in Russian). I am grateful to Ms Melanie McKittrick for translating these publications for me.

   Similar to the long recension of 2 Enoch, *Pirķê de Rabbi Eliezer* (trans. G. Friedlander (New York, 1916, repr. 1965—81)), a ninth-century composition, depended heavily on the Pseudepigrapha of the Old Testament, but deliberately rejected the solar calendar defended by the authors of 1 Enoch and Jubilees. Friedlander (p. xxii—xxiii) even considers the calendrical question the motive for composing *PRE*. The editor of the long recension of 2 Enoch and the compiler of *PRE* both tried to shape the old documents in the Pseudepigrapha and bring them into line with post first-century Judaism.

20   The Greek quotations are collected conveniently by A.-M. Denis in his *Fragmenta pseudepigraphorum quae supersunt graeca* (PVTG 3; Leiden, 1970). Apparently *horate, pòs legei·* in EBar 15:8 should be translated, 'see how (or where) it says'. The punctuation in Greek should probably not signify a quotation mark (*pace* K. Lake's *legei*; translated by him as 'Do you see what he means?' See K. Lake, *The Apostolic Fathers* (LCL; London, Cambridge, Mass., 1912, repr. 1914—65), pp. 394—5).

21   G. Vermes, 'The Impact of the Dead Sea Scrolls on Jewish Studies During the Last Twenty-Five Years', *JJS* 26 (1975), 1—14; repr. in W. S. Green (ed.), *Approaches to Ancient Judaism: Theory and Practice* (BJS 1; Missoula, Montana, 1978) pp. 201—14 and in *Jesus and the World of Judaism* (London, 1983), pp. 110—14.

22   The Aramaic fragments — but unfortunately *not all* of them — are published by J. T. Milik in *The Books of Enoch: Aramaic Fragments of Qumrân Cave 4* (Oxford, 1976).

23 A Book of Noah apparently existed by the middle of the second century B.C.E.; Jubilees refers to a *spr nḥ* (10:13), and the author of the Testament of Levi (MS *e*) mentions a writing of the *biblou tou Nōe* (18:2). See 'Book of Noah', in Charlesworth, *The Pseudepigrapha and Modern Research with a Supplement*, pp. 166–7.

24 The proceedings of the *SNTS* seminars were reported in Charlesworth, 'The SNTS Pseudepigrapha Seminars at Tübingen and Paris on the Books of Enoch', *NTS* 25 (1979), 315–23. Two papers presented in the seminar were published in the same volume: G. W. Nickelsburg, 'Riches, the Rich, and God's Judgment in 1 Enoch 92–105 and the Gospel According to Luke', *NTS* 25 (1979), 324–44; M. A. Knibb, 'The Date of the Parables of Enoch: A Critical Review', *NTS* 25 (1979), 345–59. See the Appendix, pp. 102–10.

25 See the text and translation published by J. A. Fitzmyer and D. J. Harrington in *A Manual of Palestinian Aramaic Texts (Second Century B.C. – Second Century A.D.)* (BibO 34; Rome, 1978), pp. 80–91. Other fragments of *a* Testament of Judah have been recovered; I am convinced they are in Hebrew and from TJud 24:5–25:3. In the near future I plan to publish my findings; meanwhile see the facsimile in M. Baillet, *Qumrân Grotte 4. III (4Q482–4Q520)* (DJD 7; Oxford, 1982), plate 1.

26 There are two recensions of the Greek. 4QTestament of Levi is longer than most Greek versions of the Testament of Levi, but it is paralleled in a Greek recension represented by a manuscript on Mount Athos, Koutloumous 39 (eleventh-century MS *e*), which has a longer version in TLevi 2:3. For the Greek see R. H. Charles, *The Greek Versions of the Testaments of the Twelve Patriarchs* (Oxford, 1908; repr. 1960), p. 29, in the critical apparatus; and in M. De Jonge (ed.), *The Testaments of the Twelve Patriarchs: A Critical Edition of the Greek Text*, in co-operation with H. W. Hollander, H. J. de Jonge, Th. Korteweg, (PVTG 1.2; Leiden, 1978), p. 25, in the critical apparatus.

27 M. de Jonge, *Studies on the Testaments of the Twelve Patriarchs: Text and Interpretation* (SVTP 3; Leiden, 1975), p. 257.

28 J. T. Milik, *Ten Years of Discovery in the Wilderness of Judaea*, trans. J. Strugnell (SBT 26; London, 1959), p. 34.

29 A. Hultgård – a specialist in the history of religions, especially in the hellenistic period – has devoted his research to the T12P. He has concluded that behind all twelve of the testaments lies a Jewish writing. He dates the Jewish Testaments of the Twelve Patriarchs (with Kee) to the early decades of the first century B.C.E. For him the most important features of the T12P for dating the Jewish core are the anti-Hasmonean polemics: 'Or, la tendance polémique des *Testaments* fournit les traits les plus révélateurs pour la datation de l'ouvrage. Nous avons à plusieurs reprises indiqué que la polémique des *Testaments* se situe dans le contexte politique et social des derniers Hasmonéens .. En conclusion, la date de composition des *Testaments des Douze Patriarches* doit être située dans la première moitié du Ier siècle av. J.-C., et probablement

avant 63'; see Hultgård's meticulous and insightful *L'eschatologie des Testaments des Douze Patriarches* (2 vols. AUPHR 6, 7; Uppsala, 1977–82); the quoted passage is found in vol. 2, pp. 226–7.

30 Charlesworth, 'Reflections on the SNTS Pseudepigrapha Seminar at Duke on the Testaments of the Twelve Patriarchs', *NTS* 23 (1977), 296–304. See Appendix pp. 94–102. J. J. Collins points to the Testament of Naphtali 5:8 and argues correctly that the fact that the passage refers to the Assyrians, Medes, Persians and Chaldeans, but not to the Romans reveals that it 'must at least be dated before Pompey and it was probably written before the expulsion of the Syrians in 141 BCE. It cannot be earlier than 200 BCE since it presupposes Syrian, not Ptolemaic rule in Palestine' (p. 155). *Between Athens and Jerusalem: Jewish Identity in the Hellenistic Diaspora* (New York, 1983).

31 H. C. Kee, 'Testaments of the Twelve Patriarchs', *The Old Testament Pseudepigrapha*, vol. 1, p. 777.

32 Hultgård opens his two-volumed work with the following perception: 'L'importance des *Testaments des Douze Patriarches* pour l'histoire des religions ne saurait être surestimée. Cet écrit, d'un contenu d'une extrême richesse présente un arrière-plan immédiat pour la genèse du christianisme. Les *Testaments* apparaissent en outre comme l'une des plus intéressantes productions littéraires du judaïsme antique', *L'eschatologie des Testaments des Douze Patriarches*, vol. 1, p. 11.

33 In *Paul and Palestinian Judaism* Sanders, for example, did not include in his 'comparison' the Testaments of the Twelve Patriarchs, 'because of the vexing problems of date and Christian interpolations' (p. 25). Sanders also does not use 1 En 37–71, preferring to judge the Son of Man passages as post-Christian because they have a 'Christian ring' (p. 348). This judgment unfortunately is not explained, and today must be assessed as too cavalier, as we shall see in chapter 3, pp. 53–5.

34 Nickelsburg rightly emphasizes that judging the Testaments to be a Jewish document demands the recognition that 'the present Greek collection has been interpolated with explicit christological references and in other ways expanded, compressed, and edited by Christians', *Jewish Literature Between the Bible and the Mishnah: A Historical and Literary Introduction* (Philadelphia, 1981), p. 234. Nickelsburg (pp. 231, 234), however, hesitates to choose between the options regarding the character of the Testaments.

35 Kee, 'The Ethical Dimensions of the Testaments of the XII as a Clue to Provenance', *NTS* 24 (1978), 259–70. Kee concludes that 'a likely date for the composition of the basic Jewish document is 100 B.C.' (p. 269), and that 'it is certain' that the 'Test XII was produced in a Jewish community that both spoke and thought in Greek' (p. 270). Without diminishing my support for this conclusion, I wish to stress that H. D. Slingerland is correct to point out that 'the fact that the material is Jewish does not mean it is not Christian' (p. 110).

Obviously Christians used the 'Old Testament' as scripture because of the presuppositions brought to these Jewish texts. For them they were 'Christian' texts. See the discussion of similar points by Slingerland, *The Testaments of the Twelve Patriarchs: A Critical History of Research* (SBLMS 21; Missoula, Montana, 1977), esp. see pp. 106–14.

36 For texts see D. Barthélemy and J. T. Milik, *Qumran Cave 1* (DJD 1; Oxford, 1955), pp. 82–4, plate XVI (1QJub[a,b]); M. Baillet, J. T. Milik and R. de Vaux, *Les 'Petites Grottes' de Qumrân* (2 vols., DJD 3; Oxford, 1962), pp. 77–8, plate XV (2QJub[a]); pp. 78–9, plate XV (2QJub[b]); pp. 96–8, plate XVIII (3QJub). For an identification of 3QJub see R. Deichgräber, 'Fragmente einer Jubiläen – Handschrift aus Höhle 3 von Qumran', *RQ* 5 (1964–5), 415–22, A. Rolfé, 'Further Manuscript Fragments of the Jubilees in the Third Cave of Qumran', *Tarbiz* 34 (1965), 333–6 (in Hebrew), and Baillet, 'Remarques sur le manuscrit du livre des Jubilés de la grotte 3 de Qumran', *RQ* 5 (1964–6), 423–33. Regarding 4QJub[e] and 4QJub[f], see respectively DJD 3, p. 226, and Milik, 'Fragment d'une source du Psautier (4QPs 89) et fragments des Jubilés, du Document de Damas, d'un phylactère dans la grotte 4 de Qumran', *RB* 73 (1966), 104 and plate II*a*; these fragments are now published by M. Baillet, *Qumrân Grotte 4: III (4Q482–4Q520)* (DJD 7; Oxford, 1982) pp. 1–2, plate I. For 11QJub 1, 11QJub 2, 11QJub 3, 11QJub 4, 11QJub 5 see A. S. van der Woude, 'Fragmente des Buches Jubiläen aus Qumran Höhle XI (11QJub)', *Tradition und Glaube: Das frühe Christentum in seiner Umwelt*, eds. G. Jeremias, H. W. Kuhn and H. Stegemann (Göttingen, 1971), pp. 142–3, plate VIII. Milik published 11QJub M 2 and 11QJub M 3 in 'A propos de 11QJub', *Biblica* 54 (1973), 78. The most recent and thorough examination of all these fragments, except the ones recently edited by Baillet, is by J. C. VanderKam, *Textual and Historical Studies in the Book of Jubilees* (Harvard Semitic Museum, HSM 14; Missoula, Montana, 1977), pp. 18–101.

37 In a deeper sense no text in Ethiopic (or Slavonic or Armenian) can be entirely free from some form of Christian influence. These languages, in their written form, were invented and shaped by Christian missionaries. This linguistic phenomenon is categorically different from interpolations and redactions.

38 Most scholars now conclude that the Qumran scrolls represent a type of Essene community, see Charlesworth, 'The Origin and Subsequent History of the Authors of the Dead Sea Scrolls: Four Transitional Phases Among the Qumran Essenes', *RQ* 38 (1980), 215–33.

39 J. C. VanderKam, *Textual and Historical Studies in the Book of Jubilees*, see esp. pp. 283–5.

40 O. Wintermute, 'Jubilees', *The Old Testament Pseudepigrapha*, vol. 2, in press.

41 R. H. Charles, *The Book of Jubilees or the Little Genesis* (London, 1902), pp. lxxxiii–lxxxv. Charles argued that in many places the

authors of the New Testament documents are dependent upon, presuppose, or closely parallel passages in Jubilees. Of these only five appear to warrant careful examination: Lk 11:49 (Jub 1:12), Jn 14:26 (Jub 32:25), Acts 7:53 (Jub 1:27), Jas 2:23 (Jub 14:6), Rev 1:6 (Jub 16:18).

42 Wintermute in *The Old Testament Pseudepigrapha*, vol. 2, in press.

43 These categories are derived from the sections in *The Old Testament Pseudepigrapha*.

44 For discussions of the dates of these documents see the introductions to them in *The Old Testament Pseudepigrapha*, the brief comments in Charlesworth, *The Pseudepigrapha and Modern Research with a Supplement*, the introductions in Nickelsburg, *Jewish Literature*, the succinct, but informed, comments in M. E. Stone, *Scriptures, Sects and Visions: A Profile of Judaism from Ezra to the Jewish Revolts* (Philadelphia, 1980), see esp. 'Key to Ancient Writings', pp. 131–43, and the comments in M. McNamara, *Palestinian Judaism and the New Testament* (GNS 4; Wilmington, Delaware, 1983).

45 I am convinced this document dates from the first century B.C.E., but other scholars may wish to argue against this early date.

46 Jewish prayers, in a redacted form, are probably hidden behind books seven and eight of the Apostolic Constitutions. See my comments in *The Pseudepigrapha and Modern Research with a Supplement*, pp. 288–9. I try to develop these ideas in 'Christian and Jewish Self-Definition in Light of the Christian Additions to the Apocryphal Writings', in *Jewish and Christian Self-Definition*, eds. E. P. Sanders, A. I. Baumgarten and A. Mendelson (Philadelphia, 1981), vol. 2, pp. 27–55, 310–15. Also see D. A. Fiensy and D. R. Darnell, 'Hellenistic Synagogal Prayers', in *The Old Testament Pseudepigrapha*, vol. 2, and Fiensy's 'A Redactional Examination of Prayers Alleged to be Jewish in the Constitutiones Apostolorum', Duke Ph.D., 1980.

47 I know of no Qumran document that can be dated between 50, the earliest writing in the New Testament (namely 1 Thes), and 68, when the Qumran community was destroyed by the Romans.

48 M. McNamara, whose name is naturally associated with the Targums and the New Testament, has recently surveyed the work on this issue, and concludes that with the use of critical criteria, still in need of refinement, New Testament scholars 'are justified in turning to this tradition in seeking to recreate the world in which the Gospel message was born and developed' (p. 89). McNamara readily admits that the rabbinic and targumic writings cannot be dated before 70 in the same 'sense that the age of Qumran material or most apocryphal texts can' (p. 88). See McNamara, 'Letteratura rabbinica e i Targumim', *Problemi e prospettive di Scienze Bibliche*, ed. R. Rabris (Brescia, 1982), pp. 67–109; ET: 'Some Recent Writings on Rabbinic Literature and the Targums', *Milltown Studies* 9 (1982), 59–101.

49 In the *New Testament Apocrypha and Pseudepigrapha* I discuss

the recent successful attempts to find early traditions, even *ipsissima verba Jesu*, in some NTAP, including the Gospel of Thomas.

50 The Qumran Scrolls were found neither in the Dead Sea nor at Qumran. The Nag Hammadi Codices were not found at Nag Hammadi but nearby at Jabal al-Tārif. Our nomenclature has been shaped far too much by popular journalists and the *hoi polloi*. Even 'Pseudepigrapha' is really an offensive label that tends to misrepresent documents.

51 P. Benoit rightly urges us not to forget 'que la littérature de Qumrân est un îlot d'écrits rescapés au milieu d'une mer d'autres écrits perdus' (p. 369). Benoit, 'Le Judaisme Rabbinique', *Bulletin du Comité des Études* 51 (1967), 8–25; repr. in Benoit, *Exégèse et Théologie* (Paris, 1982), vol. 4, pp. 347–70. Similarly we should always remember that the Pseudepigrapha is but a fraction of the ancient Jewish literature. See Charlesworth, 'The Search for Lost Writings', in *The Old Testament Pseudepigrapha*, vol. 1, pp. xxi–xxiii.

52 Charlesworth, 'A History of Pseudepigrapha Research: The Reemerging Importance of the Pseudepigrapha', *ANRW* 2.19.1 (1979), pp. 54–88.

53 See Charlesworth, 'Introduction for the General Reader', *The Old Testament Pseudepigrapha*, vol. 1, pp. xxi–xxxiv; also see Charlesworth, 'Introduction', *The Pseudepigrapha and Modern Research with a Supplement*, pp. 15–32, and 'Bibliography' nos. 1–92.

54 J. Daniélou, *Les manuscrits de la mer morte et les origines du Christianisme* (Paris, 1957), p. 123; ET: *The Dead Sea Scrolls and Primitive Christianity*, trans. S. Attanasio (Baltimore, Maryland, 1958), p. 128. This comment is cited with approval at the conclusion of A. Dupont-Sommer's monumental *Les écrits esséniens découverts près de la mer morte* (Paris, 1959[1], 1960[2], 1964[3], 1980[4]; ET 1962, p. 378). The ET exaggerates Daniélou's words, which now are: 'It can therefore be said that this is the most sensational discovery ever made.'

55 Sanders, *Paul and Palestinian Judaism: A Comparison of Patterns of Religion*, see esp. pp. 1–59. Sanders' book will be cited by referring in the body of this chapter to pages within parentheses.

56 In an article just published W. Horbury argues that the proscription against the *Minim* clearly condemns the Nazarenes, the Christians. See his 'The Benediction of the *Minim* and Early Jewish-Christian Controversy', *JTS* 31 (1982), 19–61. However, the *Noṣrim* were added later to the malediction, and *Minim* may not have originally included the Christians. The amazingly erudite rabbinic specialist, E. E. Urbach writes:

> We are not told who the *minim* were. In the times of R. Gamaliel this term may have denoted various sects. After the Bar Kokhba revolt, when the separation of the Christians of various groups became final, they were

included among the *minim*, and to emphasize their inclusion the *noṣrim* are mentioned explicitly.

See Urbach's 'Self-Isolation or Self-Affirmation in Judaism in the First Three Centuries: Theory and Practice', *Jewish and Christian Self-Definition*, vol. 2, pp. 269–98, 413–17. In the same volume R. Kimelman in 'Birkat Ha-Minim and the Lack of Evidence for an Anti-Christian Jewish Prayer in Late Antiquity' (pp. 226–44, 391–403) argues, *inter alia*, that there 'is no unambiguous evidence that Jews cursed Christians during the statutory prayers' (p. 244). J. Maier also argues that the *Minim* probably did not include the Jewish Christians, who anyway would not have considered themselves *Minim*. Maier, *Jüdische Auseinandersetzung mit dem Christentum in der Antike* (EF 177; Darmstadt, 1982), pp. 136–41.

57 The translation is according to the Old Palestinian rite in the Cairo Genizah fragments. For the Hebrew see S. Schechter, 'Genizah Specimens: Liturgy', *JQR* O.S. 10 (1898), 654–9. The translation given above is from J. Heinemann, *Prayer in the Talmud: Forms and Patterns*, trans. R. S. Sarason (SJ 9; Berlin, New York, 1977), p. 27.

58 Sanders correctly states that our efforts to demolish this historical reconstruction is simply and solely because it is 'based on a massive perversion and misunderstanding of the material' (*Paul and Palestinian Judaism*, p. 59).

59 Moore's full paragraph (vol. 3, p. 151): 'How a Jew of Paul's antecedents could ignore, and by implication deny, the great prophetic doctrine of repentance, which, individualized and interiorized, was a cardinal doctrine of Judaism, namely, that God, out of love, freely forgives the sincerely penitent sinner and restores him to his favor — that seems from the Jewish point of view inexplicable.' The next paragraph begins: 'From that point of view it is in fact inexplicable.' *Judaism in the First Centuries of the Christian Era: The Age of the Tannaim* (3 vols.; Cambridge, Mass., 1927–30, repr. repeatedly). Sanders, *Paul and Palestinian Judaism*, p. 6, drew my attention to this significant quotation.

60 Sanders states, quite appropriately, that 'one cannot avoid the suspicion that, in fact, Paul's own polemic against Judaism serves to define Judaism which is then contrasted with Paul's thought', *Paul and Palestinian Judaism*, p. 4.

61 Thirteen documents in the Apocrypha, fifty-two in the Pseudepigrapha proper, and thirteen in its Supplement.

62 Sanders has been more concerned than I am to implant 'a better understanding of Rabbinism in New Testament scholarship' (p. xiii). I am interested in Early Judaism, that is the full religious phenomena from circa the third century B.C.E. to around 200 C.E. Sanders should be sympathetic with my goal, because his first 'general aim' is 'to argue a case concerning Palestinian Judaism (that is, Judaism as reflected in material of Palestinian provenance) as a whole', *Paul and Palestinian Judaism*, p. xii.

63 Sanders, *Paul and Palestinian Judaism*, pp. 12–13.
64 In addition to Sanders' book *Paul and Palestinian Judaism*, pp. 12–18, also see his 'Patterns of Religion in Paul and Rabbinic Judaism: A Holistic Method of Comparison', *HTR* 66 (1973), 455–78.
65 Davies also draws attention to the inadequate nature of the term 'essence' when describing phenomena in Early Judaism and in Early Christianity. *The Territorial Dimension of Judaism*, p. 123.
66 In this quotation Sanders is, of course, explaining why he will begin by considering 'Rabbinic (Tannaitic) Literature'; his justification is because 'this literature has been primarily in mind in most major comparisons of Paul and Judaism which have been carried out by New Testament scholars (for example, Davies and Schoeps)' (p. 25). He is clearly also revealing his main interest, rabbinic Judaism. Significantly, when Sanders tries to 'reassess some of my proposals about Judaism' he entitles the publication, 'Puzzling Out Rabbinic Judaism', (in *Approaches to Ancient Judaism*, ed. W. S. Green; BJS 9; Chico, California, 1980; vol. 2, pp. 65–79).
67 As W. A. Meeks wrote, Sanders' book 'shows how powerful are the habits of our religious and scholarly traditions' (p. 27). See Meeks' 'Toward a Social Description of Pauline Christianity', in *Approaches to Ancient Judaism*, vol. 2, pp. 27–47. As N. A. Dahl claimed, Sanders' definition of a 'pattern of religion' is drawn from Western, especially Protestant, theology much more than from Judaism understood on its own terms' (p. 157). See Dahl's review essay in *RSR* 4 (1978), 153–7.
68 J. Neusner, 'The Use of the Later Rabbinic Evidence for the Study of First-Century Pharisaism', in *Approaches to Ancient Judaism* (BJS 1; Missoula, Montana, 1978), pp. 215–28, esp. see p. 221. Also see Neusner's 'Comparing Judaisms', *HR* 18 (1978), 177–91; and his 'The Use of the Later Rabbinic Evidence for the Study of Paul', *Approaches to Ancient Judaism*, vol. 3, pp. 43–63.
69 Neusner, 'The Talmud as Anthropology', *Annual Samuel Friedland Lecture, The Jewish Theological Seminary of America* (New York, 1979), see esp. p. 31.
70 I cannot imagine how Sanders can use the adverb 'presumably'. Jubilees is *assuredly* earlier than the Tannaitic literature. Also, Sanders must have slipped when he wrote that 'Jubilees and the various portions of 1 Enoch' are 'relatively short' (p. 25). They are massive documents; I cannot at the moment think of any biblical book or noncanonical book that is much longer.
71 Dahl, (in *RSR* 4 (1978) 157) also refers to Sanders' methodogy as 'abstract'.
72 Dahl, *RSR* 4 (1978), 155.
73 In the following pages I take up the problems we have with no-menclature. Neusner combines such concerns with insights related to the above imagined dialogue: 'What generates this fairly wide-spread failure of definition and resort to undefended categories is the problem of dealing with a definitive category essentially

asymmetrical to the evidence. That is, a deeply philosophical construct, "Juda-ism", is imposed upon wildly mythological or totally unphilosophical evidence, deriving from many kinds of social groups, and testifying to the state of mind and way of life of many sorts of Jews, who in their own day would scarcely have understood one another, let alone have known they all evidenced the same -ism, for instance, the Teacher of Righteousness and Aqiba, or Josephus and Bar Kokhba'; Neusner, *Judaism: The Evidence of the Mishnah* (Chicago, London, 1981), p. 22.

74 Sanders has recently clarified the purpose of *Paul and Palestinian Judaism*: 'Despite the length of that book, the subject was limited to how "getting in and staying in" were understood by Paul and his near contemporaries in Judaism'. The quotation is from the 'Preface' of Sanders' *Paul, the Law, and the Jewish People* (Philadelphia, 1983), p. ix.

75 J. Z. Smith, after discussing many documents of Early Judaism adds a significant judgment: 'It is striking that most of the scholars from G. F. Moore to E. P. Sanders who have pursued the will-o'-the-wisp of "normative Judaism" have failed to cite or consider most of the passages and positions described above' (p. 24). See Smith's brilliant article entitled 'Fences and Neighbors: Some Contours of Early Judaism', in *Approaches to Ancient Judaism*, vol. 2, pp. 1–25. A celebration of and critical reflection on Moore's work, and of Strack-Billerbeck's *Kommentar*, is F. C. Porter's 'Judaism in New Testament Times', *JR* 8 (1928), 30–62. A much more insightful critique of Moore's volumes is M. Smith's 'The Work of George Foot Moore', *Harvard Library Bulletin* 15 (1967), 169–79. Especially noteworthy are the valid judgments that in Moore's study 'Christianity appears by contrast [to 'normative' Judaism] as a heretical sect, engendered by apocalyptic enthusiasm' (p. 177), and that the use of documents of a minority party from a later time to portray earlier phenomena presents 'a seriously false picture of earlier times' (p. 177). Neusner, while recognizing the masterful nature of Moore's work, nevertheless rightly perceives that the kind of Judaism 'represented in the Mishnah, the Talmuds, and other rabbinic writings of late antiquity' simply '*did not*' (italics mine, p. 1) exist 'in the period before the turn of the first century' (p. 1). Neusner has set out with a 'completely different approach' from that of Moore to 'describe the evidence of the Mishnah on Judaism in the "Tannaitic" Age' (p. 3). Neusner, *Judaism: The Evidence of the Mishnah*; for a perspicacious critique of Moore, see pp. 5–24. Also, see note 84 below.

76 Meeks in *Approaches to Ancient Judaism*, vol. 2, p. 27.

77 M. D. Hooker, 'Paul and "Covenantal Nomism"', in *Paul and Paulinism: Essays in Honour of C. K. Barrett*, ed. M. D. Hooker and S. G. Wilson (London, 1982), pp. 47–56, esp. p. 47.

78 S. Sandmel in *RSR* 4 (1978), 160.

79 F. Dexinger insightfully states, 'Die jüdische Erwählungsvorstellung ist der biblischen Grundlage entsprechend (vgl. Dtn 7, 6–8) von

zentraler Bedeutung für das jüdische Selbstverständnis' (p. 189). He goes on to add, 'Schon die Terminologie lässt einen wesentlichen strukturellen Aspekt des Erwählungsbewusstseins erkennen. Es handelt sich um keinen statisch ontologischen Zustand, sondern um einen heilsgeschichtlichen Prozess' (p. 189). Dexinger, 'Erwählung: Judentum', *Theologische Realenzyklopädie* 10, pp. 189–92.

80 In his most recent book, *The Territorial Dimension of Judaism,* Davies felt compelled to state that 'the term "Judaism" itself cannot be understood as representing a monolithic faith in which there has been a simplistic uniformity of doctrine – whether demanded, imposed, or recognized – about The Land, as about other elements of belief. Certainly this was so at all periods and in all sections of the Jewish community before 70 C.E.' (p. 54, see also pp. 122–3).

81 In the first century C.E. there was probably one legal institution headed by the high priest. See the discussions by H. D. Mantel and Vermes, *et al.*: H.D. Mantel, 'The High Priesthood and the Sanhedrin in the Time of the Second Temple', in *The Herodian Period*, ed. M. Avi-Yonah and Z. Baras (The World History of the Jewish People 1.7; Jerusalem, New Brunswick, 1975), pp. 265–81. E. Schürer, *The History of the Jewish People in the Age of Jesus Christ*, eds. G. Vermes, F. Millar, *et al.* (Edinburgh, 1979), vol. 2, p. 208.

82 Herod the Great restored Samaria and far from restoring the Samaritan temple renamed the city Sebaste (*Sebastos* is the Gk for Augustus, the Emperor) and constructed there, as in Caesarea, a temple to Augustus (and in Sebaste Herod erected a temple, *naon … megethei kai kallei tōn ellogimōtatōn*; Josephus, *Ant* 15.8.5). See the discussion by A. Schalit, *König Herodes: Der Mann und sein Werk*, trans. J. Amir (SJ 4; Berlin, 1969), pp. 358–65.

83 B. A. Levine has described Psalm 46 in terms of 'the potent presence' of God in 'On the Presence of God in Biblical Religion', *Religions in Antiquity: Essays in Memory of Erwin Ramsdell Goodenough*, ed. J. Neusner (SHR 14; Leiden, 1968), pp. 71–87. Levine readily acknowledges, of course, that the prophets – especially Micah and Jeremiah – attacked the notion that God's 'residence' in Jerusalem guaranteed the city's security (cf. also 4 Ezra and 2 Bar).

The concept of the presence of God in biblical theologies must be balanced with a perception of the 'hiddenness' of God, which according to S. E. Balentine was not a minor problem for Israel and denoted not only divine judgment but also 'inexplicable divine hiddenness'. See Balentine, *The Hidden God: The Hiding of the Face of God in the Old Testament* (OTM; Oxford, 1983).

84 See the definitive study by R. de Vaux, *Ancient Israel: Its Life and Institutions*, trans. J. McHugh (New York, London, 1961), esp. pp. 320–1. Also, see the attempts to define the essence and describe the phenomena of the Temple by M. Haran, *Temples and Temple-Service in Ancient Israel: An Inquiry into the Character of Cult Phenomena and the Historical Setting of the Priestly School* (Oxford, 1978).

85 These differing views are very ancient and can be traced in part to the prophets. Zechariah and Ezekiel saw a Temple in restored Jerusalem, but the latter emphasized that Yahweh not the Temple was central (*wᵉshēm-hā'îr miyyôm yᵉwāh shāmmāh*, Ezek 48:35). For Jeremiah ark, Temple and Jerusalem tended to be separated conceptually; the latter dominated: 'In those days ... men shall speak no more of the Ark of the Covenant of the Lord ... it will be needed no more. At that time Jerusalem shall be called the Throne of the Lord' (Jer 3:16–17; NEB).

86 Long ago O. Cullmann drew attention to Jewish opposition to the Temple: 'L'Opposition contre le Temple de Jérusalem, motif commun de la théologie johannique et du monde ambiant', *NTS* 5 (1959), 157–73. ET: 'A New Approach to the Interpretation of the Fourth Gospel', *ExpT* 71 (1959), 8–12, 35–43.

87 V. Eppstein attempted to demonstrate the reliable history behind Jesus' action in the Temple (*Purgatio templi*: Mk 11: 15–17, Mat 21:12–13, Lk 19:45–46, Jn 2:13–17). Eppstein, 'The Historicity of the Gospel Account of the Cleansing of the Temple', *ZNW* 55 (1964), 42–8. E. Haenchen seriously questioned Eppstein's main hypothesis, that the High Priest Caiaphas, probably a Sadducee, terminated 'the custom of cordial cooperation between the Rabbis and the Temple priesthood' (p. 55) and possibly banished the Sanhedrin from the Temple. See Haenchen, *Das Johannes Evangelium: Ein Kommentar*, ed. U. Busse (Tübingen, 1980), pp. 199–200.

88 I have no difficulty with Neusner's argument that the Mishnah preserves a *system* regarding the rules of purity, and that prior to 70 there was 'a cultic system'. There probably was a system for performing the daily sacrifices in the Temple. See Neusner, *A History of the Mishnaic Law of Holy Things*, Part VI: *The Mishnaic System of Sacrifice and Sanctuary* (SJLA 30.6; Leiden, 1980), esp. see pp. 16–19. A cultic system is certainly different from, and not to be confused with, a systematic normative Jewish theology.

89 P.D. Hanson, *The Dawn of Apocalyptic* (Philadelphia, 1975, 1979²). See chapter 1, esp. no. 22.

90 The importance of the Temple and the high priesthood becomes clear when we think about Judaism after 70. This point has been emphasized many times; long ago A. Momigliano wrote, 'The most serious measure of all remains to be mentioned: by abolishing the Sanhedrin and the High Priesthood and by forbidding the resumption of the worship of the Temple at Jerusalem the Romans destroyed the political and religious centre of Judaism' (p. 864). *The Cambridge Ancient History*, vol. 10: 'The Augustan Period 44 B.C. – A.D. 70', eds. S.A. Cook, F.E. Adcock and M.P. Charlesworth (Cambridge, New York, 1934).

91 I am indebted to the discussions by Büchler, *Der galiläische 'Am-ha'areṣ des zweiten Jahrhunderts*, pp. 91–3, 158–9, and by Oppenheimer, *The 'Am Ha-aretz*, pp. 78–9, 126, 132. If the *'am ha-aretz* is one who is unclean and impure then how can Oppenheimer state that there were rules to prohibit a *khn 'm h'rṣ* from eating

priestly gifts 'when not in a state of purity' (p. 79, cf. p. 132)? See the discussion in chapter 1 and nn. 24–9.

92 It should be obvious that I side fully with D.E. Aune against any endeavour to discard documents as insignificant and construct, as N.J. McEleney attempted, an 'orthodox' Judaism. As Aune stated, any such thesis is 'both fallacious and a serious distortion of the religious integrity and structure of first century Judaism' (pp. 1–2). See Aune, 'Orthodoxy in First Century Judaism? A Response to N.J. McEleney', *JSJ* 7 (1976), 1–10.

93 One of the great minds of our century, Käsemann, looking back over five decades of writing and lecturing, claims: 'Echte und tiefe menschliche Bindungen führen stets in Konflikte, müssen sich gerade in ihnen bewähren. Auf meinem Wege haben sie sich gehäuft' (p. 7). See Käsemann's *Kirchliche Konflikte*, vol. 1 (Göttingen, 1982). For Käsemann the Bible is 'ein subversives Buch' and 'Autorität wird allein durch Dienst legitimiert' (p. 5).

94 R. Murray, 'Jews, Hebrews and Christians: Some Needed Distinctions', *NovT* 24 (1982), 194–208.

95 In Early Judaism the 'discontinuity' is greater than Murray's terms allow. Early Judaism cannot be bifurcated into two groups: the group he labels 'Jews' because they 'looked to Jerusalem' (here Temple, cult, and Jerusalem are too readily identified) for 'their focus of identity and devotion' (p. 199); and the one he defines as 'Hebrews' because they dissented (a paradigm that disguises a preconceived normative Judaism). This model will not withstand careful examination. Paul refers to himself as *Hebraios ex Hebraiōn* (Phil 3:5) and this term cannot be dismissed as referring to the Semitic language (p. 204). To begin with Josephus' terms (*Ant* 11.8.6) as 'a starting point' (p. 198) and to exclude the Samaritans as Jews tends to ignore Josephus' personal opinions and desire to cast pre-70 Judaism so that it is appealing to Romans. These brief comments should disclose that I have taken Murray seriously when he wrote, 'What follows is a basis for discussion rather than a thesis to be defended' (p. 198, cf. p. 208).

96 Murray, *NovT* 24 (1982), 202.

97 See the discussion of 'Spätjudentum' and 'Frühjudentum' in K. Hoheisel's *Das antike Judentum in Christlicher Sicht: Ein Beitrag zur neueren Forschungsgeschichte* (SOR 2; Wiesbaden, 1978). As Hoheisel (pp. 7–60) clarifies, *Spätjudentum* tends to be a pejorative term: Judaism is not dying out as Christianity is being launched. That misconception derives from Christian apologetics, if not polemics.

98 M.E. Stone, *Scriptures, Sects and Visions: A Profile of Judaism from Ezra to the Jewish Revolts* (Philadelphia, 1980), p. 35. Stone rightly emphasizes that the circles of scholars who produced 1 Enoch were 'well learned' (p. 44). See the Preface above and 'The Cosmic Theology of Early Judaism' at the end of the present chapter, pp. 65–7.

99 I am in full agreement with M. Smith's argument that 'hellenistic' denotes a 'cultural classification distinct both from "Greek" and

from "oriental",,' and that it represents 'various groups of a single cultural continuum – the Hellenistic' (p. 81). Hengel also correctly states that 'we may term Judaism of the Hellenistic Roman period, both in the home country and the Diaspora, "Hellenistic Judaism"' (pp. 125–6). See their books: M. Smith, *Palestinian Parties and Politics that Shaped the Old Testament* (New York, London, 1974). M. Hengel, *Jews, Greeks and Barbarians: Aspects of the Hellenization of Judaism in the Pre-Christian Period*, trans. J. Bowden (Philadelphia, 1980).

100 In 'Das Neue Testament als jüdische Schrift' G. Stemberger emphasizes that 'Das Neue Testament ist voll und ganz aus den Judentum des 1. und beginnenden 2. Jahrhunderts erwachsen, steht in der reichen jüdischen Tradition und ist in ständigem Gespräch mit ihr auch dort, wo es von ihr abweicht' *Geschichte der jüdischen Literatur: Eine Einführung* (Munich, 1977), p. 65. It is certainly true that portions of some New Testament writings *may* be originally Jewish, namely James and Revelation, but Stemberger's claim is too sweeping and fails to note that some writings in the New Testament, notably Acts and Paul's writings, are also influenced by Greek philosophical ideas. On the other hand, C. C. Torrey in *Documents of the Primitive Church* (New York, London, 1941) erred when he contended that Tosephta Yadayim 2:13 indicated that Jews thought the gospels would be equal in authority to the scriptures. Zeitlin correctly replied that 'it is quite impossible to assume that some Pharisees felt that the Gospels should be put on a par with the *Ketubim*' (*JQR* 32 (1942), repr. in *Solomon Zeitlin's Studies in the Early History of Judaism*, vol. 3, p. 431). Tosephta Yadayim 2:13 is translated by Neusner as follows: 'The Gospels (*gylymnyn*) and books of heretics do not impart uncleanness to hands' (p. 333). *The Tosefta Translated from the Hebrew*. Sixth Division: *Tohorot (The Order of Purities)* (New York, 1977). While Neusner does not comment on this debate between Torrey and Zeitlin (cf. *A History of the Mishnaic Law of Purities*. Part XIX: *Tebul Yom and Yadayim* (SJLA 6.19; Leiden, 1977), it seems clear to me that he agrees with Torrey that the gospels are mentioned in Yadayim 2:13 but would side with Zeitlin in interpreting the passage.

101 As J. Z. Smith (in *Approaches to Ancient Judaism*, vol. 2, p. 15) contends, 'we cannot sustain the impossible construct of *a* normative, Jewish understanding. We must conceive of a variety of early Judaism*s*, which cluster in varying configurations' (his italics). M. Smith rightly claims that the Jamnia court 'effectuated a reorganization of Jewish law and life that effectively marked the beginnings of a distinctive, new form of the religion, "rabbinic Judaism", of which the center was a distinctive, new rabbinic organization' (p. 43). M. Smith, 'Early Christianity and Judaism', in *Great Confrontations in Jewish History*, ed. S. Wagner and A. Breck (Denver, 1977), pp. 41–61.

A monolith has no life; hence 'monolithic' Judaism, a concept shared by most New Testament scholars before approximately 1960, when the Dead Sea Scrolls made a permanent impact on scholarship, probably reflects the idea that piety had died out in Early Judaism, as Schürer had argued – most incorrectly – in 'Das Leben unter dem Gesetz', *Geschichte des Jüdischen Volkes im Zeitalter Jesu Christi* (Leipzig, 1886²), Part II, pp. 387–416.

102 The one document that has misled some recent and excellent scholars into thinking it may belong to one of the sects is the Psalms of Solomon. For further elaboration on this point see my 'Introduction for the General Reader', *The Old Testament Pseudepigrapha*, vol. 1, pp. xi–xxxiv. H. Cousin, incorrectly, labels both the Psalms of Solomon and 4 Ezra as Pharisaic. See his *Vies d'Adam et Eve, des patriarches et des prophètes* (Paris, 1980). Also, we must *no longer* tolerate the misrepresentation of pre-70 Judaism that speaks about the Pharisees as the popular, 'normative sect'. See M. Smith's clarification that this conception derives from Josephus' post-70 political apologia found especially in the *Antiquities* (93–4 C.E.). Smith, 'Palestinian Judaism in the First Century', in *Israel: Its Role in Civilization*, ed. M. Davis (New York, 1956), pp. 67–81. Neusner has further developed Smith's insight; see Neusner's 'Josephus' Pharisees: A Complete Repertoire', *Formative Judaism: Religious, Historical and Literary Studies*, Third Series (Chico, California, 1983), pp. 61–82. Also, see note 110.

103 Unfortunately Bultmann's 'Das Urchristentum' was translated as 'Primitive Christianity'; see note 10 above. Perhaps also, our understanding of the term 'primitive' has altered significantly since the fifties. Also, see the ET of Daniélou's *Les origines* (cf. n. 54).

104 See chapter 1, '"Christian Origins", Perspective, and Appreciation', pp. 13–14.

105 As Stone argues, in *Scriptures, Sects and Visions*, '*Later* configurations of Judaism and Christianity may have only a peripheral importance in determining the actual situation that existed' (p. 115). Stone also correctly stresses two important points: First, the 'Christian sources form a valuable body of evidence about Judaism in the first century' (p. 115). Second, 'a whole range of speculative interests is missing from the New Testament' (p. 115, also see p. 43).

106 'Die inneren Notwendigkeiten, die zu diesem völligen Wandel in der Geschichtsbetrachtung geführt haben, können wir, wie gesagt, nicht aufzeigen.' G. von Rad, *Weisheit in Israel* (Neukirchen-Vluyn, 1970), p. 354; ET: *Wisdom in Israel* (Nashville, New York, 1972), p. 276. G. von Rad also wrote that in 'the course of this completely altered idea (völlig veränderten Vorstellung) of divine salvation, the interpretation of history was, so to speak, subjected to a revolution of a hundred and eighty degrees, for now it was interpreted not from the past but from the eschaton' (p. 282); 'denn nun wurde sie nicht von der Vergangenheit, sondern von den Eschata her interpretiert' (p. 362). While this position is significant, I think that von Rad has tended to exaggerate the alterations of older ideas in Early Judaism.

107 J. Neusner, *Judaism: The Evidence of the Mishnah* (Chicago, London, 1981), p. 7.

108 For the Greek see H. Jacobson, *The* Exagoge *of Ezekiel* (Cambridge, 1983), p. 56.

109 I am focusing upon the mind of the early Jew, not the causes of revolt! Certainly many factors in the latter concern must be emphasized, not the least significant of which is the repressiveness and clumsiness of Rome.

110 See my comments in *JAAR* 50 (1982), 292–3 (a review of J. Schüpphaus, *Die Psalmen Salomos* (Leiden, 1977). Also, see the discussion above and chapter 1, 'New Opportunities and Challenges', pp. 18–25.

111 J. Heinemann, *Prayer in the Talmud*, pp. 26–7. The Hebrew of the last sentence, according to Schechter in *JQR* O.S. 10 (1898), 656: *brwk 'th yy mthyh hmtym*.

3. The Pseudepigrapha and the New Testament

1 Before the discovery of the Dead Sea Scrolls, compared to the Hebrew, the LXX of Jeremiah was considered unimportant. Now, thanks to the recovery of the fragments of Jeremiah found in the Qumran caves we know *two* recensions are ancient; one lies behind the MT, the other behind the LXX. Long ago F. M. Cross pointed this out: 'In Chapter 10, for example, the Septuagint omits no fewer than four verses, and shifts the order of a fifth. The Qumrân Jeremiah (4QJer[b]) omits the four verses and shifts the order in identical fashion', *The Ancient Library of Qumran and Modern Biblical Studies* (Garden City, New York, 1961 (revised edition)), p. 187.

2 The translations are my own; they are designed to be faithful to the Hebrew and the Greek and also to clarify the parallels. A comparison of the RSV translations of Jeremiah 31:15 and Matthew 2:17–18 suggests a wide difference between the two that simply does not exist.

3 For introduction, transcription and facsimile see J. T. Milik, *The Books of Enoch: Aramaic Fragments of Qumrân Cave 4*, with the collaboration of M. Black (Oxford, 1976). Milik dates 4QEn[c] to 'the early Herodian period or the last third of the first century B.C.E.' (p. 178).

4 C. D. Osborn concludes an analysis of Aramaic Enoch and Jude with the statement that 'not only is Jude quoting 1 Enoch i.9, but specifically from an Aramaic Enoch' (p. 338). Osborn, 'The Christological Use of 1 Enoch i.9 in Jude 14, 15', *NTS* 23 (1977), 334–41. Bauckham, in *Jude, 2 Peter* (WBC 50; Waco, Texas, 1983), concluded that 'the simplest explanation is that Jude *knew* the Greek version, but made his own translation from the Aramaic' (p. 96, cf. p. 47).

5 The translation is essentially (see following notes) Isaac's, in '1 Enoch', *The Old Testament Pseudepigrapha*, vol. 1, pp. 13–14.

6 My translation is from the facsimile in Milik, *Books of Enoch*, plate IX. The Ethiopic (Knibb's translation), the Greek of Codex Panopolitanus and Jude, and the Latin according to Pseudo-Cyprian

are conveniently placed in parallel columns in R. J. Bauckham, *Jude, 2 Peter*, p. 95.

7 Isaac notes: 'All of Charles's MSS, except *e*, read *maṣ'a* "he came"'. Ethiopian commentators who follow this reading argue that the perfect tense is used to emphasize that "he will certainly come".' See Isaac, '1 Enoch', *The Old Testament Pseudepigrapha*, vol. 1, p. 13. M. A. Knibb translates the verse with the English present: 'He comes'. See Knibb, *The Ethiopic Book of Enoch: A New Edition in the Light of the Aramaic Dead Sea Fragments*, in consultation with E. Ullendorff (2 vols., Oxford, 1978), vol. 2, p. 60.

8 Isaac: 'with ten million', Knibb (p. 60): 'was with ten thousand holy ones'; I choose 'myriad' for the Ethiopic here to avoid confusing comparisons.

9 The Ethiopic does not have the possessive pronoun, but the Greek of Jude clearly does (*autou*). It is important to see if the pronoun is in the Aramaic fragment. Not the transcription, but the facsimile (Milik, plate IX) clearly shows *qd.sh.*[...], the third and fifth letters are either two Waws, two Yodhs, or one of each; it is difficult to be certain. Milik reads *qaddîshô*[*hî*], '[hi]s holy ones'. This reading is possible, but so are two others. Another possibility is *qaddîshî*[*n*], 'the holy one[s]'. The third possibility is the first impression I received when looking at the facsimile: *qᵉdhôshî*[*n*], 'the holy one[s]'; in that case we have a Hebraism, which is not strange in this type of Aramaic. In favour of this rendering is not only the first impression, but also a comparison of the Waws and Yodhs in 4QEnᶜ. They are either indistinguishable, or the Waws seem to be occasionally a little longer. Here the third consonant is longer than the fifth. In Herodian scripts, as in 1QM, Waws often have a longer stem than Yodhs. On balance, I tend to think we are faced, therefore, with 'the holy ones', which agrees with the Ethiopic. Against the Aramaic, and Ethiopic, would then be the reading 'his holy ones', which is behind Jude, followed by Codex Panopolitanus (*autou*) and Ps-Cyprian (*suorum*).

10 Osborn perceptively concludes that 'Jude has made a decidedly Christian adaptation of 1 Enoch i.9 by the unique addition of *kurios*' (*NTS* 23 (1977), 338). Bauckham, in *Jude, 2 Peter*, correctly judges that *kurios* 'is probably Jude's interpretative gloss on the text ... by which he applies a prophecy of the eschatological coming of God (1 *Enoch* 1:4) to the Parousia of the Lord Jesus' (p. 96, cf. 94). I am not convinced, however, that the prophecy is employed only with regard to the parousia of Jesus; it is more natural in the light of the omissions from 1 Enoch, especially the deletions of 'destroy', because they were not fulfilled by the so-called advent; and the 'past' tense of the aorist may suggest that the first coming, with subtle allusions to the second, was in the mind of the author of Jude. The *parousia* was portrayed in terms of the *advent*. Both, from prophetic insight, have been fulfilled. For further observations regarding

interpolations and redactions that are christologically motivated, see Charlesworth, *Jewish and Christian Self-Definition*, vol. 2, pp. 27−55, 310−15.

11 Bauckham claims that early Christian readers would understand *tais muriasin autou* 'as a reference to the angels', and *tois hagiois autou* 'as a reference to Christians' (p. 138); 'A Note on a Problem in the Greek Version of 1 Enoch i.9', *JTS* N.S. 32 (1981), 136−8. I take this argument to be rather speculative.

12 See the comments by Osborn, '1 Enoch i.9 in Jude 14, 15', *NTS* 23 (1977), 334−41, esp. 340−1. Bauckham agrees that 'the modifications of the text' are in 'accordance with early Christian practice' (*Jude, 2 Peter*, pp. 93−4). For a penetrating discussion of this issue in a wider context, see C. F. D. Moule, *The Birth of the New Testament*, third edition, revised and rewritten (San Francisco, Cambridge, 1982), pp. 84−5.

13 Osborn, although not using our technical terms, correctly states, 'Jude's citation is not literally word for word, nor on the other hand is it merely a reminiscence or allusion. He has rather *adapted* the 1 Enoch text to the new historical situation in view of his eschatological purposes and his christological understanding', '1 Enoch i.9 in Jude 14, 15', p. 340.

14 While I do not agree with Bauckham that we can use the term 'midrash' when referring to Jude, I do agree with his assessment of the importance and the meaning of the quotation from 1 Enoch in Jude:

> The quotation from Enoch is probably to be seen as Jude's key text in his midrash. Interpreted by the addition of the word 'Lord', it speaks of the coming of the Lord Jesus to judge the wicked. Its emphatic repetition of the word 'ungodly' hammers home the message of Jude's whole midrash: that those who indulge in 'ungodly' conduct, as the false teachers do, are those on whom judgment will fall.   (*Jude, 2 Peter*, p. 100)

15 Bauckham in *Jude, 2 Peter*, perceptively states that while the verb *eprophēteusen* 'indicates that Jude regarded the prophecies in 1 Enoch as inspired by God, it need not imply that he regarded the book as canonical Scripture' (p. 96).

16 B. Reicke in *The Epistles of James, Peter, and Jude* (The Anchor Bible; Garden City, New York, 1964) rightly emphasizes that while 1 Enoch 'was not accepted by the Jews or the Christians as a canonical scripture', yet 'it is clear that Jude regarded this writing as inspired. In fact, due to its presumed antiquity, First Enoch is placed on an even higher level than the Old Testament prophets' (p. 209). K. H. Schelkle, in *Die Petrusbriefe; der Judasbrief* (HTKNT 13.2; Freiburg, Basel, Vienna, 1980⁵), judiciously argues that Jude had a high estimate of 1 Enoch, and 'without question' believed 'dass es wirklich vom Patriarchen Henoch stamme. Darum zitiert er es hier also prophetisches Buch und spielt an anderen Stellen

(Jud 6.12) darauf an' (p. 164). W. Grundmann in *Der Brief des Judas und der zweite Brief des Petrus* (THNT 15; Berlin, 1979²) states only that 'in dem Kreis des Judas und auch seiner Leser [1 Enoch] hochgeschätzt wurde' (p. 43); but earlier (p. 16) he asked, thinking about the provenance of Jude: 'Wo hat apokalyptische Literatur neben den Schriften des Alten Bundes gleichwertiges Gewicht?'

17 See the comments at the close of chapter 1, p. 25.

18 In K. Aland, *et al.* (ed.), *The Greek New Testament*, Jude 9 is in bold type, but Jude 14–15 is in ordinary type. The 'Index of Quotations' in this edition is intended to include almost all conceivable 'quotations'; it can be *very misleading* if taken in any other sense.

19 Bauckham, 'Excursus: The Background and Source of Jude 9', *Jude, 2 Peter*, pp. 65–76. J. R. Busto Sáiz in 'La carta de Judas a la luz de algunos escritos judíos', (*EB* 39 (1981), 83–105) also thinks that Jude depended directly not only on 1 Enoch but also on the Testament of Moses. *The Palaea Historica* also contains the account of Moses' death, the struggle between Michael and Samael (the Devil), and the saying, 'the Lord rebuke you'. D. Flusser thinks that this story 'originates from the "Assumption of Moses"' (p. 73). Flusser's interest, however, was in searching for possible Jewish sources in the *Palaea Historica*. See Flusser, '*Palaea Historica*: An Unknown Source of Biblical Legends', *Studies in Aggadah and Folk-Literature*, ed. J. Heinemann and Dov Noy (SH 22; Jerusalem, 1971), pp. 48–79.

20 See J. Priest, 'Testament of Moses', *The Old Testament Pseudepigrapha*, vol. 1, pp. 919–34; and the critical studies published in G. W. E. Nickelsburg (ed.), *Studies on the Testament of Moses: Seminar Papers* (SCS 4; Cambridge, Mass., 1973).

21 K. Berger, in a detailed and well-researched article, rightly draws attention to numerous texts (many of which postdate Jude) that contain traditions parallel to Jude 9 and 4Q'Amramᵇ. He concludes that the tradition 'über den Engelstreit' has a long and complex development. 'Ihr ältestes Dokument ist 4Q Amrᵇ. In Judas (und in dem im ganzen ursprünglicheren Palaia-Bericht) hatte sie bereits eine formgeschichtlich sekundäre Verwendung gefunden. Die späteren Zeugnisse sind kaum literarisch abhängig, sondern dokumentieren, dass es sich hier um eine relativ feste Tradition gehandelt hat' (p. 18). Berger, 'Der Streit des guten and des bösen Engels um die Seele: Beobachtungen zu 4Q Amrᵇ und Judas 9', *JSJ* 4 (1973), 1–18.

22 Bauckham in *Jude, 2 Peter*, p. 67.

23 Bauckham in *Jude, 2 Peter*, p. 67.

24 Translation by H. C. Kee in *The Old Testament Pseudepigrapha*, vol. 1, p. 828.

25 Bauckham in *Jude, 2 Peter*, p. 67.

26 For the citations extant in Greek, see A.-M. Denis, *Fragmenta pseudepigraphorum quae supersunt Graeca* (PVTG 3; Leiden, 1970), pp. 63–7.

27 The Latin text: 'Adversarii hujus contemplationis praescribunt

praesenti epistolae et Moyseos Assumptioni propter eum locum ubi significatur verbum Archangeli de corpore Moyseos ad diabolum factum.' This text is taken from Charles, *The Assumption of Moses* (London, 1897), p. 108.

28 These lists are conveniently collected by A.-M. Denis, *Introduction aux pseudépigraphes Grecs d'Ancien Testament* (SVTP 1; Leiden, 1970), pp. xiv–xv. For the texts see: J.-P. Migne, 'Nicephori confessoris aliquot canones', *Patrologiae Graecae* 100 (1865), 852–64; and T. Zahn, 'Die sogenannte Synopsis des Athanasius', *Geschichte des Neutestamentlichen Kanons* (Erlangen, Leipzig, 1890), vol. 2, first half, pp. 302–18.

29 Charles, *The Assumption of Moses*, p. xlvi. Charles argued that these two separate works were 'subsequently put together and edited in one' (p. xlvi). If so, what has been lost, how different were they originally, and what alterations were made by the editor?

30 M. R. James was incorrect to attribute it to Jubilees; see *The Testament of Abraham* (T&S 2.2; Cambridge, 1892), esp. p. 17: 'The book is of course the "Lepto genesis" = Book of Jubilees = *Diathēkē Mōuseōs*' (transliteration is mine).

31 This work was cited by Gelasius Cyzicenus (fl. 475) in *Hist. Eccl.* 2.17.18; for the Greek, see Denis, *Fragmenta*, p. 65. Traditions about Moses were varied; Philo of Byblos, according to Helladius, stated that 'Moses is called Alpha (*alpha*), because his body was afflicted with leprosy (*alphois*).' See the text and translation by H. W. Attridge and R. A. Oden, Jr., *Philo of Byblos: The Phoenician History. Introduction, Critical Text, Translation, Notes* (CBQ Monograph Series 9; Washington, D.C., 1981) pp. 100–1. See the general discussion by J. G. Gager, *Moses in Greco-Roman Paganism* (SBLMS 16; New York, 1972).

32 The Latin: 'Et primo quidem in Genesi serpens Evam seduxisse describitur, de quo in Adscensione Mosis, cujus libelli meminit in epistola sua apostolus Judas, Michael archangelus cum diabolo disputans de corpore Mosis ait, a diabolo inspiratum serpentum causam exstitisse praevaricationis Adae et Evae.' The Latin is taken from Charles, *Assumption*, p. 108.

33 I have taken the Greek from James, *The Testament of Abraham*, p. 17.

34 Translated by M. A. Knibb in *The Old Testament Pseudepigrapha*, vol. 2, in press.

35 Translated by Robert Wright in *The Old Testament Pseudepigrapha*, vol. 2, in press.

36 R. T. Lutz and A. Pietersma in *The Old Testament Pseudepigrapha*, (vol. 2, in press) correctly conclude that the author of 2 Timothy knew the *tradition* about Jannes and Jambres, but he imparts 'no information apart from their names'.

37 CD 5.17–19, 'For formerly Moses and Aaron stood (*'md*) by the Prince of Lights (*śr h'wrym*), but Belial (*bly'l*) in his licentiousness raised up (*wyqm*) Jannes (*yḥnh*) and his brother when Israel was saved the first (time).' Facsimile in S. Zeitlin, *The Zadokite*

Fragments (JQR Monograph Series 1; Philadelphia, 1952).

38 For bibliography see Charlesworth, with Mueller, *The New Testament Apocrypha and Pseudepigrapha: A Guide to Publications with Excurses on Apocalypses* (Metuchen, N.J., London, 1985) *ad loc. cit.* ActsPil 5:1, after mentioning Moses' many signs (*sēmeia polla*) in Egypt, we read: 'And there were there servants of Pharaoh, Jannes and Jambres (*Iannēs kai Iambrēs*); and they also accomplished signs (*sēmeia*), not a few of which Moses had accomplished. And the Egyptians held them, Jannes and Jambres, as gods (*hōs theous*).' Translated from the Greek edition of C. Tischendorf, *Evangelia Apocrypha* (Leipzig, 1853), p. 223.

39 My comments here do not refer to the *shebe'al peh*; for a discussion of the Oral Torah, see Neusner, 'Oral Torah and Oral Tradition: Defining the Problematic', in *Method and Meaning in Ancient Judaism* (BJS 10; Missoula, Montana, 1979), pp. 59–75; 'The Meaning of Torah Shebe'al Peh with Special Reference to Mishnah-Tractates Kelim and Ohalot', in *Formative Judaism: Religious, Historical and Literary Studies*; Third Series: *Torah, Pharisees, and Rabbis* (BJS 46; Chico, California, 1983), pp. 13–33.

40 Three books have just appeared that will clarify our methodological approach to oral traditions and perception of oral psychodynamics. These are: W. H. Kelber, *The Oral and the Written Gospel: The Hermeneutics of Speaking and Writing in the Synoptic Tradition, Mark, Paul, and Q* (Philadelphia, 1983); and W. J. Ong, *Orality and Literacy: The Technologizing of the Word* (New Accents; London, New York, 1982), see esp. pp. 65–8, 156–79; and R. Riesner, *Jesus als Lehrer: Eine Untersuchung zum Ursprung der Evangelien-Überlieferung* (WUNT 2.7; Tübingen, 1981).

41 In an encyclopedic work, *Song of Songs: A New Translation with Introduction and Commentary* (Anchor Bible; Garden City, New York, 1977), M. H. Pope demonstrates that 'the cultic interpretation' is 'best able to account for the erotic imagery' (p. 17, cf. pp. 145–53, 228–9). He writes, 'There is no doubt whatever about the general idea of these poems, which is the same as that treated of in Canticles – the mutual love of the sexes. In monologues and dialogues are described the reciprocal love and longing of the male and female for each other' (p. 57). Pope sees the Song of Songs in the light of the 'funeral feasts celebrated with wine, women, and song' (p. 228).

42 The fragments of 4QWiles are published by J. M. Allegro, *Qumrân Cave 4: I (4Q158–4Q186)*, with the collaboration of A.-A. Anderson (DJD 5; Oxford, 1968), pp. 82–5. J. Strugnell disagrees with some restorations and readings, see his 'Notes en marge du volume V des "Discoveries in the Judaean Desert of Jordan"', *RQ* 26 (1970), 163–276, esp. pp. 263–8.

43 Bauckham, *Jude, 2 Peter*, p. 46.

44 Perhaps the presupposition that better ideas must mean later ideas reflects the anachronistic polemic against a type of Judaism that was perceived to be 'decadent'.

45 For Moule, 'development' means 'something ... like the growth,

Notes to pages 81–2   *172*

from immaturity to maturity, of a single specimen from within itself', *The Origins of Christology* (Cambridge, 1977), p. 2.

Marxsen correctly perceives a *continuity* between Christology before and after Easter, 'the continuity, which reaches all the way back into the time prior to Easter, exists in the fact that Jesus is always the one who is proclaimed – even when he himself appears as the proclaimer' (p. 81). Marxsen, *The Beginnings of Christology, Together with the Lord's Supper as a Christological Problem*, trans. P. J. Achtemeier and L. Nieting, with an introduction by J. Reumann (Philadelphia, 1979). Marxsen also speaks about 'development', and although he does not contrast development with evolution, he stands with Moule on the side of the debate which emphasizes *continuity* and development of ideas vis-à-vis the alteration through mutation of different ideas.

46 As Meeks contended, the 'Pauline Christians believe in one God', and they 'also accord to the crucified and resurrected Messiah, Jesus, some titles and functions that in the Bible and Jewish tradition were attributed only to God', *The First Urban Christians* (New Haven, London, 1983), p. 190.

47 There is much in Bultmann's work that reflects astounding brilliance; other sections are simply initiated by an antipathy to and ignorance of Early Jewish thought. Bultmann was definitely incorrect to *deny* that the earliest Church entitled Jesus 'Lord'. He argued that 'the Kyrios-cult originated on Hellenistic soil' (vol. 1, p. 51). See Bultmann's magisterial *Theology of the New Testament*, trans. K. Grobel (2 vols., New York, 1951, 1955).

48 In the early 70s R. J. Bull and his team of archaeologists excavated a vault that was originally 96 feet long. It had been constructed by Herod as a warehouse for the harbour at Caesarea. This warehouse was 'turned into a Mithraeum in the third century A.D. The walls of this vault had been plastered and were at one time completely covered with elaborate frescoes from the life of Mithra. The ceiling was painted blue. Beside the altar at the end of the vault were three scenes from the life of Mithra' (p. 36). Moreover, a marble medallion was recovered; it depicts scenes honouring Mithra. See the account, with beautiful illustrations and photographs, by Bull in 'Caesarea Maritima – The Search for Herod's City', *BAR* 8 (1982), 24–40.

49 S. Lieberman argues that for the Jews 'the mysteries represented no danger. A Jew had to become an idol worshipper before he could be initiated into the mysteries. In the first centuries C.E. the Jews were so far removed from clear-cut idolatry that there was not the slightest need to argue and to preach against it' (pp. 120–1). Lieberman, *Hellenism in Jewish Palestine* (TSJTSA 18; New York, 1950). D. Sänger in *Antikes Judentum und die Mysterien: Religionsgeschichtliche Untersuchungen zu Joseph und Aseneth* (WUNT 2, series 5; Tübingen, 1980) concludes that his 'wesentlicher Ertrag' is 'dass JosAs weder aufgrund formaler noch auch inhaltlicher Kriterien als Mysterienroman bezeichnet werden darf, ja dass wir

nicht einmal einen den Mysterieninitiationen vergleichbaren Eintrittsritus hier finden' (p. 216). For a recent discussion of the mystery religions see M. J. Vermaseren (ed.) *Die orientalischen Religionen im Römerreich (OrRR)* (EPROER 93; Leiden, 1981).

50 Hengel, *Judaism and Hellenism: Studies in their Encounter in Palestine During the Early Hellenistic Period*, trans. J. Bowden (2 vols., Philadelphia, 1974), vol. 1, p. 202.

51 A heavenly voice was heard proclaiming daily during the life of Ḥanina ben Dosa the following:

> The whole universe is sustained on account of *my son* Hanina; but *my son* Hanina is satisfied with one kab of carob from one Sabbath eve to another.
>
> (bTa'an 24*b*; bBer 17*b*; bḤull 86*a*)

Translation and italics are according to Vermes, *Jesus the Jew: A Historian's Reading of the Gospels* (London, 1973), p. 206.

52 Chrysostom wrote in *Hom. adv. Jud.* (847) that Christians 'go to these places [the synagogues] as though they were sacred shrines. I am not imagining such things. I know them from my own experience.' See the excellent translation in Meeks and R. L. Wilken, *Jews and Christians in Antioch in the First Four Centuries of the Common Era* (SBLBS 13; Missoula, Montana, 1978) the quotation is on p. 90.

53 J. L. Martyn, *History and Theology in the Fourth Gospel* (Nashville, 1979[2]). Also see his *The Gospel of John in Christian History: Essays for Interpreters* (New York, 1978), esp. 'Persecution and Martyrdom' on pp. 55–89.

54 As is well known H. D. Betz argues that Galatians was directed to Gauls, not Jews. Davies replied that it was addressed to Jews and former proselytes. Despite their great differences regarding the audience to which Galatians is directed, it is remarkable that both Betz and Davies speak about a sophisticated and well-educated audience. See Betz's *Galatians: A Commentary on Paul's Letter to the Churches in Galatia* (Hermenia; Philadelphia, 1979), p. 2 and Davies' review of Betz's *Galatians* in *RSR* 7 (1981), 310–18, esp. p. 312.

55 Hengel, *The Son of God: The Origin of Christology and the History of Jewish-Hellenistic Religion*, trans. J. Bowden (Philadelphia, 1976), p. 2. With Moule and Marxsen, Hengel argues for a 'consistent development and completion' of early ideas and concepts. My personal judgment is that these scholars are entirely correct. Hengel develops his perception of earliest Christianity in *Between Jesus and Paul: Studies in the Earliest History of Christianity*, trans. J. Bowden (London, 1983). In chapter 2, entitled 'Christology and New Testament Chronology', Hengel argues astutely that Paul's Christology was 'largely complete' before 48, the time of the so-called apostolic council (p. 39). He raises a most important question: 'Is it not historically more appropriate here to explain the christological development up to the Apostolic Council intrinsically on Jewish presuppositions, which of course are richer and more

varied than the fathers of the history-of-religions school could have supposed?' (p. 35) For one who has thoroughly perused the pre-Christian documents in the Pseudepigrapha the answer can only be an emphatic 'yes'. I would go on to add that the Jewish erudition and sophistication is 'richer and more varied' than New Testament specialists have supposed.

56 Kümmel, *Introduction to the New Testament*, revised edition, trans. H. C. Kee (Nashville, New York, 1973), p. 403. J. A. T. Robinson in *Redating the New Testament* (London, 1976) was surprised to discover how many 'Introductions' argued for a late date for Hebrews; but he also noted 'a detectable swing' to an earlier dating by recent research specialists on Hebrews (pp. 200–1).

57 Kümmel, *Introduction*, p. 403. Hebrews 2:3 does not, as Kümmel argues, indicate a time of 'the second Christian generation'. It simply means that the author did not know Jesus personally. As Robinson states (*Redating*, p. 219) the words 'would suit Barnabas admirably'.

58 One of the merits of J. Swetnam's *Jesus and Isaac: A Study of the Epistle to The Hebrews in the Light of the Aqedah* (AB 94; Rome, 1981) is his wide use of Jewish sources.

59 D. R. Darnell has speculated that Hebrews 3:7–4:13, before its present redactional form, may have been a synagogal sermon given by the author of Hebrews. See Darnell's 'Rebellion, Rest, and the Word of God (An Exegetical Study of Hebrews 3:1–4:13)' Duke University Ph.D., 1973.

60 See the erudite discussion by P. W. van der Horst entitled 'Moses' Throne Vision in Ezekiel the Dramatist', *JSJ* 34 (1983), 21–9.

61 Translation, with emendation by van der Horst in *JSJ* 34 (1983), 23. He has worked from the edition of B. Snell, *Tragicorum graecorum fragmenta I* (Göttingen, 1971), pp. 288–301. For a different interpretation of the dream-vision, see H. Jacobson's *The Exagoge of Ezekiel* (Cambridge, 1983); according to him the dream 'amounts to a prophecy of Moses' future deeds and greatness' (p. 94).

62 See Philo's Allegorical Interpretation 3.79–82, and The Preliminary Studies 98–9. Also, see Josephus' *War* 6.438 and Jewish *Ant* 1.180–1. Neither Philo nor Josephus preserves traditions about Melchisedek that approximate so close to those of Hebrews as the ones in 2 Enoch. Josephus, for example, is content to refer to him as *basileus dikaios*, 'righteous (or good) king'.

63 See chapter 1, 'The Original Ending of 2 Enoch', pp. 23–4, for an excerpt of this ending.

64 D. Flusser, who is unusually gifted linguistically and a revered specialist on ancient texts, concludes – and I concur – that 2 Enoch 'could have been written originally in Hebrew or Aramaic, probably in the 1st century C.E.' (p. 936). Flusser, 'Intertestamental Literature', *The New Encyclopaedia Britannica: Micropaedia* 2 (1973), 931–8. Andersen, who has pioneered a new approach to 2 Enoch, is judiciously cautious about any sweeping conclusions now about 2 Enoch; but he admits the 'text abounds in Semitisms', that the

original may be Hebrew (or Aramaic), and it is not impossible that the original composition is early and Jewish. See Andersen, '2 Enoch', *The Old Testament Pseudepigrapha*, vol. 1, pp. 91–100.

65 Andersen argues, quite wisely, that the story of Melchisedek's birth 'is certainly not an imitation of the account of Jesus' birth found in Matthew and Luke. No Christian could have developed such a blasphemy (and we can imagine a scribe refusing to copy this part); and why should a Jew answer the Christians in this way when a more obvious and more scurrilous explanation of Mary's pregnancy was at hand?' Andersen goes on to point to the importance of the ending of 2 Enoch for Hebrews. Andersen, in *The Old Testament Pseud-epigrapha*, vol. 1, p. 97. A. Caquot also argues for a Jewish substratum to the story of Melchisedek's birth in 2 Enoch; see Caquot, 'La pérennité du sacerdoce', *Paganisme, judaïsme, christianisme: Influences et affrontements dans le monde antique. Mélanges offerts à Marcel Simon* (Paris, 1978), pp. 109–16.

66 Moule, *The Birth of the New Testament*, p. 68; also see pp. 68–106, 'The Use of the Jewish Scriptures'. Robinson (*Redating*, p. 215) dates Hebrews 'tentatively c. 67'. G.W. Buchanan, in *To The Hebrews: Translation, Comment and Conclusions* (Anchor Bible; Garden City, N.Y., 1972), places Hebrews 1–12 in Jerusalem 'and before the destruction of the temple (A.D. 70)' (p. 263). These scholars do not see the significance of the Pseudepigrapha for corroborating their position. J.K. Watson, however, perceives the importance of 2 Enoch's account of the birth of Melchisedek for understanding Hebrews, which he dates before the burning of the Temple. See Watson, 'Melkisédec et le fils de Dieu', *Cahiers du Cercle Ernest-Renan* 124 (1982), 49–60.

67 Kümmel, *Introduction*, p. 414.

68 Kümmel, *Introduction*, p. 412.

69 See my discussions in *The Pseudepigrapha and Modern Research with a Supplement, ad loc. cit.*

70 Robinson dates James to 'the second decade of the Christian mission, as the first surviving finished document of the church', *Redating*, p. 139. For bibliography on scholarly publications see Robinson's impressive notes, pp. 118–39.

71 I develop this idea in 'The Apocalypse of John: Its Theology and Impact on Subsequent Apocalypses', *The New Testament Apocrypha and Pseudepigrapha*, in press.

72 One of my doctoral seminars was devoted to this search. A scrutiny of the published arguments for an earlier Jewish layer, or even an earlier Christian layer, and a search for seams in the Semitized Greek of Revelation were fruitless.

73 Robinson (*Redating*, p. 248) seems to date Revelation 'late in 68'; but the force of his argument appears to be that the author experienced the catastrophes in Rome, 68–70, and 'in exile' wrote his visions as he reflected 'upon the terrible events of the latter 60s' (p. 253).

74 G.K. Beale sees some of the similarities between 4 Ezra and Revelation as caused by a *development* of traditions related to

Daniel. See his recent, 'The Problem of the Man from the Sea in IV Ezra 13 and its Relation to the Messianic Concept in John's Apocalypse', *NovT* 25 (1983), 182–8.

75 It is puzzling that the author of Revelation (in contrast to Mk 13:8, Mat 24:7, Lk 21:11) refers to 'thunders' and 'voices' but always (6:12; 8:5; 11:13 [*bis*], 11:19; 16:18 [*bis*]) to *only one* earthquake: 'and there were thunders and voices [not 'peals of thunder' as in NEB] and lightnings [not 'lightning' as in NEB] and an earthquake' (8:5, cf. 11:19). The author of Revelation is probably influenced here by the 'lists' in apocalyptic language. The Apocalypse of Abraham in 30:8 has the nouns in the same order but mentions 'earthquakes': 'The tenth: thunder, voices, and destroying earthquakes' (trans. R. Rubinkiewicz in *The Old Testament Pseudepigrapha*, vol. 1, p. 704).

76 See the bibliography and discussion in Charlesworth, *The Apocrypha and Pseudepigrapha of the New Testament: A Guide to Publications with Excurses on the Apocalypses*, in press. The list of the tribes in Revelation 7:1–8 does not include 'Dan'. A similar tradition is found in Pseudo-Philo, in which the list of 'twelve' tribes does not contain 'Dan' and 'Naphtali' (cf. *LAB* 25:1–6; in 25:9 and 10:3 they are mentioned).

77 Matthew had a definite purpose in shaping and framing his traditions, especially the miracle stories. G. Bornkamm long ago demonstrated Matthew's emphasis on 'faith'. H. J. Held also showed that in Matthew the climax of a miracle story was the importance of *faith*, a full dynamic commitment to Jesus. See G. Bornkamm, G. Barth and H. J. Held, *Tradition and Interpretation in Matthew*, trans. P. Scott (Philadelphia, 1963). While it is clear that Matthew emphasizes the importance of faith, *pistis* in Matthew 8:10 must predate Matthew, since it is also found in the parallel text, Luke 7:9. Matthew here inherits *pistis*, emphasizes it and adds the dimension of judgment in verses 11–12. E. Schweizer correctly states that 'Q contained only the dialogue in verses 8–10' (pp. 212–13), and that 'what matters to Matthew is not the miracle as such, but the correspondence between faith and its fulfillment' (p. 215). Schweizer, *The Good News According to Matthew*, trans. D. E. Green (Atlanta, 1975).

78 Hooker, for example, can tend to ignore 1 Enoch 37–71, because she receives the impression from Milik and others that this section of 1 Enoch is too late for her consideration of 'Son of Man' in Mark and for the historical Jesus. See Hooker, 'Is the Son of Man Problem Really Insoluble?' in *Text and Interpretation: Studies in the New Testament Presented to Matthew Black*, ed. E. Best and R. McL. Wilson (Cambridge, London, New York, 1979), pp. 155–68, see esp. p. 156.

79 Charles, *APOT*, vol. 2, p. 237.

80 At the beginning of 1 Enoch 70 Charles added this note: 'The writer awkwardly makes Enoch describe his own translation. Otherwise this chapter is in keeping with the Parables', *APOT*, vol. 2, p. 235.

81 Fitzmyer, 'Implications of the New Enoch Literature from Qumran', *TS* 38 (1977), 332–45.

82 For bibliographical references to the publications by these scholars see my *The Pseudepigrapha and Modern Research with a Supplement*, pp. 100–3, 278–83; also see the *SNTS* seminar report in *NTS* 25 (1979), 315–23 (and in the Appendix) pp. 106–10. Also, see the recent publication by VanderKam, 'Some Major Issues in the Contemporary Study of 1 Enoch: Reflections on J. T. Milik's *The Books of Enoch: Aramaic Fragments of Qumrân Cave 4*', *Maarav* 3 (1982), 85–97. VanderKam correctly concludes that 1 Enoch 37–71 was written in a Semitic language by a Jew in the first century C.E. (p. 93). M. Black's dating of 1 Enoch 37–71 has shifted markedly. In 1976 he wrote, 'The negative arguments, in particular the silence of Qumran and of versional and patristic tradition seem absolutely decisive for the mediaeval origins and composition of the Book' (p. 6). Black, 'The "Parables" of Enoch (1En 37–71) and the "Son of Man"',' *ExpT* 88 (1976), 5–8. Black *now* argues (correctly) that 'Halévy and Charles were right in proposing a Hebrew *Urschrift* for the Book of the Parables, which I would date to the early Roman period, probably pre-70 A.D.' (p. 28). Black, 'The Composition, Character, and Date of the "Second Vision of Enoch"', in *Text – Wort – Glaube (K. Aland Festschrift)* (AK 50; Berlin, New York, 1980), pp. 19–30. A few years ago Harrington could assess the *status quo* as follows: 'An emerging consensus places them [1En 37–71] in the first-century A.D. Judaism' (p. 152). Harrington, 'Research on the Jewish Pseudepigrapha During the 1970s', *CBQ* 42 (1980), 147–59. Since Harrington's article the agreement has become even much more impressive; the Parables of Enoch (1 En 37–71) were composed in a Semitic language in Palestine by a Jew before 70 C.E. Flusser, in fact argues that 1 Enoch 37–71 was composed in Hebrew by a Palestinian Jew of the first century B.C.E. See Flusser's, *The New Encyclopaedia Britannica: Micropaedia* 2 (1973), 937. M. Casey in *Son of Man: The Interpretation and Influence of Daniel 7* (London, 1979) argues that 1 Enoch 37–71 'should probably be dated c. 100 B.C. – A.D. 70, since its ideas can be made intelligible against the background of this period' (p. 99).

83 Casey, 'The Use of the Term "Son of Man" in the Similitudes of Enoch', *JSJ* 7 (1976), 11–29.

84 Moule, 'Neglected Features in the Problem of "the Son of Man"', in *Neues Testament und Kirche (Festschrift für R. Schnackenburg)*, ed. J. Gnilka (Freiburg, 1974), pp. 413–28.

Conclusion

1 M. Philonenko judiciously argues that Bauer's *Lexicon* must be expanded with copious references to the works in the Pseudepigrapha that are preserved in Greek. See Philonenko, 'La littérature intertestamentaire et le Nouveau Testament', *RevSR* 47 (1973), 270–9, esp. see p. 276. Many terms in the Greek text of

Joseph and Aseneth, which is clearly Jewish and predates 150 C.E., are very important for research in the Greek New Testament.

2 I have tried to demonstrate elsewhere some of the great significance of daily religious prayers, especially the statutory prayers, for research upon Jesus and his early followers. See 'A Prolegomenon to a New Study of the Jewish Background of the Hymns and Prayers in the New Testament', *JJS* 32 (1982), 265–85 (= *Essays in Honour of Yigael Yadin*, eds. Vermes and Neusner (Oxford, 1982), pp. 265–85); 'Jewish Liturgies: Hymns and Prayers (c. 167 B.C.E. – 135 C.E.)', *Early Post-Biblical Judaism and its Modern Interpreters*, eds. R. A. Kraft and G. W. E. Nickelsburg (SBL Centennial Publications Series 2; Chico, California, in press). Also, see the informative bibliographical essay by J. Hennig, 'Liturgie und das Judentum', *ALW* 24 (1982), 113–30.

3 Our comments above have been limited to the Testaments of the Twelve Patriarchs. Many other pseudepigrapha are also important, viz. Pseudo-Phocylides. Now see P. W. van der Horst, 'Pseudo-Phocylides and the New Testament', *ZNW* 69 (1978), 187–202.

4 In a forthcoming book I attempt to show that Jesus' parables are strikingly similar to some in the Pseudepigrapha, especially the eschatological 'parable' in the Apocryphon of Ezekiel 1:1–2:11.

5 These ideas are developed in Charlesworth, 'The Historical Jesus in Light of Writings Contemporaneous with Him', *ANRW* 2.25.1 (1982), pp. 451–76.

6 The delay of the eschaton for the Jews, and the crucifixion of Jesus, the (apparently new) means of salvation argued by Paul, and the delay of the parousia for the Christians created a need to argue (against the critics) that God continues to be righteous. This insight deserves intensive examination.

7 In Early Judaism there was often a preoccupation with theodicy, as illustrated by the tortured language of 4 Ezra. In Early Christianity this concern is noticeably absent, especially in Paul's letters. As Meeks writes, 'Pauline Christianity seems, at least in the extant letters, to offer no general theodicy', *The First Urban Christians*, p. 189. I would argue that theodicy was replaced by Easter proclamation; but see n. 6 above.

8 See the following publications: the introduction to 'Expansions of the "Old Testament"' in *The Old Testament Pseudepigrapha*, vol. 2, in press. Vermes, 'The Qumran Interpretation of Scripture in its Historical Setting', *ALUOS* 6 (1966–8), 85–97. Vermes, 'Bible and Midrash: Early Old Testament Exegesis', *The Cambridge History of the Bible*, ed. P. R. Ackroyd and C. F. Evans (Cambridge, 1970), vol. 1, pp. 199–231. A. Shinan, *The Aqqadah in the Aramaic Targums to the Pentateuch* (2 vols. Jerusalem, 1979) (in modern Hebrew).

9 Fitzmyer emphasizes that one of the areas in which the Dead Sea Scrolls have proved to be significant for New Testament research is in the area of Christology and Christological titles. See Fitzmyer, 'The Dead Sea Scrolls and the New Testament After Thirty Years', *TD* 29 (1981), 351–67.

10 W. Wrede, *Das Messiasgeheimnis in den Evangelien: Zugleich ein Beitrag zum Verständnis des Markusevangeliums* (Göttingen, 1901, repr. 1963). ET: *The Messianic Secret*, trans. J. C. G. Greig (Cambridge, 1971).

11 See Charlesworth, 'The Concept of the Messiah in the Pseudepigrapha', *ANRW* 2.19.1 (1979), pp. 188–218.

12 I recall that J. C. O'Neill in 'The Silence of Jesus' (*NTS* (1969), 153–67) made a point similar to mine, but his was in a different context. I fully agree with O'Neill that the 'Messiah does not [according to some Jewish traditions] admit his identity until God has crowned him' (p. 166). The bracketed words are my own.

13 M.-J. Lagrange, *Le Judaïsme avant Jésus-Christ* (EtB; Paris, 1931), p. 587.

14 Lagrange, *Le Judaïsme avant Jésus-Christ*, p. 588.

15 For brief surveys of the varieties of thought in Early Judaism see my 'Literature in Early Judaism' and 'Astrology, Astronomy, and Magic'; both are separate, slide-illustrated lectures available in the series entitled *Judaism, 200 B.C. – A.D. 200*, ed. Charlesworth (Evanston, Illinois, 1983).

16 Einstein's words to Max Born in 1949. See A. Pais, *Subtle is the Lord* (Oxford, New York, 1982), p. 467.

17 'Raffiniert ist der Herrgott aber boshaft ist er nicht.' Asked what he had meant by these words Einstein replied, 'Nature hides her secret because of her essential loftiness, but not by means of ruse' ('Die Natur verbirgt ihr Geheimnis durch die Erhabenheit ihres Wesens, aber nicht durch List'). In this certain sense history can be perceived as an aspect of Nature. See Pais, *Subtle is the Lord*, the opening pages.

18 Price, *A Palpable God*, p. 6. My last footnote is a return to the book noted in my first footnote; and so, as in apocalyptic thought, Die Endzeit wird zur Urzeit.

NOTES TO THE APPENDIXES

1976

1 *Untersuchungen zur Entstehungsgeschichte der Testamente der zwölf Patriarchen* (AGAJU 8; Leiden, 1970); *idem, Die Testamente der zwölf Patriarchen* (JSHRZ 3.1; Gütersloh, 1974). For an updated bibliography and *Arbeitsbericht* on the T12P see J.H. Charlesworth, *The Pseudepigrapha and Modern Research with a Supplement* (SBL SCS 7S; Chico, California, 1981), *loc. cit.*

2 *Studien zu den Testamenten der zwölf Patriarchen* (BZNW 36; Berlin, 1969). Articles are by Chr. Burchard, J. Jervell and J. Thomas.

3 *Studies on the Testaments of the Twelve Patriarchs* (SVTP 3; Leiden, 1975). Seven chapters are by M. de Jonge, six by H.J. de Jonge, three by Th. Korteweg and one each by H.W. Hollander and H.E. Gaylord, Jr.

4 The volume appeared two years after the *SNTS* seminar. See M. de Jonge, with H.W. Hollander, H.J. de Jonge and Th. Korteweg, *The Testaments of the Twelve Patriarchs: A Critical Edition of the Greek Text* (PVTG 1.2; Leiden, 1978).

5 In attendance at least one of the three sessions were the following: J. Priest, H.C. Kee, W. Harrelson, M. de Jonge, K.H. Rengstorf, R.A. Kraft, A.B. Kolenkow, G.W.E. Nickelsburg, Jr., P.W. van der Horst, P. Dykers, E.G. Martin, J. Trafton, B. Kanael, R. Price, B. Sandays, S. Robinson, C. Wilson, J.R. Mueller and E. Stuckenbruck.

6 *The Greek Versions of the Testaments of the Twelve Patriarchs*, (Oxford, 1908).

7 *Studies*, p. 64.

8 *The Greek Versions*, pp. xii–xiv.

9 See M.E. Stone, 'The Armenian Version of the Testaments of the Twelve Patriarchs: Selection of Manuscripts', *Sion* 49 (1975), 207–14; *idem*, 'New Evidence for the Armenian Version of the Testaments of the Twelve Patriarchs', *RB* 84 (1977), 94–197; *idem*, *The Armenian Version of the Testament of Joseph* (T&T, Pseudepigrapha Series, 5; Missoula, Montana, 1975). The critical edition has now appeared: Stone (ed. and trans.), *The Armenian Version of IV Ezra* (University of Pennsylvania Armenian Texts and Studies 1; Missoula, Montana, 1979). Cf. M. de Jonge, 'The Greek Testaments

of the Twelve Patriarchs and the Armenian Version', *Studies*, pp. 120–39; and Chr. Burchard, 'Zur armenischen Überlieferung des Testamente der zwölf Patriarchen', *Studien*, pp. 1–29.

10 *Studien*, p. 15.

11 *JBL* 89 (1970), 487.

12 *Studies*, pp. 144–60.

13 *Studies*, pp. 63–86.

14 *Studies*, p. 64.

15 Kee cautions that this statement is not always representative. Often material missing from A is 'explicitly Christian, and indeed, christological'.

16 β is no longer a family, only 'a' remains from Charles' textual studies as a sub-family.

17 Becker perceives three distinct strata in the T12P: an early second-century B.C.E. hellenistic-Jewish *Grundschrift*, hellenistic-Jewish expansions to the core during the first centuries B.C.E. and C.E., and a Christian redaction. His method and suggestions are published in his *Untersuchungen* and demonstrated in the reconstruction of the Greek text underlying his translation.

18 The Greek is from M. de Jonge's *Testamenta XII Patriarcharum*, (PVTG 1; Leiden 1972). English translations of the T12P are taken from H. C. Kee's contribution to *The Old Testament Pseudepigrapha*.

19 Kee asks, 'Why was the original writer or compiler *more* inconsistent?'

20 During the discussion I drew attention to the interesting parallels between TIss 2:3 ('For he perceived that she wanted to lie with Jacob for the sake of children and not merely for sexual gratification. For on the morrow also she again gave up Jacob.') and the History of the Rechabites ('Neither are there among us any who take wives for themselves except until they produce two children [ἕως οὗ ποιήσωσιν δύο τέκνα], and after they have produced two children they separate from each other and continue in chastity [ἐν ἁγνείᾳ ...]').

21 ΑΠΛΟΤΗΣ: *Eine begriffsgeschichtliche Studie zum jüdisch-christlichen Griechisch* (Theophaneia 19; Bonn, 1968). M. de Jonge stated that Amstutz correctly emphasizes the unifying nature of paraenesis in the T12P.

22 Kee responds by arguing that 'there is no objective reason for excluding the possibility of redactions'.

23 Kee claims that the only clear instance where removal of a phrase affects the whole context is in TJos 19:8. Nothing essential depends on the presence in T12P of the brief christological phrases. Each tribe's disobedience and subsequent judgment remains fixed in the text after the interpolations are removed.

24 See M. de Jonge, 'Testament Issachar als "Typisches" Testament', *Studies*, pp. 291–316.

25 Cf. G. W. E. Nickelsburg, Jr., *Studies on the Testament of Joseph* (SCS 5; Missoula, Montana, 1975).

26 The language is mine not Nickelsburg's. The question has concerned

me since we discussued it in a Duke graduate seminar in 1974. Nevertheless, I am indebted to Nickelsburg's insights.

27 *Ten Years of Discovery in the Wilderness of Judaea*, trans. J. Strugnell (SBT 26; London 1959), p. 34. The French original appeared in 1957.

28 M. de Jonge has pursued his research and developed his position in an admirable fashion; yet I am impressed by the fact that Naphtali is not a significant figure in the Pentateuch and that in Genesis 49 he is no more blest than Zebulun, Dan, Asher and Benjamin and far less than Judah and Joseph. In Genesis 49 Naphtali is certainly presented a little more favourably than Issachar and Gad, and far more approvingly than Reuben, Simeon and Levi. It is not inconceivable that a Jewish author chose to dedicate a testament to Naphtali; however, is it probable? We must observe, however, that the author of a pseudepigraphon is often focusing upon a self-contained passage and composing a 'midrash' upon it.

29 Kee published his paper in *NTS*, hence the account above is greatly abbreviated. See Kee, 'The Ethical Dimensions of the Testaments of the XII as a Clue to Provenance', *NTS* 24 (1978), 259–70.

30 *Wisdom in Israel*, trans. J. Martin (Nashville, 1972), esp. see pp. 263–83.

31 Professor Rengstorf rejected the claim that ἁπλότης in the T12P is influenced by Stoicism; he denied that there is any Stoic influence in the T12P. M. de Jonge emphasized that in hellenistic-Jewish paraenetic literature as well as in early Christian documents notions derived from or influenced by the ethics found in hellenistic philosophical writings occupied a prominent place.

32 See J. H. Charlesworth, 'A Critical Comparison of the Dualism in 1QS 3:13–4:26 and the "Dualism" Contained in the Gospel of John', *John and Qumran* (London, 1972), pp. 76–106.

33 M. Hengel has drawn attention to affinities between Stoicism and several types of thought in late Judaism. *Judaism and Hellenism*, trans. J. Bowden (2 vols., Philadelphia, 1974). I note, however, that Hengel does not mention possible influences from Stoicism upon Qumran thought. He does, however, seek to show the influence of hellenistic philosophy on apocalypticism.

34 See de Jonge's arguments in *The Testaments of the Twelve Patriarchs* (Assen, 1953, repr. 1975), pp. 123–4, and in *Ned. Theol. Tijdschrift* 21 (1966/67), 267–76.

35 'Problèmes de la littérature hénochique à la lumière des fragments araméens de Qumrân', *HTR* 64 (1971), 333–78, esp. see p. 345.

36 I am indebted to de Jonge and Kee, who read this report and helped me correct it.

37 The title was 'The Christianity of the Pseudepigrapha'.

38 The members of the seminar admitted that they could think of Christian ethical lists, especially in the second century C.E., that were not peculiarly 'Christian'. This confession raises a virtually unanswerable question: 'then how do we know they are Christian?'.

It is sobering to observe that James 5:10–11, 17 contains a paraenesis that points not to Jesus as the pious man but to the OT prophets.

39 J.T. Milik with M. Black, *The Books of Enoch: Aramaic Fragments of Qumran Cave 4* (Oxford, 1976).

1977

1 The first session was in August 1976 at Duke University. See the preceding pages. I wish to express my appreciation to Andersen, Isaac, Knibb and Nickelsburg for correcting the present report and helping me accurately to summarize their own arguments.

2 Many of these Ethiopic manuscripts are recent copies; but some may be very old. As chairman I began the sessions with an appeal for a refinement in our nomenclature. 1 Enoch should not be used indiscriminately to represent both Ethiopic Enoch and the Qumranic Aramaic fragments. Otherwise, significant variants and the omission of 37–71, the Parables of Enoch, among the Aramaic fragments are either ignored or articulated in imprecise, potentially confusing terms. 1 (Ethiopic) Enoch should denote the full book of 1 Enoch as extant in Ethiopic manuscripts, with a recognition of the important variants therein. Aramaic Enoch should refer to the Qumranic fragments. By analogy reference can then be made to the Greek, Coptic and Syriac texts, that is 1 (Greek) Enoch, etc. 1 Enoch, without these parentheses, should refer to the conjectured original document (not necessarily the *Urtext*). These terms should help clarify discussions about the traditions embodied in 1 Enoch in distinction to the later 2 (Slavonic) Enoch and the much later 3 (Hebrew) Enoch.

3 This manuscript was microfilmed by E. Hammerschmidt in 1968 in the Church of Holy Gabriel on the island of Kebran in Lake Tana. Cf. E. Hammerschmidt, *Äthiopische Handschriften vom TānāSee I: Reisebericht und Beschreibung der Handschriften in dem Kloster des Heiligen Gabriel auf der Inseln Kebrän* (Wiesbaden, 1973). Knibb has subsequently informed me that he has used this manuscript in his edition of Ethiopic Enoch which is to be published by the Clarendon Press in 1978; and that he has included in an appendix a list of all significant, previously unknown, variants attested by this manuscript. Now see, M. A. Knibb, with E. Ullendorff, *The Ethiopic Book of Enoch: A New Edition in the Light of the Aramaic Dead Sea Fragments* (2 vols., Oxford, 1978).

4 EMML represents the Ethiopian Manuscript Microfilm Library which is catalogued by W. M. Macomber and published by the Monastic Manuscript Microfilm Library of St John's Abbey and University in Collegeville, Minnesota.

5 J. H. Charlesworth, E. Isaac, V. MacDermott, Chr. Burchard, Th. Korteweg, H.-W. Kuhn, R. Kearns, I. A. Moir, A. Böhlig, J. P. Heil, L. Hartman, F. I. Andersen, A. B. Kolenkow, B. Schaller, G. Nickelsburg, H. P. Kingdon, G. W. MacRae, M. A. Knibb, D. R. Catchpole, M. de Jonge, H. Lichtenberger, R. Maddox, P. W.

van der Horst, F. van Menxel, N. Walter, A.R.C. Leaney, G. Davenport, A.-M. Denis, and S. Agourides.

6 These and other observations are now found in Nickelsburg's review of Milik's *Books of Enoch* in *CBQ* 40 (1978), 411–18.

7 Andersen and I wish to express our deep appreciation to the Library of the Academy of Sciences of the USSR in Leningrad for supplying microfilms of these manuscripts. Our attention was drawn to these manuscripts by N. A. Meshchersky; see his publications listed in my *The Pseudepigrapha and Modern Research with a Supplement*, pp. 103–6.

8 *Le livre des secrets d'Hénoch: Texte slave et traduction française* (Textes publiés par l'institut d'études slaves 4; Paris, 1952; reprinted 1976).

9 Andersen knows of the arguments along similar lines by S. Pines in 'Eschatology and the Concept of Time in the Slavonic Book of Enoch', *Types of Redemption: Contributions to the Theme of the Study-Conference Held at Jerusalem, 14th to 19th July 1968*, eds. R.J.Z. Werblowsky and C.J. Bleeker (Sup *Numen* 18; Leiden, 1970), pp. 72–87 (esp. see p. 72, note 1).

10 *Qumran Texts* (Moscow, 1971), p. 297 (in Russian).

1978

1 In attendance were J.H. Charlesworth, G. Nickelsburg, M.A. Knibb, D.R. Catchpole, M. de Jonge, L. Hartman, H. Lichtenberger, R. Maddox, I.A. Moir, P.W. van der Horst, F. van Menxel, N. Walter, A.R.C. Leaney, G.L. Davenport, E. Isaac, S. Benetreau and A.-M. Denis.

2 Other scholars, not necessarily specialists on 1 (Ethiopic) Enoch, are preparing or have recently published translations of this document: E. Hammershaimb into Danish, Rau into German, S. Agourides into modern Greek, A. Caquot into French, T. Muraoka into Japanese, and F. Carriente into Spanish. See my 'Translating the Apocrypha and Pseudepigrapha: A Report of International Projects', *BIOSCS* 10 (1977), 11–21; 'New Developments in the Study of the *Ecrits Intertestamentaires*', *BIOSCS* 11 (1978), 14–18; and 'A History of Pseudepigrapha Research: The Re-Emerging Importance of the Pseudepigrapha', *ANRW* 2.19.1 (1979), pp. 54–88.

3 M. Black (ed.), *Apocalypsis Henochi Graece* (PVTG 3; Leiden, 1970).

4 See *NTS* 25 (1979), 324–44.

5 'St Luke's Gospel and the Last Chapters of 1 Enoch', *NTS* 13 (1966), 1–13.

6 See *NTS* 25 (1979), 345–59. Also see C.L. Mearns, 'Dating the Similitudes of Enoch', *NTS* 25 (1979), 360–9. Mearns suggests that the Parables antedate 70 and may have been composed in the late 40s.

7 'In conclusion it is around the year A.D. 270 or shortly afterwards that I would place the composition of the Book of Parables.' Milik,

Books of Enoch, p. 96.

8 Knibb suggested later (see *NTS* 25 (1979), 359 n. 47) that the Parables of Enoch and the Gospel of John may be contemporaneous.

9 'The "Parables" of Enoch (1 En 37–71) and the "Son of Man"'', *ExpT* 88 (1976), 5–8.

10 'The Parables of Enoch – Origin and Date', *ExpT* 89 (1978), 118–19.

11 Black (correctly) argues that the Parables are Semitic and predate 70 (see my discussion in chapter 3, especially n. 82).

12 Translation by R. H. Charles, *The Book of Enoch* (Oxford, 1912), p. 110.

13 'Thus the date of the Parables could not have been earlier than 94 B.C. or later than 64 B.C.' Charles, *The Book of Enoch*, p. liv.

1979

1 Scholars attending at least one of the sessions in 1979 were the following: D. R. Catchpole, J. H. Charlesworth, J. M. Court, W. V. Crockett, A. D. Edwards, T. F. Glasson, D. Y. Hadidian, L. Hartman, J. P. Heil, M. Hooker, W. Horbury, M. de Jonge, H. P. Kingdon, M. A. Knibb, K. H. Kuhn, R. Leivestad, L. Leloir, C. L. Mearns, A. P. O'Hagan, J. C. O'Neill, R. Pesch, R. Rubinkiewicz, B. Schaller, N. Walter, B. M. Metzger, G. A. Wells, and E. P. Sanders.

2 N. A. Dahl, 'The Messiahship of Jesus in Paul', in *The Crucified Messiah and Other Essays* (Minneapolis, Minnesota, 1974), p. 40.

3 See my comments in the 'Conclusion' to the present book, pp. 91–3.

4 See 1 Cor 15:3 ὅτι χριστὸς ἀπέθανεν ὑπὲρ τῶν ἁμαρτιῶν ἡμῶν κατὰ τὰς γραφάς.

5 Attempting to summarize the presentations and discussions in these seminars brings home how redactional is my present writing, and how the thoughts of others must be expressed in what in the last analysis is really one's own use of language. Sketchy notes aid a failing memory; and there is a connection between what I am attempting to do and what the earliest Christian authors were struggling to achieve, although the traditions here are not supported by a community and are relatively insignificant (the christological discussion is not evolving out of soteriology).

6 Dahl confronts this question and answers 'yes'. 'That the title Messiah was inextricably bound up with the name of Jesus can only be explained by presupposing that Jesus was actually crucified as the Messiah. Otherwise one falls into great difficulties and cannot make historically understandable the title's Christian meaning and its wide use as another name of Jesus' (*The Crucified Messiah and Other Essays*, p. 24).

7 I have taken the Greek from L. H. Feldman, *Josephus: Jewish Antiquities* (LCL; London, Cambridge, Mass., 1965), p. 440. Feldman (p. 440, n. *b*) points out that γόης 'refers' to a sorcerer or a wizard (later a juggler or a cheat) in classical Greek literature'.

He also points out that in 'Philo, *Spec. Leg.* i. 315, the term is used in the sense of false prophet and is the very antithesis of προφήτης'.

Also among the imposters (οἱ δὲ γόητες *Ant* 20.167) is a man from Egypt (τις ἐξ Αἰγύπτου, *Ant* 20.169) whom Josephus reports claimed that he was a προφήτης (*Ant* 20.169).

8 Cf. Feldman, *Josephus*, p. 50.

9 D. J. Harrington (text) and J. Cadeaux (trans.), *Pseudo-Philon: Les Antiquités Bibliques* (2 vols., Sources Chrétiennes 229 and 230; Paris, 1976), vol. 1, p. 336. Italics by Harrington.

10 Harrington, *Pseudo-Philon*, vol. 1, p. 364; italics by Harrington.

11 Harrington, *Pseudo-Philon*, vol. 1, p. 366.

12 Translated by Isaac in *The Old Testament Pseudepigrapha*, vol. 1, p. 36.

13 Translated by Isaac in *The Old Testament Pseudepigrapha*, vol. 1, p. 37.

14 For the Syriac see R. J. Bidawid (ed.), '4 Esdras', in *The Old Testament in Syriac* (Leiden, 1973), Part IV, fascicle 3.

15 See B. Violet (ed.), *Die Esra-Apokalypse (IV Esra): Die Überlieferung* (GCS 18; Leipzig, 1910), p. 356.

16 Translated by A. F. J. Klijn in *The Old Testament Pseudepigrapha*, vol. 1, p. 633. All translations of 2 Baruch are by Klijn.

17 See M. de Jonge, 'The Role of Intermediaries in God's Final Intervention in the Future According to the Qumran Scrolls', in *Studies on the Jewish Background of the New Testament*, ed. O. Michel, *et al.* (Assen, 1969), pp. 44–63, see esp. pp. 50–1.

18 See Charlesworth, 'The Concept of the Messiah in the Pseudepigrapha', *ANRW* 2.19.1 (1979), pp. 188–218.

1980

1 F. C. Grant, 'Modern Study of the Jewish Liturgy', *ZAW* 65 (1953), 59–77; the quotation is on p. 60.

1981

1 In attendance for most of the discussions were the following scholars: M. Scopello, L. Cirillo, A.-M. Denis, T. F. Glasson, H. A. Lombanse, M. E. Boring, W. Popkes, B. M. Metzger, A. Kowalski, R. Hamerton-Kelly, A. Geyser, R. Pesch, J. H. Charlesworth and G. MacRae.

2 See my *The Apocrypha and Pseudepigrapha of the New Testament: A Guide to Publications with Excurses on the Apocalypses*, in press.

3 Translated from the Greek; see O. Wahl (ed.), *Apocalypsis Sedrach* (PVTG 4; Leiden, 1977), pp. 38–9.

4 Translated by R. Rubinkiewicz and H. G. Lunt, in *The Old Testament Pseudepigrapha*, vol. 1, p. 693. I have capitalized 'Voice'.

5 Translated from the Syriac; see S. Dedering (ed.), 'Apocalypse of Baruch', *The Old Testament in Syriac*, part IV, fascicle 3, p. 6.

6 Translated from the Greek; see S. P. Brock (ed.), *Testamentum Iobi* (PVTG 2; Leiden, 1967), p. 20.

1982

1 Scholars present for most of the discussions were J. H. Charlesworth, Chr. Burchard, H. C. Kee, A.-M. Denis, M. de Jonge, J. Ashton, R. M. Casey and Barnabas Lindars.

2 Burchard in *The Old Testament Pseudepigrapha*, vol. 2 (in press). I sent a copy of Burchard's typescript to Kee; hence some of Kee's reactions were to Burchard's numerous publications on Joseph and Aseneth (see *The Pseudepigrapha and Modern Research with a Supplement* pp. 137–40, 291–2) and also to his forthcoming contribution in *The Old Testament Pseudepigrapha*.

3 See R. H. Charles, *Eschatology: The Doctrine of a Future Life in Israel, Judaism and Christianity: A Critical History* (Oxford, 1913²; reprinted by Schocken Books in New York, 1963), pp. 304–5.

1983

1 Scholars in attendance were J. H. Charlesworth, A.-M. Denis, R. Murray, C. S. Rodd, L. J. Kreitzer, T. F. Glasson, M. Glasswell, J. L. North, J. Ashton, C. H. Cave, M. Casey, S. Schagen, W. Baker, D. G. Meade, Morton Smith, J. Cahill, B. Dehandschutter, R. J. Bauckham and Chr. Burchard.

2 Translated by Isaac in *The Old Testament Pseudepigrapha*, vol. 1, p. 14.

3 See R. J. Bauckham, 'Excursus: The Background and Source of Jude 9', *Jude, 2 Peter* (WBC 50; Waco, Texas, 1983), pp. 65–76.

4 See the discussion in chapter 3, 'Quintus (Jude and the Death of Moses)', pp. 75–7.

5 The chairman will be living in Tübingen during the 1983 and 1984 academic year, and will be returning to the United States in August 1984.

GLOSSARY

Parts of the preceding chapters were originally plenary addresses for two learned societies. While polishing and expanding them for publication I noted that the non-specialist might be hindered by the necessary scholarly jargon. I have removed, therefore, some technical terms, but to delete all of them would undermine the intent and clarity of my writing. To facilitate the reading of this monograph I have now added a glossary of terms or phrases that may be unfamiliar to the non-specialist. These technical words are explained or defined in the following pages according to the ways in which I have employed them.

I wish to emphasize that in the present work — as in ancient writings themselves — we are dealing not with concepts or terms but with words used in sentences by an individual attempting to communicate with another. This perception was eloquently articulated by J. Barr in *The Semantics of Biblical Language* (Oxford, 1961; esp. see pp. 206–19) and in *Biblical Words for Time* (SBT, first series 33; London, 1969[2]; esp. see pp. 50–67).

Finally, I also wish to clarify that modern 'English' has expanded astronomically; linguists estimate that the number of words now exceeds one million. In *Language of the Specialists: A Communication Guide to Twenty Different Fields* (New York, 1966) M. Pei argues that the average cultured person 'probably uses about 30,000 (words), and may be able to recognize and understand 60,000 more' (p. ix). Educated English-speaking individuals, therefore, understand less than 10% of the words in their own language. The fear that we have become isolated in specialized-language worlds is heightened by the observation that while Pei includes such fields as philosophy, sociology, music, anthropology and psychology, he has no section for biblical studies or even religion.

In the latter fields of research advances have often been made using *termini technici* derived primarily from Latin, Greek, Hebrew, German and French, because of the languages through which we attempt to see the ancients and because of the hundreds of years of 'modern' research on antiquity by specialists in Germany, France and elsewhere. The following insignificant glossary attempts to form a bridge to a world of thought, fascinating and exciting to many, in which some of the best minds have laboured for over 2,000 years. The commitment to clarity in communication demands precision (hence scholarly jargon) and definition (and so the following glossary).

'am ha-aretz	(Hebrew) literally: 'the people of the land'; see chapter 1 and notes 24–31
'ar^ebhîth w^eshah^arîth	(Hebrew) 'evening and morning'
axis mundi	(Latin) denotes the central sacred place on earth: the geographical point at which heaven touches earth
b^enei Israel	(Hebrew) 'sons (or children) of Israel'; the term can denote the nation Israel or parts of it
Birkath hām-Mînîm	(Hebrew) signifies the condemnation of the Minim through the alteration of the twelfth of the Eighteen Benedictions; see chapter 3 and references
bruta facta	(Latin) indicates brute, uninterpreted facts
consensus communis	(Latin) denotes the common mind, judgment, or conclusion of international specialists
deus ex machina	(Latin) describes the attitude or idea that God must and does respond as a machine to human behaviour, especially righteous deeds or prayers
Early Judaism	See chapter 2: 'Nomenclature: New Definitions and Discarded Terms', pp. 59–62
editio princeps	(Latin) 'first edition'
Festschrift	(German) categorizes a publication that honours a distinguished person
Geschichte	(German) primarily 'history', but also 'story'
Grundschrift	(German) designates the supposed manuscript from which another manuscript has been copied or translated, perhaps through one or more other manuscripts
Halakah, Halakoth	(Hebrew) represent the focus of rabbinic literature and life upon daily conduct, or how one should 'walk' (*hālāk*) each day
Heilsgeschichte	(German) signifies the history of salvation; most of the biblical authors – except those who produced the wisdom literature – focused not upon ideas, doctrine, or theology, but upon a recitation of the acts of God in history
hellenistic	See chapter 2: 'Nomenclature: New Definitions and Discarded Terms', pp. 59–62
heresy	See chapter 2: 'Nomenclature: New Definitions and Discarded Terms', pp. 59–62
hoi polloi	(Greek) 'the people', the uneducated or unperceptive people
inter alia	(Latin) 'among other things'
interpolations	See Appendix – 1976, p. 100
intertestamental	See chapter 2: 'Nomenclature: New Definitions and Discarded Terms', pp. 59–62
ipsissima verba Jesu	(Latin) denotes the authentic unadulterated words of Jesus
Jews, Jewish, Judaism	See chapter 2: 'Nomenclature: New Definitions and Discarded Terms', pp. 59–62

Lebenswelt	(German) literally: 'life-world'
logos	(Greek) the divine word or Word (see Jn 1:1–18)
melleᵗhâ	(Syriac) almost always is the only accepted Syriac term for *logos*
Messiah, 'Christos', 'the Anointed One'	See pp. 87–90 andAppendix – 1979, pp. 111–23
Mithraeum	(Latin) a room usually rectangular with benches and an altar; in this place men, especially Roman troops, worshipped Mithra, a god of light (sun) and truth
Môrēh haṣ-Ṣedek	(Hebrew) either 'The Teacher of Righteousness' or better 'The Righteous Teacher'; specifies the unnamed founder of the Jewish community at Qumran that produced the Dead Sea Scrolls
normative	See chapter 2: 'Nomenclature: New Definitions and Discarded Terms', pp. 59–62, and 'Synthesis: No Normative Judaism', pp. 63–5
orthodoxy	See chapter 2: 'Nomenclature: New Definitions and Discarded Terms'
papyri	(Latin) denotes manuscripts composed of soaked, pressed and dried strips of the pith of the plant Cyperus Papyrus usually from the Nile valley
paraenesis	(Greek) ethical admonition
peᵗhghāmâ	(Syriac) 'word', 'saying': in the Odes of Solomon it can denote the Word, i.e. Jesus Christ
primitive Christianity	See chapter 2: 'Nomenclature: New Definitions and Discarded Terms', pp. 59–62
redactions	See Appendix – 1976, pp. 100–1
redivivus	(Latin) specifies the reappearance of something or someone virtually unchanged
rēma	(Greek) 'word', 'saying', 'subject of speech'
sect, sects	This term has often been used in relation to a supposed monolithic Judaism. The noun 'sect' – according to *The Random House Dictionary of the English Language: The Unabridged Edition*, eds. J. Stein and L. Urdang (New York, 1973), p. 1289 – can be used to denote 'a group regarded as heretical or as deviating from a generally accepted religious tradition'. This sense is obviously inappropriate for describing the religious groups, like the Pharisees, in pre-70 Judaism. As argued in chapter 1, I contend we should cease using this word to define phenomena in Early Judaism. Also see chapter 2: 'Nomenclature: New Definitions and Discarded Terms', pp. 59–62
shebe'al peh	(Hebrew) the oral Torah recorded in the Mishnah
Shema	(Hebrew) is the name of the popular Jewish prayer derived from Deuteronomy 6:4 (5) – 'Hear (*sheᵐmaʻ*), O Israel, the Lord our God (is) the only Lord.'
sicarii	(Latin) specifies the 'bandits' who think and aҫt

through the use of the *sica*, 'a dagger'; the Jewish revolutionaries, not to be equated with the Zealots. See D. M. Rhoads, *Israel in Revolution 6–74 C.E.: A Political History Based on the Writings of Josephus* (Philadelphia, 1976), pp. 94–122.

sine qua non   (Latin) literally: 'without which not', denotes something essential

Sitzfleisch   (German) denotes the ability to sit and concentrate for an inordinate amount of time

Sitz im Glauben   (German) signifies that a tradition or document originated or was decisively shaped by the faith or belief of a community

Sitz im Leben   (German) denotes the 'life-situation' or actual conditions out of which a tradition or document has come and has been paradigmatically influenced

Tanach   specifies the 'Old Testament'; it is an acronym created from the Hebrew names of the three divisions in the *Biblia Hebraica: twrh* (Law), *nby'ym* (Prophets), *wctwbym* (and Writings)

teleological   is a term created from two Greek words, *telos* (end) and *logos* (word or discourse); it denotes the idea that history is not only linear but also has a definite end that is determined by God

Tendenz, Tendenzen   (German) these terms are singular and plural nouns that denote the tendency or tendencies characteristic of and often peculiar to a writer or a document

terminus a quo   (Latin) literally: 'the limit from which', specifies the earliest possible date

terminus ad quem   (Latin) literally: 'the limit to which', signifies the latest possible date

termini technici   (Latin) 'technical terms'

terminus technicus   (Latin) 'technical term'

tetragrammaton   (Latin) designates the four (*tetra*) consonants in God's ineffable name in Hebrew (*yhwh*)

Torah   (Hebrew) the Law; see Tanach

Torah shebikhtabh   (Hebrew) the written Torah recorded in the Mishnah

Untertext   (German) is the term used to refer to the text directly beneath or behind a manuscript, i.e. the one from which it derives directly

Urgemeinde   (German) is a term given to the early community of believers, almost all Jews, in Jerusalem before 70 C.E., who accepted as definitive the life and teachings of Jesus

Urtext   (German) denotes the lost and conjectured original manuscript behind one or more manuscripts

Yahweh   (Hebrew) is more of a transliteration than a translation of the four Hebrew consonants often translated 'Lord'; see also tetragrammaton defined above

Zeitgeist   (German) is the term used to convey the spirit or mind of a particular period in time

In this work I have tried to avoid simply listing alternatives, and have wrestled with difficult positions, *'yn hbwyyshn lmd* (Masseket Derek Erez II.7, ed. M. Higger, vol. 1, p. 93), 'A timid person cannot learn.' The source of this quotation is mAbot 2.5, *w^{e}lo' habbayshān lāmēdh*.

SELECT BIBLIOGRAPHY

Guides for Research on the Old Testament Pseudepigrapha and the New Testament

The footnotes to the foregoing discussion draw attention to and evaluate the major introductions to Early Judaism, the relevant texts and translations, and the best contemporary studies. Here in this selected bibliography attention will be drawn to (what I consider) the best bibliographies, the most reliable texts and translations, and the available concordances; finally, further guidance will be provided to the recent and excellent studies. Owing to limited space the bibliography is not complete and tends to favour works in English.

Bibliographies

Recent publications on Early Judaism and the New Testament are reviewed in numerous periodicals, especially *RSR*, and are summarized in *Internationale Zeitschriftenschau für Bibelwissenschaft und Grenzgebiete, Elenchus bibliographicus biblicus* and *NTA*.

For publications on Early Judaism that predate this century study the following three major works:

(1) J. Fürst, *Bibliotheca Judaica: Bibliographisches Handbuch der gesamten Jüdischen Literatur mit Einschluss der Schriften über Juden und Judenthum und einer Geschichte der jüdischen Bibliographie* (3 vols., Leipzig, 1849–63; reprinted by Olms in 1960). The arrangement of publications is not consistent, sometimes the reader must look under editions – so see Fabricius, at other times data is listed under pseudonyms – so under 'Salomo b. David' is the PssSol, OdesSol, WisSol, TSol, Sir, the canonical Solomonic works, and other Solomonic literature.

(2) M. Steinschneider, *Hebräische Bibliographie: Blätter für neuere und ältere Literatur des Judenthums* (4 vols., Berlin, 1858–82; reprinted by Olms in 1972). Again, it is difficult to locate publications within the running commentary.

(3) E. Schürer, *Geschichte des jüdischen Volkes im Zeitalter Jesu Christi* (3 vols., Leipzig, 1901–9$^{3/4}$). The English translation, *A History of the Jewish People in the Time of Jesus Christ*, is from the second edition, and is translated by J. MacPherson in 5 vols. (Edinburgh, 1897–8). The fifth German edition of 1920 is a reprinting of the so-called third and fourth edition.

Guidance to bibliographies has been provided in several works. See especially S. Shunami, *Bibliography of Jewish Bibliographies* (Jerusalem,

1965[2]) and J. A. Fitzmyer, 'Bibliographies', *An Introductory Bibliography for the Study of Scripture*, revised edition (Subsidia Biblica 3; Rome, 1981), pp. 1–9. Shunami's bibliography has a modern bias, but see 'Dead Sea Scrolls' (967, 4547), 'Talmudic and Midrashic Lit.' (975, 4549*a*); L. Finkelstein's bibliography on the Pharisees (2088) should have been listed under 'Sects'.

For modern publications on Early Judaism consult the following five publications:

(1) Schürer's masterpiece, the crowning achievement of the nineteenth century, is now reworked and commonly called the new Schürer. See E. Schürer, *The History of the Jewish People in the Age of Jesus Christ (175 B.C.–A.D. 135): A New English Edition*, eds. G. Vermes, F. Millar, P. Vermes and M. Black (2 vols., Edinburgh, 1973, 1979–).

(2) G. Kisch, *Judaistische Bibliographie: Ein Verzeichnis der in Deutschland und der Schweiz von 1956 bis 1970 erschienenen Dissertationen und Habilitationschriften* (Basel, Stuttgart, 1972), see pp. 45–54.

(3) A helpful list of current publications appears annually or semi-annually in *Index of Articles on Jewish Studies* (Jerusalem, a publication of the Hebrew University through the Magnes Press).

(4) Publications on the Targums, including 'Targum and the New Testament', are listed in B. Grossfeld, *A Bibliography of Targum Literature* (2 vols., New York, 1972, 1977).

(5) J. H. Hospers (ed.), *A Basic Bibliography for the Study of the Semitic Languages* (2 vols., Leiden, 1973–4). See especially in vol. 1: B. Jongeling, 'Qumran, Murabba'at, Masada, etc.', and T. de Bruin, 'Mishnaic and Talmudical Hebrew'.

Old Testament. For bibliographical guides to research on the Old Testament consult *Old Testament Abstracts*, H. H. Rowley (ed.), *Eleven Years of Bible Bibliography: The Book Lists of the Society of Old Testament Study 1945–56* (Indian Hills, Colorado, 1957), G. W. Anderson, *A Decade of Bible Bibliography: The Book Lists of the Society for Old Testament Study 1957–1966* (Oxford, 1967), P. R. Ackroyd, *Bible Bibliography 1967–1973: Old Testament* (Oxford, 1974), and P. É. Langevin, *Bibliographie Biblique* (2 vols., Quebec, 1972, 1978). For a study of the history of critical research read H.-J. Kraus, *Geschichte der historisch-kritischen Erforschung des Alten Testaments* (Neukirchen-Vluyn, 1982[3]). See the publications in D. O. Via's series *Guides to Biblical Scholarship*.

Old Testament Pseudepigrapha. A bibliography of publications from 1960 to 1979 on the Old Testament Pseudepigrapha was published by me in *The Pseudepigrapha and Modern Research with a Supplement* (SCS 7S; Chico, California, 1981). For earlier publications and also bibliographical information on other Jewish writings, including Philo and Josephus, see G. Delling's valuable *Bibliographie zur jüdisch-hellenistischen und intertestamentarischen Literatur 1900–1970* (TU 106.2; Berlin, 1975).

Old Testament Apocrypha. See the works cited in Langevin's *Bibliographie Biblique*, and S. P. Brock, C. T. Fritsch and S. Jellicoe, *A Classified Bibliography of the Septuagint* (ALGHJ 6; Leiden, 1973).

Dead Sea Scrolls. For publications on the Dead Sea Scrolls see the bibliographies published by Ch. Burchard, J. A. Fitzmyer, A. M. Habermann, B. Jongeling, W. S. LaSor, J. Sanders and M. Yizhar. For bibliographical information on the publications on the Qumran Scrolls themselves see J. A. Fitzmyer, *The Dead Sea Scrolls: Major Publications and Tools for Study* (Sources for Biblical Study 8; Missoula, Montana, 1975).

Philo and Josephus. For works on Philo and Josephus, besides Delling's *Bibliographie*, consult L. H. Feldman, *Studies in Judaica: Scholarship on Philo and Josephus (1937–1962)* (New York, 1963).

For publications on Philo see H. L. Goodhart and E. R. Goodenough, *The Politics of Philo Judaeus* (New Haven, 1938; this work contains a comprehensive bibliography on Philo up to 1937/8), J. Allenbach, *et al.* (eds.), *Biblia Patristica: Supplément, Philon d'Alexandrie* (Centre d'Analyse et Documentation Patristiques; Paris, 1982), E. Hilgert, 'Bibliographia Philoniana 1935–1975', *ANRW* 2.21 (in press), and P. Borgen, 'Philo of Alexandria: A Critical and Synthetical Survey of Research Since World War II', *ANRW* 2.21 (in press).

For recent works on Josephus see H. Schreckenberg, *Bibliographie zu Flavius Josephus (1470–1968)* (ALGHJ 1; Leiden, 1968), and Schreckenberg, *Bibliographie zu Flavius Josephus: Supplementband mit Gesamtregister* (ALGHJ 14; Leiden, 1979). Also see O. Betz, K. Haacker and M. Hengel (eds.), *Josephus-Studien: Untersuchungen zu Josephus, dem antiken Judentum und dem Neuen Testament (O. Michel zum 70. Geburtstag gewidmet)* (Göttingen, 1974), and L. H. Feldman, *Josephus and Modern Scholarship (1937–1980)*, ed. W. Haase (Berlin, 1984). Major works on Josephus are cited in G. Vermes, *et al.* (eds.), *The History of the Jewish People*, pp. 61–3.

New Testament. There are numerous reliable bibliographical guides to publications on the documents in the New Testament. An especially good one, with sections on Early Judaism, is Fitzmyer's *An Introductory Bibliography for the Study of Scripture*. Also see *NTA*, Langevin, *Bibliographie Biblique*, and the publications in Via's series *Guides to Biblical Scholarship*. For an introduction to the history of New Testament research see the critical introductions, especially W. G. Kümmel's *Einleitung in das Neue Testament* (Heidelberg, 1978[19]; ET of 17th edition: Nashville, 1975), and his *Das Neue Testament: Geschichte der Erforschung seiner Probleme* (Freiburg, 1970[2], ET: Nashville, 1972).

Mishnah and Tosephta. See the bibliographies cited at the beginning of this selected bibliography, the citations in *Kirjath Sepher*, and the relevant sections of *EncyJud*; for older works see the sections of *JE*, and the bibliographical notes in G. Vermes, *et al.* (eds.), *The History of the Jewish People*, pp. 68–9, 80–90. Finally see Shunami's *Bibliography of Jewish Bibliographies*.

Texts and Translations
Old Testament.
> *Text.* K. Elliger, W. Rudolph *et al.* (eds.), *Biblia Hebraica Stuttgartensia* (Stuttgart, 1967/77).
> *Translation.* RSV.

Old Testament Pseudepigrapha.
> *Text.* No collection available, see the editions cited in the *Pseudepigrapha and Modern Research with a Supplement* (esp. see the editions in SBL T&T, Pseudepigrapha Series and in PVTG).
> *Translation.* J. H. Charlesworth (ed.), *The Old Testament Pseudepigrapha* (2 vols., Garden City, New York, 1983–5).

W. G. Kümmel (ed.), *Jüdische Schriften aus hellenistisch-römischer Zeit* (Gütersloh, 1973–).

P. Sacchi (ed.), *Apocrifi dell'Antico Testamento* (Classici Delle Religioni; Turin, 1981).

Old Testament Apocrypha.

Text. Peruse the Cambridge and Göttingen editions of the Septuagint. A pocket edition is A. Rahlfs' *Septuaginta* (2 vols., Stuttgart, 1935; reprinted 1965[8], reprinted in one volume by *Biblikē Etaipia*, Athens (n.d.)). Also, it is now necessary to consult and use the non-Greek texts of some of the Apocrypha.

Translation. RSV.

Dead Sea Scrolls.

Text. The *editiones principes* usually appear in the series published by the Clarendon Press in Oxford; it is called Discoveries in the Judaean Desert (of Jordan) and is at present edited by P. Benoit. A student collection (without some major documents), with Massoretic punctuation, is published by E. Lohse, *Die Texte aus Qumran, Hebräisch und Deutsch* (Munich, 1981[3]).

Translation. A. Dupont-Sommer, *Les écrits esséniens découverts près de la Mer Morte* (Bibliothèque Historique; Paris, 1959[2]), ET: *The Essene Writings from Qumran*, trans. G. Vermes (Oxford, 1961: reprinted 1973).

G. Vermes, *The Dead Sea Scrolls in English* (Harmondsworth, 1962, revised 1965, 1968, 1975[2] reprinted 1982).

L. Moraldi, *I. Manoscritti di Qumrân* (Turin, 1971).

Philo.

Text and Translation. LCL.

R. Arnaldez, J. Pouilloux, C. Mondésert (eds.), *Les Oeuvres de Philon d'Alexandrie* (35 vols., Paris, 1961–79).

L. Cohn, *et al.* (eds.), *Philo von Alexandria: Die Werke in Deutscher Übersetzung* (7 vols., Berlin, 1964[2]).

L. Cohn, and P. Wendland (eds.), *Philonis alexandrini opera supersunt* (7 vols. (the *editio maior*), Berlin, 1896–1930; reprinted 1962).

Josephus.

Text and Translation. LCL.

S. A. Naber, *Flavii Josephi Opera Omnia* (6 vols., Leipzig, 1888–96).

B. Niese, *Flavii Ioesphi Opera* (7 vols., Berlin, 1885–95, reprinted 1955).

H. Clementz, *Der Flavius Josephus: Jüdische Altertümer. Übersetzt und mit Einleitung und Anmerkungen versehen* (2 vols., Berlin, Vienna, 1923; reprinted (without date) by Fourier Verlag in Wiesbaden).

Th. Reinach and L. Blum, *Flavius Josèphe: Contre Apion* (Paris, 1930).

Th. Reinach (ed.), *Oeuvres complètes de Flavius Josèphe* (7 vols., Paris, 1900–32).

O. Michel and O. Bauernfeind (eds.), *Flavius Josephus: De Bello Judaico; Der Jüdische Krieg: Griechisch und Deutsch* (4 vols., Munich, 1962[2]–9[2]).

A. Schalit (trans.), *Qadmoniyot ha-Yehudim* (3 vols., Jerusalem,

1955–63). This work contains an introduction to and modern Hebrew translation of *Ant.*

A. D'Andilly and J. A. C. Buchon (trans.), *Flavius Josèphe: Histoire ancienne des Juifs & la guerre des Juifs contre les Romains 66–70 ap. J.-C.; Autobiographie,* with a preface by V. Nikipowetzky (Paris, 1968–73).

New Testament.

Text. K. Aland, *et al.* (eds.), *The Greek New Testament* (New York, London, Edinburgh, Amsterdam, Stuttgart, 1975³).

Translation. RSV.

Mishnah.

Text. Ch. Albeck and H. Yalon (eds.), *ShShShH SDRY MShNH* (6 vols., Jerusalem, 1954–8).

Translation. H. Danby, *The Mishnah* (London, 1933, reprinted 1964).

P. Blackman, *Mishnayoth: Pointed Hebrew Text, Introductions, Translation, Notes, Supplements, Appendix, Indices* (7 vols., London, 1951–6).

P. Fiebig, *Ausgewählte Mischnatraktate in deutscher Übersetzung* (2 vols., Tübingen, 1906–12).

G. Beer and O. Holtzmann (eds.), *Die Mischna: Text, Übersetzung und ausführliche Erklärungen* (Berlin, Giessen 1912–; it is still continuing).

C. del Valle (ed., trans.), *La Misna* (Clásicos para una Biblioteca Contemporánea 6; Madrid, 1981).

Tosephta.

Text. M. S. Zuckermandel, *Tosephta, Based on the Erfurt and Vienna Codices with Parallels and Variants* (Halberstadt, 1881, reprinted in Jerusalem, 1963).

S. Lieberman (ed.), *The Tosefta. According to Codex Vienna, with Variants from Codices Erfurt, Genizah MSS., and Editio Princeps (Venice, 1521)* (4 vols., New York, 1955–73).

Translation. J. Neusner, *The Tosefta* (6 vols., New York, 1977–).

D. W. Windfuhr, G. Lisowsky, K. H. Rengstorf, *et al.* (eds.), *Die Tosefta: Übersetzung und Erklärung* (5 vols., Stuttgart, 1960–7).

K. H. Rengstorf (ed.), *Die Tosefta: Text* (2 vols., Stuttgart, Berlin, 1967, 1983). Only two tractates, Ţoharot and Zeraim, have appeared.

Concordances

Old Testament. S. Mandelkern, *Veteris Testamenti Concordantiae Hebraicae Atque Chaldaicae* (2 vols., Leipzig, 1925–37, reprinted Graz. 1955, reprinted Tel Aviv, 1969).

G. Lisowsky, *Konkordanz zum Hebräischen Alten Testament* (Stuttgart, 1958, the second edition is also dated 1958).

S. E. Loewenstamm (ed.), *Thesaurus of the Language of the Bible: Complete Concordance, Hebrew Bible Dictionary, Hebrew-English Dictionary* (3 vols., Jerusalem, 1957–).

A. Even-Shoshan (ed.), *Qônqôrdanṣeyāh Ḥᵃdhāshāh. ᶫTôrāh Nᵉbhî'îm uKᵉthûbhîm: A New Concordance of the Bible* (4 vols., Jerusalem, 1977–80).

Old Testament Pseudepigrapha.
No collection; see the editions or individual publications (esp. A.-M. Denis, *Concordance Latine du Liber Jubilaeorum sive Parva Genesis* (Informatique et étude de textes, collection dirigée par Paul Tombeur 4; Louvain, 1973). A.-M. Denis has almost completed a concordance to the Greek pseudepigrapha. Consult J. B. Bauer (ed.), *Index Verborum in Libris Pseudepigraphis Usurpatorum*, appended to C. A. Wahl reprint (see next entry).

Old Testament Apocrypha. C. A. Wahl, *Clavis Librorum Veteris Testamenti Apocryphorum Philologica* (Leipzig, 1853, reprinted Graz, 1972).
E. Hatch, H. A. Redpath *et al.* (eds.), *A Concordance to the Septuagint and the Other Greek Versions of the Old Testament (Including the Apocryphal Books)* (Oxford, 1897; reprinted Graz, 1974).
E. C. Dos Santos, *An Expanded Hebrew Index for the Hatch-Redpath Concordance to the Septuagint* (Jerusalem, n.d.).

Dead Sea Scrolls.
K. G. Kuhn *et al.* (eds.), *Kondordanz zu den Qumrantexten* (Göttingen, 1960); see the 'Nachträge zur Konkordanz zu den Qumrantexten', *RQ* 4 (1963/4), 163–234.
A. M. Habermann, *Megilloth Midhbar Yehuda: The Scrolls from the Jordan Desert, with Vocalization, Introduction, Notes and Concordance* (Israel, 1959).
Also see the concordances often appended to some of the critical editions (esp. 11QTemple).

Philo.
G. Mayer (ed.), *Index Philoneus* (Berlin, New York, 1974).
I. Leisegang, *Philonis Alexandrini: Opera Quae Supersunt. Indices ad Philonis Alexandrini Opera* (2 vols., Berlin, 1926, 1930).
R. Marcus, 'An Armenian-Greek Index to Philo's *Quaestiones* and *De Vita Contemplativa*', *JAOS* 53 (1933), 251–82.

Josephus.
K. H. Rengstorf (ed.), *A Complete Concordance to Flavius Josephus* (4 vols., Leiden, 1973–83).
A. Schalit, *Namenwörterbuch zu Flavius Josephus* (Leiden, 1968; a supplement to Rengstorf).
H. St. J. Thackeray and R. Marcus, *A Lexicon to Josephus*, 4 fascicles (Paris, 1930; incomplete).

New Testament.
K. Aland, *Vollständige Konkordanz zum*

Griechischen Neuen Testament (3 vols., Berlin, New York, 1978–83).

W. F. Moulton and A. S. Geden, *A Concordance to the Greek Testament According to the Texts of Westcott and Hort, Tischendorf and the English Revisers* (Edinburgh, 1897, 1978[5]).

R. Morgenthaler, *Statistik des neutestamentlichen Wortschatzes* (Zürich, Frankfurt, 1958; not a concordance, but a significant research tool, if used after studying the text).

Mishnah. Ch. J. Kasowski (or Kassovsky), '*Oṣar leshon ham-Mishnah. Concordantiae Totius Mischnae* (2 vols., Frankfort, 1927; second edition: *Thesaurus Mishnae*, 4 vols., Jerusalem, 1956–60).

Tosephta. Ch. J. Kasowski (or Kassovsky), '*Oṣar leshon hat-Tosephta. Thesaurus Thosephthae: Concordantiae verborum quae in sex Thosephthae ordinibus reperiuntur* (6 vols., Jerusalem, 1932–61).

Studies

The major publications on the ancient texts we have been focusing upon are so numerous that a mere listing of them would fill volumes. Fortunately there are introductions to each collection and current periodicals concentrate on one or more of them. These reference works and reports of research are well known, and most have been discussed throughout the present book, and are abbreviated in the list of abbreviations. They are also easily found by using the bibliographical guides cited at the beginning of this selected bibliography. For further guidance I append these minor notes. Especially helpful are the short and prompt reviews in *RSR, OTA (Old Testament Abstracts)*, the *Book List* of the Society for Old Testament Study, and *NTA*.

Old Testament. See especially the reviews and articles in *RB, JBL, ZAW* and *RB*. Excellent summaries of recent publications appear in *RSR, OTA*, and the *Book List*.

Old Testament Pseudepigrapha. Research is published in many periodicals, especially, *JJS, JTS, JSJ, RQ, JBL, CBQ, NTS*, and *HTR*, and series notably SVTP, SJLA and SCS. See the reviews in *JSJ* and *RSR*. Publications on the Old Testament Pseudepigrapha and the documents themselves have been summarized and assessed in works mentioned in the footnotes to the chapters in this book; note especially the books by Stone, Nickelsburg, Collins, McNamara, Denis, and myself. Finally see the volume on the Old Testament Pseudepigrapha edited by Charlesworth and H. Lichtenberger in the series Wege der Forschung.

Old Testament Apocrypha. See *APOT*, vol. 1; the many introductions, notably B. M. Metzger's *An Introduction to the Apocrypha* (New York, 1957), the relevant fascicles in JSHRZ, the sections of *JBC*, Nickelsburg's introduction (cited frequently above), the volumes on the Apocrypha in the Anchor Bible, and the Dropsie University series, Jewish Apocryphal Literature.

Dead Sea Scrolls. See the helpful summaries of contemporary research published in *RSR, RB, RQ, JSJ* and A. Malamat and H. Reviv, *A Bibliography of the Biblical Period, with Emphasis on Publications in Modern Hebrew*, revised edition (Jerusalem, 1973, in modern Hebrew). Also see K. E. Grözinger, *et al.* (eds.), *Qumran* (Wege der Forschung 410; Darmstadt, 1981). Surveys have been published by Vermes, Fitzmyer, Sanders, Cross, and others (see esp. *DBSup* and *JBC*); there are many good collections of articles, see, for example, M. Delcor (ed.), *Qumrân: Sa piété, sa théologie et son milieu* (Bibliotheca Ephemeridum Theologicarum Lovaniensium 46; Paris, Leuven, 1978).

Philo. Consult, *JSJ, JJS*, the significant studies in *ANRW* 2.21 (in press), and *Studia Philonica*; obviously one must study the classics on Philo, primarily A. P. Wolfson's *Philo: Foundations of Religious Philosophy in Judaism, Christianity, and Islam* (2 vols., Cambridge, Mass., 1948) and E. R. Goodenough's *By Light, Light: The Mystic Gospel of Hellenistic Judaism* (New Haven, 1935).

Josephus. See *JSJ, JJS*, the series ALGHJ, the Michel Festschrift mentioned at the beginning of this selected bibliography (p. 195); H. Schreckenberg, *Rezeptionsgeschichtliche und Textkritische Untersuchungen zu Flavius Josephus* (ALGHJ 10; Leiden, 1977); A. Schalit (ed.), *Zur Josephus-Forschung* (Wege der Forschung 84; Darmstadt, 1973); the numerous publications in *ANRW* 2.21 (in press); T. Rajak, *Josephus: The Historian and His Society* (London, 1983), and *A Symposium: Josephus Flavius – Historian of Eretz-Israel in the Hellenistic-Roman Period*, published *sans* editor (noted) by the University of Haifa and The Center for the Study of Eretz Israel and Its Yishuv (1981).

New Testament. Read the articles in the major periodicals, notably *NTS, ZNW, JBL, NovT, CBQ* and *RB*. Especially helpful are *NTA* and Metzger's series entitled NTTS.

Mishnah. Study the research published in *JSJ, JJS,* Urbach's classic (mentioned in the notes to the chapters above), Neusner's vast publications, and P. Schäfer's *Studien zur Geschichte und Theologie des Rabbinischen Judentums* (AGAJU 15; Leiden, 1978).

Tosephta. See S. Lieberman, *Tosefta Ki-Fshuṭah: A Comprehensive Commentary on the Tosefta* (8 vols., New York, 1955–73; in Hebrew), Neusner's publications and translation, Urbach's classic and T. Kronholm, 'Tosefta, Yom hak-Kippurim and the Art of Publishing Rabbinic Texts', *SEA* 46 (1981), 130–52 (in Swedish); this review article focuses on the Tosephta but also includes the Mishnah.

INDEXES

All Indexes in this book have been prepared by M. J. H. Charlesworth.
References are first to the document itself and then to passages cited from it.

INDEX OF ANCIENT DOCUMENTS

Index of Scriptural Passages

Genesis   25, 170 n. 32
5   78
6   33
30:14−18   96
34:2   11
49:7, 21   97
49   182 n. 28

Exodus
7:11   79
20:17   78
24   127

Leviticus
6:5−8   11

Numbers
26:59   76

Deuteronomy   56
5:21   78
7:6−11   56
34   77
35:6   76

Joshua
7:16−26   54

Judges
11:30−40   25

2 Samuel   25
7:16   126,127

1 Kings   79

Ezra   163 n. 98

Esther   74

Job   25

Psalms
2:2   114
46:5   57
110:1 (LXX 109:1)   71, 112

Ecclesiastes   62
12:14   124

Song of Songs   79, 171 n. 41

Isaiah
5:10   86
24:23   127

Jeremiah
3:16−17   162 n. 85
31:15 (BH)   72
31:15 (RSV)   166 n. 2
35   24
38:15 (LXX)   72

Ezekiel
37   126
48:35   162 n. 85

Daniel   13, 14, 88, 116, 126
7   123, 127, 177 n. 82
7:1   65
12   124

Joel
3   123

Zechariah
3:2   77

Malachi
1:6−8   57

Tobit
1:4   57

Wisdom of Solomon
4:10   84

Sirach   80
25:23   84
36:13   57
44:16   84
44:21   84

1 Baruch   56

Letter of Jeremiah   79

Susanna   79

1 Maccabees   126

2 Maccabees   68

Matthew   48, 81, 175 n. 65
2   73
2:16   72
2:17–18   72, 166 n. 2
5: 33–7   35
8:6–9   88
8:10–12   176 n. 77
16:13   88
22:32   78
24:7   176 n. 75

Mark   80, 81, 92, 107, 119, 125, 126, 171
          n. 40, 176 n. 78
1:1   111
8:27   88
8:29, 34–8   112
12:35–7   112, 113, 114
13:8   176 n. 75
13:32   118
14:22–4   133
14:61   112
15:32   112

Luke   41, 81, 83, 84, 106, 107, 110, 125, 126,
          153 n. 24, 175 n. 65, 184 n. 5
11:21–2   79
11:49   156 n. 41
20:42   71
21:11

John   31, 48, 82, 83, 120, 121, 125, 126, 150
          n. 12, 162 n. 86, 173 n. 53, 182 n. 32,
          185 n. 8
1:1–8   190
1:14   49
5:27   108
6   133, 134
6:35, 48   131
7:53–8:11   70
14:2   35
14:26   156 n. 41

Acts   x, xi, 41, 83, 84, 107, 125, 126, 136,
          164 n. 100

7:53   156 n. 41
17:28   78, 140
24:14   19, 145 n. 20

Romans   23, 91
2:6–16   124
7:7   78

1 Corinthians
9–11, 10:31   134
15:3   185 n. 4
15:33   78

Galatians   x, 173 n. 54

Philippians
2:6–11   120
3:5   54, 163 n. 95

1 Thessalonians   13

2 Timothy   79

Titus
1:12   78, 140

Hebrews   24, 41, 83, 87, 105, 174 nn. 56,
          58
1–12   175 nn. 65, 66
2:3   174 n. 57
3:3   84
3:7–4:13   174 n. 59
5:5–10   84
6:14, 20   84
7:3   85
7:23–8   84
8:1   84
8:4   85
9:8–10   85
10:1–4   85
11:5   78, 84
11:31*b*   79
11:37   78, 84
12:12   84
13:10   85

James   7, 41, 83, 86, 107, 125, 126, 164
          n. 100, 168 n. 16, 175 n. 70
2:23   156 n. 41
5:10–11, 17   183 n. 38

1 Peter   125, 126

2 Peter   41, 166 n. 4, 167 nn. 6, 10, 168
          nn. 12, 14, 15, 169 nn. 16, 19, 22,
          23, 25, 171 n. 43, 187 n. 3

Jude   8, 25, 37, 68, 94, 140, 166 n. 6, 167
          n. 6, 167 nn. 9, 10, 168 nn. 14–16,

169 nn. 22, 23, 25, 170 n. 32, 171
    n. 43
5–7   80
6:12   169 n. 16
9   75, 76, 77, 139, 169 nn. 18, 19, 21, 187
    nn. 3–4
12   169 n. 16
14–15   72–4, 137, 138, 166 n. 4, 168
    nn. 12–13, 169 n. 18

Revelation   14, 33, 48, 83, 87, 121, 126, 127,
    129, 164 n. 100, 175 nn. 71, 72, 74,
    176 n. 75
1   130
1:6   156 n. 41
1:10–11   128
1:10   130
1:12   128
3:1–2   130
4:1   125
5:6   130
6:12   176 n. 75
7:1–8   176 n. 76
8:15   176 n. 75
11:13   176 n. 75
11:19   176 n. 75
14:4   132
16:18   176 n. 75
19:9   125
20:11–15   123

Index of Pseudepigraphal Passages

Old Testament Pseudepigrapha   3, 6, 16, 22,
    28, 40, 63, 86, 94, 103, 106, 143 n. 5,
    145 n. 15, 148 n. 36, 150 n. 14, 156
    nn. 42, 44, 46, 164 n. 102, 166 n. 5,
    169 nn. 20, 24, 170 nn. 34–6, 175 n. 65,
    176 n. 75, 178 n. 8, 181 n. 16, 186 nn.
    12–13, 16, n. 4, 187 n. 2, n. 2

Apocalypse of Abraham   14, 15, 32, 34, 79,
    87, 91
9:1–4   129
30:8   176 n. 75

Testament of Abraham   124, 170 nn. 30, 33
13   68

Apocalypse of Adam   14, 42, 46

Testament of Adam   32, 65, 150 n. 13

Life of Adam and Eve   42, 86, 165 n. 102

Ahiqar   43

Letter of Aristeas   42, 45

Aristeas the Exegete   43, 45

Aristobulus   43

Artapanus   44

2 (Syriac Apocalypse of) Baruch   9, 14, 37,
    42, 53, 55, 56, 58, 87, 91, 108, 116,
    118, 161 n. 83, 186 n. 16, n. 5
10:6–19   120
11:1–7   120
13:1   130
14:8–10   120
15:1   130
16:1   130
17:1   130
29:3–30:1   115
35:1–37:1   115
35:2–5   120
38:1–4   120
39:7   115
40:3   115
48:2–24   120
53:7   10
54:1–22   120
68:6–7   57
70:9   115
72:2–3   115
73:1   115
75:1–8   120
83   123

3 (Greek Apocalypse of) Baruch   14, 42, 105

4 Baruch   42
6:6–10   120
6:12–14   120
9:3–6   120

Cleodemus Malchus   44

Apocalypse of Daniel   14, 32

Demetrius   43

Eldad and Modad   37, 42

Apocalypse of Elijah   14, 37, 42

1 (Ethiopic Apocalypse of) Enoch   4, 8, 9,
    12, 14, 25, 31, 33, 37, 38, 40, 41, 44,
    53, 63, 72, 74, 78, 86, 102, 116, 118,
    127, 138, 140, 152 n. 19, 159 n. 70,
    163 n. 98, 166 nn. 5, 6, 167 nn. 7–9,
    168 nn. 14, 15, 16, 184 nn. 6, 8–9 nn.
    2–3, 5–6, 185 n. 7
1:1–2   65
1:4   167 nn. 7–10
1:9   73, 166 nn. 4–6, 168 nn. 11–13
1:9, 15   137
9:61   2

1 (Ethiopic Apocalypse of) Enoch (cont.)
14:8–25 66
22   124
37–71   18, 88, 89, 90, 94, 103, 108, 109, 123,
       154 n. 33, 176 n. 78, 177 nn. 82–4,
       183 nn. 2–3, 185 nn. 8–13
48:10   114
52:4   114
56:1–36   109
56:5–8   108
56:5–57:3   108
56:7   109
61:1   103
69:9–10   2
70   176 n. 80
70:1–4   84
71:14   18, 88
84:1–6   120
89:62–4   2
89:73–4   56
92   107
92:1   107
92–105   106, 107, 110, 153 n. 24
97:107   103
104:7–13   2
106:10–12   24
106:11   148 n. 37

2 (Slavonic Apocalypse of) Enoch   14, 32, 34,
       53, 63, 85, 87, 103, 105, 110, 150 n.
       14, 152 n. 19, 174 nn. 62–4, 175 nn.
       65–6, 183 n. 2, 184 nn. 8–9
1–22   65
1:6–3:3   65
49:1   35
51:4   57
61:2   35
68, 69–73   23
71:2–28 [A]   24

3 (Hebrew Apocalypse of) Enoch   14, 32, 63,
       65, 84, 150 n. 13, 183 n. 2

Eupolemus   44

Pseudo-Eupolemus   44

Apocryphon of Ezekiel   14, 25, 37, 41
1:1–2:11   178 n. 4

Ezekiel the Tragedian   43, 66, 85, 166 n. 108,
       174 nn. 60, 61

4 Ezra   7, 14, 15, 24, 36, 37, 42, 48, 53, 58,
       87, 91, 117, 127, 141, 161 n. 83, 163 n.
       98, 165 n. 102, 178 n. 7, 180 n. 9, 186
       nn. 14–15
3–14   108
3:20   67
4:27   56
6:26   114

7:26–30   114
7:28   114
7:29   115
7:30   114
11:1–12:3   114
12:31–4   114
12:32   114
13   114, 116, 175 n. 74
13:52   114, 118
14:9   114
14:44–7   2
7:30–140   123
8:20–36   120

Greek Apocalypse of Ezra   14

Questions of Ezra   14, 32

Revelation of Ezra   14, 32

Vision of Ezra   14, 32

Pseudo-Hecataeus   44

Hellenistic Synagogal Prayers   25, 36, 43, 120

Testament of Isaac   32

Ascension of Isaiah   24, 36, 37, 65
5:11–14   84

Martyrdom of Isaiah   36, 42
5:1   78

Ladder of Jacob   32, 34

Prayer of Jacob   37, 43

Testament of Jacob   32

Jannes and Jambres   42, 79, 170 nn. 36, 37,
       171 n. 38

Testament of Job   15, 25, 42, 186 n. 6
3:1–2   130

Joseph and Aseneth   15, 24, 42, 79, 137, 172
       n. 49, 177 n. 1, 187 n. 2
4:7   132
8:5   131
9   131
12:5   47
12:12   47
15:5   131
15:13–17:4   133
16   133
16:14   134
18:11   136
20:5   136
21:4   136

History of Joseph 32

Prayer of Joseph 43

Jubilees 9, 12, 16, 40, 41, 42, 44, 53, 58, 77,
 80, 86, 127, 152 n. 19, 153 n. 23, 155
 nn. 36, 39–41, 159 n. 70, 170 n. 30
1:12 156 n. 41
1:27 156 n. 41
8:19 67
14:6 156 n. 41
16:18 156 n. 41
32:25 156 n. 41

Liber Antiquitatum Biblicarum 77, 114, 116,
 119
10:3 176 n. 76
25:1–6 176 n. 76
25:9 176 n. 76
51:6–7 114
59:3 114

3 Maccabees 7, 15, 16, 43, 45, 79, 80, 86,
 143 n. 3

4 Maccabees 6, 15, 43, 86
2:5 78
7:19 78

Prayer of Manasseh 6, 15, 16, 37, 43, 47

Syriac Menander 25, 32, 86

Apocalypse of Moses 87, 88

Assumption of Moses 75, 76, 139, 169 n. 19,
 170 nn. 27, 29, 32

Testament of Moses 9, 19, 37, 42, 68, 75, 76,
 77, 139, 169 nn. 19, 20
11:6–8 76

Book of Noah 38, 153 n. 23

Pseudo-Orpheus 44

Pseudo-Philo 25, 42, 67, 86, 176 n. 76, 186
 nn. 9–11

Philo the Epic Poet 43

Pseudo-Phocylides 25, 43, 86, 178 n. 3

Fragments of Poetical Works 43

Lives of the Prophets 15, 42

History of the Rechabites 24, 36, 43, 107,
 145 n. 21, 181 n. 20

Apocalypse of Sedrach 14, 32, 186 n. 3
2:2–5 129

Treatise of Shem 14, 24, 41, 107

Sibylline Oracles 7, 14, 24, 36, 41, 110
4:41–2, 184 123
5:104–10 108
5:414–33 57

Odes of Solomon 37, 43, 49, 58, 107, 120,
 190
7:18–19 121
7, 19:4b 122

Psalms of Solomon 19, 43, 44, 58, 68, 119,
 165 n. 102, 166 n. 110
5:3–4 79
17:23, 42 92
17:32–6 57
17:32, 18 114

Testament of Solomon 32, 37, 150 n. 13

Five Apocryphal Syriac Psalms 15, 43

Theodotus 43

Apocalypse of Zephaniah 14, 41, 53
9:1–10, 12:5–10 120

Testaments of the Twelve Patriarchs 4, 12,
 20, 36, 38, 39, 40, 42, 55, 58, 63, 76,
 94, 96, 97, 98, 99, 100, 101, 102, 107,
 116, 151 n. 17, 153 nn. 26, 27, 29, 154
 nn. 30–3, 35, 178 n. 3, 180 nn. 1–4,
 6, 9, 181 nn. 17–18, 21, 23, 182 nn.
 29, 31, 34
Testament of Reuben 182 n. 28
Testament of Simeon 182 n. 28
Testament of Levi 38, 39, 153 n. 23, 182
 n. 28
2:3 153 n. 26
10:1–2 99, 100
10:26, 14:2, 10, 14–15, 16, 14:3–4 100
12:2, 14:4 98
Testament of Judah 182 n. 28
20:1 99
24:5–25:3 153 n. 25
Testament of Issachar 181 n. 24, 182 n.
 28
1 96
1:7a 96
1:14 96
2 96
2:1–3 96
2:2 96
2:3 181 n. 20
3:1–2 96
3:5 96
3–5 96
7:7b 97
Testament of Zebulun 182 n. 28
5–9 95

Testaments of the Twelve Patriarchs (cont.)
  Testament of Naphtali   39, 80, 182 n. 28
  2:1   97
  5:8   154 n. 30
  Testament of Gad   182 n. 28
  Testament of Asher   182 n. 28
  2:8   98
  Testament of Joseph   97, 180 n. 9, 182 n. 28
  19:8   181 n. 23
  30:3   99
  Testament of Benjamin   182 n. 28
  9:4   100
  12:2   76

**Index of Dead Sea Scrolls
(and Qumran Fragments)**

Dead Sea Scrolls (and Qumran Fragments)   x, 8, 12, 13, 25, 27, 28, 33, 37, 38, 39, 41, 44, 45, 46, 54, 55, 57, 63, 71, 84, 89, 92, 117, 121, 147 n. 33, 148 n. 1, 157 nn. 50, 54, 164 n. 101, 166 n. 1, 178 n. 9, 186 n. 17, 190

Cairo Damascus Document   16, 27, 55, 79, 80, 117
  5.17–19   170 n. 37

Enoch (fragments)   59, 73, 102, 152 n. 22, 166 n. 3, 167 nn. 7, 9, 183 n. 39, n. 2

Genesis Apocryphon   79

Hodayoth   120, 121

The Isaiah Commentary   127

Jeremiah   166 n. 1

Jubilees (fragments)   41, 155 n. 36

The Melkisedek Scroll   85, 105

The War Scroll   84, 167 n. 9

Apocryphon of Moses   77

The Rule of the Community   21
  3.13–4.26   33, 151 n. 16, 182 n. 32
  3.13   99
  8.1   151 n. 17

The Rule of the Congregation   20, 117

The Temple Scroll   20, 25, 38, 57, 117

Testament of Levi (1QT Levi ar)   38

Testament of Levi (4QT Levi ar^a)   38, 153 n. 26

Visions of 'Amram or 'Testament'
4Q'Amram^{b–e}   76, 169 n. 21

Wiles of the Wicked Woman   80, 171 n. 42

Index of Rabbinic Passages

Rabbinic Writings   20, 21, 28, 53, 64, 65, 146 n. 25, 149 n. 1, 156 n. 48, 159 nn. 66, 70, 160 n. 75

mAbot   16, 27
  2.5   192

Abot de-Rabbi Nathan
Version A, xli   58

t'Abodah Zarah
III.10   58

bBerakot
17b   173 n. 51

Birkath hām-Mînîm   47, 82, 157 n. 56, 158 n. 57

Eighteen Benedictions   47, 57, 82, 68, 157 n. 56, 158 n. 57

Halakah, Halakoth   21, 64, 65, 68, 84

bHullin
86a   173 n. 51

Masseket Derek Erez
I.14   58
II.7   192

Mekilta de-Rabbi Ishmael   150 n. 13

Mishnah   x, 19, 28, 64, 80, 154 n. 34, 160 n. 75, 162 n. 88, 164 n. 100, 165 n. 107, 171 n. 39, 190

bNedarim
20a   58

Pirke de-Rabbi Eliezer   152 n. 19

bSanhedrin
90b   58

mSanhedrin
1:6   56, 80

bTa'anit
b24b   173 n. 51

Tosephta   64, 146 n. 28, 164 n. 100

tYadayim
2.13   164 n. 100

Index of Other Ancient Passages

Adversus Haereses (Epiphanias) 145 n. 20
29:1 20
29:4 20
29:5 20

Aeneid
(p. 68) x

Apocrypha 28, 71, 118, 148 n. 1, 150 n. 11,
   156 n. 49, 158 n. 61

Apostolic Constitutions
Bk 7, 8 156 n. 46

1 Clement 37

Codex Panopolitanus 73, 166 n. 6

Hermas 37, 42

Hermetica 28, 71

How to Write History (Lucian) x

Jewish Magical Papyri 28

Letters (Pliny the Younger)
9:36 (p. 141) x

Life of Vergil (Suetonius)
22–3 x

Nag Hammadi Codices 28, 45, 46, 71, 157
   n. 50

On the Jews (Polyhistor) 16

Apocalypse of Paul 131

Poetics (Aristotle)
17:5–10 x

Acts of Pilate
5:1 79
5:1 171 n. 38

Preparation for the Gospel (Eusebius)
Book 9 16

De principiis (Origen)
3.2.1 77

Gospel of Thomas 46, 156 n. 49

INDEX OF AUTHORS

Index of 'Authors' Antedating 1800

Apuleius, 79
Aratus, 78
Aristotle, x
Betuleius, 6
Brenz, J., 7
Cephalaeus, 6
Chrysostom, John, 82, 173 n. 52
Cleanthes, 78
Clement of Alexandria, 37, 76, 77
    Stromata, 1.23.153, 1; 6.15.132, 2–3
    76
Didymas the Blind, *In Ep. Judae Enarratio*, 76
Fabricius, J. A., 7, 9
Epimenides, 78
Epiphanius, 20, 37, 145 n. 20
Erasmus, 6
Eusebius, 16, 37, 85
Gamaliel, 157 n. 56
Gelasius Cyzicenus, 76, 170 n. 31
Helladius, 170 n. 31
Hillel, 19, 23, 54, 68, 147 n. 29
Hippolytus, 37
Ignatius, 121
Jason of Cyrene, 77
Johanan ben Zakkai, 54
Josephus, x, 19, 20, 23, 28, 54, 56, 71, 85, 113
    140, 148 n. 1, 163 n. 95, 165 n. 102,
    174 n. 62, 185 n. 7, 186 n. 8, 191
Justin Martyr, 36
Justin of Tiberius, 77
Lactantius, 37
Laurence (Laventus), 151 n. 18
Lucian, x
Lucretius, 66
Luther, M., 6, 7
Mai, A., 7
Marcion, 60, 120
Menander, 78
Nicephoros, 76, 170 n. 28
Opsopoeus, 6
Origen, 37, 77, 105
Paul, x, 10, 23, 41, 47–9, 54, 64, 84, 113,
    124–6, 128, 134, 158 n. 60, 159 n. 66,
    160 n. 74, 163 n. 95, 164 n. 100, 173

n. 55, 178 nn. 6, 7
Philo, x, 20, 28, 54, 71, 85, 137, 148 n. 1, 174
    n. 62, 185 n. 7
Philo of Byblos, 170 n. 31
Pliny the Elder, 79
Pliny the Younger, x
Polyhistor, A., 16, 85
Pseudo-Athanasius, 76, 170 n. 28
Pseudo-Cyprian, 73, 138, 166 n. 6, 167 n. 9
Sabatier, 7
Servanthus, 6
Severus of Antioch, 77
Shammai, 19, 68
Suetonius, x
Valentinus, 121
Vergil, x

Index of Modern Authors

Aalen, S., 106
Abrahams, I., 147 n. 29
Achtemeier, P. J., 172 n. 45
Ackroyd, P. R., 178 n. 8
Adcock, F. E., 162 n. 90
Agourides, S., 15, 62, 183 n. 5, 184 n. 2
Aland, K., 75, 137, 143 n. 3, 169, n.18
Alexander, P. S., 62
Allegro, J. M., 171 n. 42
Amir, J., 161 n. 82
Amstutz, J., 96, 181 n. 21
Amusin, I. D., 105
Andersen, F. I., 23, 62, 85, 89, 103, 104, 105,
    110, 148 n. 36, 150 n. 14, 151 n. 15,
    174 n. 64, 175 n. 65, 183 nn. 1, 5, 184
    nn. 7, 9
Anderson, A.-A., 171 n. 42
Anderson, H., iv, 62
Angelov, D., 150 n. 14
Arai, S., 16
Ashton, J., 187 n. 1
Asting, R., 144 n. 11
Attanasio, S., 157 n. 54
Attridge, H. W., 62, 170 n. 31
Aune, D. E., 120, 121, 122, 163 n. 92
Avi-Yonah, M., 161 n. 81

Baarda, Tj., 62
Baeck, L., 51
Baillet, M., 153 n. 25, 155 n. 36
Baker, W., 187 n. 1
Balentine, S.E., 161 n. 83
Baras, Z., 161 n. 81
Barr, J., 188
Barrett, C.K., 160 n. 77
Barth, G., 176 n. 77
Barthélemy, D., 155 n. 36
Batiffol, P., 132
Bauer, W., 177 n. 1
Bauckham, R.J., 75, 80, 137, 138, 139, 140,
    141, 166 nn. 4, 6, 167 n. 10, 168 nn.
    11, 12, 14, 15, 169 nn. 19, 22, 23, 25,
    171 n. 43, 187 nn. 1, 3
Baumgarten, A.I., 156 n. 46
Beale, G.K., 175 n. 74
Becker, J., 94, 96, 181 n. 17
Benetreau, S., 184 n. 1
Benoit, P., 144 n. 11, 157 n. 51
Berger, K., 169 n. 21
Best, E., 176 n. 78
Betz, H.D., x, 62, 173 n. 54
Bidawid, R.J., 186 n. 14
Billerbeck, P., 31, 49, 149 n. 6, 149 n. 8, 160
    n. 75
Birdsall, N., 122
Black, M., 62, 89, 106, 108, 109, 145 n. 18,
    149 n. 4, 166 n. 3, 176 n. 78, 177 n. 82,
    183 n. 39, 184 n. 3, 185 n. 11
Bleeker, C.J., 184 n. 9
Böhlig, A., 183 n. 5
Bonhoeffer, D., 51
Bonsirven, J., 15
Boring, M.E., 186 n. 1
Borkovsky, V.I., 151 n. 18
Born, Max, 179 n. 16
Bornkamm, G., 176 n. 77
Bousset, W., ix, 31, 149 n. 6, 150 n. 9
Bowden, J., 164 n. 99, 173 nn. 50, 55, 182
    n. 33
Braaten, C.E., 143 n. 8
Brandenburger, E., 133
Brecht, M., 143 n. 3
Breck, A., 164 n. 101
Brock, S.P., 186 n. 6
Brown, R.E., 150 n. 12
Brownlee, W.H., 12
Brox, N., 148 n. 34
Buchanan, G.W., 85, 175 n. 66
Büchler, A., 20, 146 n. 24, 162 n. 91
Bull, R.J., 172 n. 48
Bultmann, R., 11, 14, 31, 81, 82, 149 n. 6,
    150 n. 10, 165 n. 103, 172 n. 47
Burchard, Chr., 62, 95, 132, 133, 134, 135,
    137, 180 nn. 2, 9, 183 n. 5, 187 nn. 1,
    2
Burrows, M., 12
Busse, U., 162 n. 87
Busto Sáiz, J.R., 169 n. 19

Cahill, J., 140, 141, 187 n. 1
Carriente, F., 184 n. 2
Caquot, A., 175 n. 65, 184 n. 2
Casey, M., 89, 138, 140, 177 nn. 82, 83,
    187 n. 1
Catchpole, D.R., 113, 119, 183 n. 5, 184 n. 1,
    185 n. 1
Cave, C.H., 187 n. 1
Cazeaux, J., 186 n. 9
Charles, R.H., 9, 10, 11, 12, 14–19, 27, 30,
    41, 63, 76, 85, 88, 94–6, 100, 103, 104,
    109, 137, 143 nn. 4, 9, 148 n. 37, 149
    n. 2, 153 n. 26, 155 n. 41, 167 n. 7,
    169 n. 27, 170 nn. 29, 32, 176 nn. 79,
    80, 177 n. 82, 181 n. 16, 185 nn.
    12–13, 187 n. 3
Charlesworth, J.H., 116–18, 120, 122, 128,
    130, 131, 137–9, 141, 142 nn. 2–3, 6,
    143 n. 1, 144 nn. 13–14, 145 nn. 17,
    21, 147 n. 33, 148 n. 34, 150 nn. 11,
    14, 151 n. 16, 153 nn. 23–4, 154 n. 30,
    155 n. 38, 156 nn. 44, 46, 49, 157
    nn. 51–3, 166 n. 110, 167 n. 10, 171
    n. 38, 175 n. 69, 176 n. 76, 177 n. 82,
    178 nn. 2, 4–5, 179 nn. 11, 15, 180
    n. 1, 182 n. 32, 183 n. 5, 184 n. 7, nn.
    1–2, 185 n. 1, 186 n. 18, nn. 1–2, 187
    nn. 1–2, n. 1
Charlesworth, M.P., 162 n. 90
Childs, B.S., 25, 148 n. 38
Christie, P., 149 n. 3
Cirillo, L., 186 n. 1
Collins, J.J., 62, 130, 154 n. 30
Cook, S.A., 162 n. 90
Court, J.M., 185 n. 1
Cousin, I.H., 165 n. 102
Crockett, W.V., 185 n. 1
Cross, F.M., 166 n. 1
Cross, S.H., 151 n. 15
Cullmann, O., 162 n. 86

Dahl, N.A., 54, 111, 113, 144 n. 11, 159
    nn. 67, 71, 72, 185 nn. 2, 6
Daniélou, J., 46, 157 n. 54, 165 n. 103
D'Arcy, C.F., 143 n. 4
Darnell, D.R., 156 n. 46, 174 n. 59
Davenport, G.L., 183 n. 5, 184 n. 1
Davies, W.D., iv, 56, 145 n. 21, 159 nn. 65,
    66, 161 n. 80, 173 n. 54
Davis M., 165 n. 102
Dedering, S., 186 n. 5
Dehandschutter, B., 137, 138, 187 n. 1
Deichgräber, R., 155 n. 36
Delitzsch, F., 149 n. 7
Delcor, M., 130
Denis, A.-M., 15, 62, 124, 132, 138, 140,
    141, 152 n. 20, 169 n. 26, 170 nn. 28,
    31, 183 n. 5, 184 n. 1, 186 n. 1, 187,
    n. 1, n. 1
Dexinger, F., 62, 160 n. 79
Díez Macho, A., 16

Dillmann, A., 8
Dunand, F., 136
Dupont-Sommer, A., 16, 157 n. 54
Düsterdieck, F., 132
Dykers, P., 180 n. 5

Edwards, A. D., 185 n. 1
Einstein, A., 92, 179 n. 16
Eltester, W., 94
Eppstein, V., 162 n. 87
Evans, C. F., 178 n. 8

Feldman, L. H., 185 n. 7, 186 n. 8
Fiensy, D. A., 156 n. 46
Fischer, G., 133
Fitzmyer, J. A., 38, 89, 153 n. 25, 178 n. 9
Flusser, D., 62, 169 n. 19, 174 n. 64, 177 n. 82
Friedland, S., 159 n. 69
Friedlander, G., 152 n. 19
Frost, S. B., 14
Fuller, R. H., 150 n. 10
Funk, R. W., 144 n. 12

Gager, J. G., 170 n. 31
Gardiner, A., 142 n. 4
Gaylord, H. E., Jr., 180 n. 3
Geyser, A. S., 125, 128, 186 n. 1
Glasson, T. F., 116, 123, 124, 125, 138, 140, 185 n. 1, 186 n. 1, 187 n. 1
Glasswell, W., 187 n. 1
Gnilka, J., 177 n. 84
Goodenough, E. R., 161 n. 83
Gray, G. B., 19
Grant, F. C., 122, 186 n. 1
Green, D. E., 176 n. 77
Green, W. S., 143 n. 7, 147 n. 33, 152 n. 21
Greenfield, J. C., 89
Greig, J. C. G., 179 n. 10
Grintz, Y. M., 148 n. 1
Grobel, K., 172 n. 47
Grundmann, W., 168 n. 16

Hadidian, D. Y., 185 n. 1
Haenchen, E., 162 n. 87
Halévy, J., 177 n. 82
Hamerton-Kelly, R. G., 131, 186 n. 1
Hammerschmidt, E., 183 n. 3
Hammershaimb, E., 15, 184 n. 2
Hammond, N. G. L., 148 n. 34
Hanson, P. D., 14, 57, 145 n. 22, 162 n. 89
Haran, M., 161 n. 84
Harnack, A., 20
Harrelson, W., 62, 180 n. 5
Harrington, D. J., 38, 62, 153 n. 25, 177 n. 82, 186 nn. 9–11
Hartman, L., 107, 113, 117, 183 n. 5, 184 n. 1, 185 n. 1
Heil, J. P., 185 n. 1
Heinemann, J., 158 n. 57, 166 n. 111, 169 n. 19
Heisenberg, W., 146 n. 26

Held, H. J., 176 n. 77
Hellendorf, E., 183 n. 3
Hengel, M., iv, xi, 13, 62, 82, 83, 142 n. 5, 145 n. 19, 163 n. 99, 173 nn. 50, 55, 182 n. 33
Hennig, J., 178 n. 2
Hermann, A., 146, n. 26
Higger, M., 58, 192
Highet, G., 148 n. 39
Hoffmann, A. G., 8
Hofius, O., 133
Hoheisel, K., 163 n. 97
Hollander, H. W., 153 n. 26, 180 nn. 3, 4, 185 n. 1
Hooker, M. D., 55, 113, 160 n. 77, 176 n. 78, 185 n. 1
Horbury, W., 157 n. 56, 185 n. 1
Horst, P. W. van der, xi, 62, 174 nn. 60, 61, 178 n. 3, 180 n. 5, 183 n. 5, 184 n. 1
Hultgård, A., 62, 153 n. 29, 154 n. 32

Isaac, E., 18, 89, 102, 103, 106, 107, 110, 142 n. 3, 145 n. 15, 166 n. 5, 167 nn. 7, 8, 18, 183 nn. 1, 5, 184 n. 1, 186 nn. 12, 13, 187 n. 2
Ivanov, I., 150 n. 14

Jacobson, H., 166 n. 108, 174 n. 61
Jaeger, W., 148 n. 39
James, M. R., 63, 170 nn. 30, 33
Janowski, B., 147 n. 33
Jastrow, M., 142 n. 7
Jeremias, G., 155 n. 36
Jeremias, J., 132, 133
Jervell, J., 180 n. 2
Jonge, H. J. de, 95, 153 n. 26, 180 nn. 3, 4
Jonge, M. de, 15, 39, 62, 94, 95, 96, 97, 98, 99, 100, 101, 107, 109, 111, 112, 113, 115, 116, 117, 118, 119, 132, 137, 141, 153 nn. 26, 27, 180 nn. 3, 4, 5, 181 nn. 18, 21, 24, 182 nn. 28, 31, 34, 35, 183 n. 5, 184 n. 1, 185 n. 1, 186 n. 17, 187 n. 1

Kähler, M., 11, 143 n. 8
Kamrat, M., 52
Kanael, B., 180 n. 5
Kant, I., 146 n. 26
Käsemann, E., 13, 14, 144 nn. 11, 12, 163 n. 93
Kautzsch, E., 9, 10, 11, 12, 27, 63, 143 n. 9
Kearns, R., 183 n. 5
Kee, H. C., 40, 62, 94, 98, 99, 100, 101, 130, 132, 134, 135, 136, 137, 153 n. 29, 154 nn. 31, 35, 169 n. 24, 174 n. 56, 180 n. 5, 181 nn. 15, 19, 22, 23, 182 nn. 29, 36, 187 nn. 1, 2
Kelber, W. H., 171 n. 40
Kierkegaard, S., 68, 142 n. 2
Kilpatrick, G. D., 132, 133
Kimelman, R., 82, 157 n. 56
Kingdon, H. P., 183 n. 5, 185 n. 1

Kittle, G., 142 n. 7, 149 n. 8
Klijn, A. F. J., 62, 143 n. 5, 186 n. 16
Knibb, M. A., 18, 62, 89, 106, 107, 108, 109,
    115, 116, 117, 145 n. 16, 153 n. 24,
    166 n. 6, 167 nn. 7–8, 170 n. 34,
    183 nn. 1, 3, 5, 184 n. 1, 185 n. 8, n. 1
Koch, K., 14
Kolenkow, A. B., 180 n. 5, 183 n. 5
Korteweg, Th., 153 n. 26, 180 nn. 3, 4, 183
    n. 5
Kowalski, A., 186 n. 1
Kraft, R. A., 62, 101, 178 n. 2, 180 n. 5
Kreitzer, L. J., 187 n. 1
Kuhn, H.-W., 155 n. 36, 183 n. 5
Kuhn, K. G., 133, 185 n. 1
Kümmel, W. G., 15, 62, 83, 86, 174 nn. 56–7,
    175 nn. 67–8
Kuznecov, P. S., 151 n. 18

Lagrange, M.-J., ix, 179 nn. 13–14
Lake, K., 152 n. 20
Lamb, G., 148 n. 39
Lombanse, H. A., 186 n. 1
Lane, W., 142 n. 7
Laurence, R., 8
Lauterbach, J. Z., 150 n. 13
Leaney, A. R. C., 107, 183 n. 5, 184 n. 1
Leivestad, R., 116, 117, 119, 185 n. 1
Leloir, L, 185 n. 1
Levine, B. A., 161 n. 83
Levine, I. H., 146 n. 27
Lichtenberger, H., 147 n. 33, 183 n. 5, 184
    n. 1
Liebermann, S., 146 n. 28, 172 n. 49
Lindars, B., 137, 187 n. 1
Lindenberger, J. M., 62
Lücke, F., 8
Lunt, H. G., 186 n. 4
Lutz, R. T., 62, 170 n. 36

MacDermott, V., 183 n. 5
Mack, B., 148 n. 39
MacRae, G. W., 62, 124, 131, 183 n. 5, 186
    n. 1
Maddox, R., 183 n. 5, 184 n. 1
Maier, J., 82, 157 n. 56
Mantel, H. D., 161 n. 81
Marrou, H. I., 148 n. 39
Martin, E. G., 180 n. 5
Martin, J., 182 n. 30
Martyn, J. L., 82, 83, 173 n. 53
Marxsen, W., 81, 83, 171 n. 45
McEleney, N. J., 163, n. 92
McHugh, J., 161 n. 84
McKittrick, M., 152 n. 19
McNamara, M., 156 nn. 44, 48
Meade, D. G., 187 n. 1
Mearns, C. L., 108, 184 n. 6, 185 n. 1
Meeks, W. A., 22, 55, 148 n. 35, 159 n. 67,
    160 n. 76, 172 n. 46, 173 n. 52,
    178 n. 7

Mendelson, A., 156 n. 46
Menxel, F. van, 183 n. 5, 184 n. 1
Merleau-Ponty, M., 142 n. 6
Meshchersky, N. A., 34, 62, 104, 150 n. 14,
    152 n. 19, 184 n. 7
Metzger, B. M., 7, 15, 62, 117, 143 n. 3, 185
    n. 1, 186 n. 1
Michel, O., 186 n. 17
Migne, J.-P., 15, 89, 170 n. 28
Milik, J. T., 18, 39, 89, 97, 100, 102, 103, 104,
    105, 106, 108, 109, 110, 138, 145
    n. 18, 152 n. 22, 153 n. 28, 155 n. 36,
    166 n. 3, 167 n. 9, 176 n. 78, 177 n. 82,
    182 n. 27, 183 n. 39, 184 nn. 6, 7
Millar, F., 149 n. 4, 161 n. 81
Moir, I. A., 183 n. 5, 184 n. 1
Momigliano, A., 162 n. 90
Montague, W. J., 144 n. 11
Moore, G. F., 30, 47, 65, 149 n. 5, 160 n. 75
Moule, C. F. D., 81, 83, 85, 89, 168 n. 12,
    171 n. 45, 175 n. 66, 177 n. 84
Mueller, J. R., 150 n. 11, 171 n. 38, 180 n. 5
Müller, U. B., 115
Muraoka, T., 184 n. 2
Murray, R., 59, 140, 163 nn. 94, 95, 96, 187
    n. 1

Nestlé, E., 137
Neusner, J., 53, 65, 120, 147 n. 31, 159 nn.
    68, 69, 73, 160 n. 75, 161 n. 83, 162
    n. 88, 164 n. 100, 165 nn. 102, 107,
    171 n. 39, 178 n. 2
Nevill, T., 146 n. 26
Nickelsburg, G. W. E., Jr., 62, 89, 97, 103,
    106, 107, 108, 142 n. 5, 153 n. 24,
    154 n. 34, 156 n. 44, 169 n. 20, 178
    n. 2, 180 n. 5, 181 n. 25, 183 nn. 1, 5,
    184 nn. 6, 1
Nieting, L., 171 n. 45
Nobel, B., 51
North, J. L., 187 n. 1
Noy, D., 169 n. 19

Obolensky, D., 150 n. 14
Oden, R. A., Jr., 170 n. 31
Oesterley, W. O. E., 30, 149 n. 2
Ong, W. J., 171 n. 40
O'Hagan, A. P., 185 n. 1
O'Neill, J. C., 118, 179 n. 12, 185 n. 1
Oppenheimer, A., 20, 21, 146 nn. 27, 28, 162
    n. 91
Osborn, C. D., 166 n. 4, 167 n. 10, 168 n. 13

Pais, A., 179 nn. 16, 17
Pei, M., 188
Perry, B. E., 134, 135
Pesch, R., 113, 119, 185 n. 1, 186 n. 1
Pfeiffer, R. H., 130
Philippi, C. F., 8
Philonenko, M., 16, 62, 130, 135, 177 n. 1
Pietersma, A., 62, 170 n. 36

Pines, S., 105
Pope, M. H., 171 n. 41
Popkes, W., 186 n. 1
Porter, F. C., 160 n. 75
Potter, C. F., 35
Price, R., 1, 142 n. 1, 179 n. 18, 180 n. 5
Priest, J., 62, 169 n. 20, 180 n. 5
Pugh, S., 151 n. 15

Rabris, R., 156 n. 48
Rad, G. von, 64, 98, 165 n. 106
Rau, E., 184 n. 2
Reicke, B., 168 n. 16
Rengstorf, K. H., 180 n. 5, 182 n. 31
Reumann, J., 171 n. 45
Rhoads, D. M., 145 n. 19, 191
Richards, K. H., 148 n. 39
Riesner, R., 171 n. 40
Riessler, P., 143 n. 9
Robinson, J. A. T., iv, 85, 86, 174 n. 56, 175
    nn. 66, 70, 73
Robinson, S. E., 180 n. 5
Rodd, C. S., 187 n. 1
Rolfé, A., 155 n. 36
Rose, H. J., 148 n. 34
Rowley, H. H., 14
Rubinkiewicz, R., 176 n. 75, 185 n. 1, 186 n. 4
Rubinstein, A., 105
Runciman, S., 150 n. 14, 151 n. 18
Russell, D. S., 14

Sacchi, P., 15
Sanders, E. P., iv, 30, 47, 49, 50–5, 62, 113,
    119, 149 n. 6, 154 n. 33, 156 n. 46,
    157 n. 55, 158 nn. 59–60, 62, 159
    nn. 63–4, 66–7, 70–1, 160 nn. 74–5,
    185 n. 1
Sanders, J. A., 62
Sandmel, S., 55, 160 n. 78
Sandays, B., 180 n. 5
Sänger, D., 172 n. 49
Santos Otero, A. de, 150 n. 14
Sarason, R. S., 147 n. 28, 158 n. 57
Sartre, J. P., 142 n. 6
Schagen, S., 187 n. 1
Schalit, A., 161 n. 82
Schaller, B., 116, 183 n. 5, 185 n. 1
Schechter, S., 58, 158 n. 57, 166 n. 111
Schelkle, K. H., 168 n. 16
Schmidt, J. M., 14
Schmidt, N., 104
Schmithals, W., 14
Schnackenburg, R., 177 n. 84
Schnedermann, G., 149 n. 7
Schoeps, H. J., 159 n. 66
Scholem, G., 105
Schreiner, J., 14
Schüpphaus, J., 166 n. 110
Schürer, E., 20, 30, 31, 145 n. 23, 149 n. 3,
    149 n. 4, 161 n. 81, 164 n. 101
Schweitzer, A., 14

Schweizer, E., 176 n. 77
Scopello, M., 186 n. 1
Scullard, H. H., 148 n. 34
Sekine, M., 16
Sherbowitz-Wetzor, O. P., 151 n. 15
Shinan, A., 178 n. 8
Shutt, R. J. H., 62
Siegele-Wenschkewitz, L., 149 n. 8
Slingerland, H. D., 154 n. 35
Smallwood, E. M., 147 n. 32
Smith, M., 62, 138, 139, 140, 160 n. 75, 163
    n. 99, 164 n. 101, 165 n. 102, 187 n. 1
Smith, J. Z., 62, 160 n. 75, 164 n. 101
Snell, B., 174 n. 61
Sodon, P. von, 134
Sokolov, M. I., 104
Spittler, R. P., 130
Spiro, S. S., 147 n. 30
Starcky, J., 116
Stegemann, H., 155 n. 36
Stemberger, G., 164 n. 100
Stone, M. E., 59, 62, 89, 95, 150 n. 14, 156
    n. 44, 163 n. 98, 165 n. 105, 180 n. 9
Strack, H. L., 49, 149 n. 8, 160 n. 75
Strugnell, J., 62, 153 n. 28, 171 n. 42, 182
    n. 27
Stuckenbruck, E., 180 n. 5
Stuhlmacher, P., 133
Suter, D. W., 89
Swetnam, J., 174 n. 58

Talbert, C. H., x
Taylor, S., 149 n. 3
Thomas, J., 180 n. 2
Tischendorf, C., 171 n. 38
Torrey, C. C., 130, 164 n. 100
Trafton, J., 180 n. 5
Trever, J. C., 12
Turdeanu, E., 150 n. 14

Ullendorff, E., 167 n. 7
Urbach, E. E., 82, 147 n. 29, 157 n. 56

Vaillant, A., 104, 105, 184 n. 8
Vanderkam, J. C., 41, 62, 89, 155 nn. 36, 39,
    177 n. 82
Vaux, R. de, 155 n. 36, 161 n. 84
Vermaseren, M. J., 172 n. 49
Vermes, G., 11, 37, 62, 82, 120, 143 nn. 7, 10,
    148 n. 1, 149 nn. 4, 8, 152 n. 21, 161
    n. 81, 173 n. 51, 178 nn. 2, 8
Vermes, P., 149 n. 4
Villieurs, P. G. R. de, 62
Violet, B., 186 n. 15

Wagner, S., 164 n. 101
Walter, N., 62, 116, 183 n. 5, 184 n. 1, 185
    n. 1
Watson, J. K., 175 n. 66
Weatherhead, B., 144 n. 11
Weber, F., 31, 47, 55, 149 n. 7

Weisse, C. H., 8
Wells, G. A., 185 n. 1
Werblowsky, R. J. Z., 184 n. 9
Wiencke, G. K., 143 n. 2
Wilken, R. L., 173 n. 52
Wilson, C., 180 n. 5
Wilson, R. McL., 176 n. 78
Wilson, S. G., 160 n. 77
Wintermute, O. S., 41, 62, 155 n. 40, 156 n. 42
Woude, A. S. van der, 155 n. 36

Wrede, W., 91, 179 n. 10
Wright, R., 170 n. 35

Yadin, Y., 178 n. 2

Zahn, T., 9, 138, 170 n. 28
Zeitlin, S., 20, 146 n. 25, 146 n. 28, 164
    n. 100, 170 n. 37
Zentner, C., 143 n. 6